Collective Capacity Building

International Issues in Adult Education

Series Editor

Peter Mayo (*University of Malta, Msida, Malta*)

Editorial Advisory Board

Stephen Brookfield (*University of St Thomas, Minnesota, USA*)
Waguida El Bakary (*American University in Cairo, Egypt*)
Budd L. Hall (*University of Victoria, BC, Canada*)
Astrid von Kotze (*University of Western Cape, South Africa*)
Alberto Melo (*University of the Algarve, Portugal*)
Lidia Puigvert-Mallart (*CREA-University of Barcelona, Spain*)
Daniel Schugurensky (*Arizona State University, USA*)
Joyce Stalker (*University of Waikato, Hamilton, New Zealand/Aotearoa*)
Juha Suoranta (*University of Tampere, Finland*)

VOLUME 30

The titles published in this series are listed at *brill.com/adul*

Collective Capacity Building

Shaping Education and Communication in Knowledge Society

Edited By

Simona Sava, Claudia Borca and Gheorghe Clitan

BRILL
SENSE

LEIDEN | BOSTON

All chapters in this book have undergone peer review.

The Library of Congress Cataloging-in-Publication Data is available online at
http://catalog.loc.gov

ISSN 2352-2372
ISBN 978-90-04-42218-6 (paperback)
ISBN 978-90-04-42219-3 (hardback)
ISBN 978-90-04-42220-9 (e-book)

Copyright 2020 by Koninklijke Brill NV, Leiden, The Netherlands.
Koninklijke Brill NV incorporates the imprints Brill, Brill Hes & De Graaf,
Brill Nijhoff, Brill Rodopi, Brill Sense, Hotei Publishing, mentis Verlag,
Verlag Ferdinand Schöningh and Wilhelm Fink Verlag.
All rights reserved. No part of this publication may be reproduced, translated,
stored in a retrieval system, or transmitted in any form or by any means, electronic,
mechanical, photocopying, recording or otherwise, without prior written
permission from the publisher.
Authorization to photocopy items for internal or personal use is granted by
Koninklijke Brill NV provided that the appropriate fees are paid directly to The
Copyright Clearance Center, 222 Rosewood Drive, Suite 910, Danvers, MA 01923,
USA. Fees are subject to change.

This book is printed on acid-free paper and produced in a sustainable manner.

CONTENTS

List of Figures and Tables	vii
Notes on Contributors	ix
Introduction: Towards Collective Capacity Building in a Transdisciplinary Perspective *Simona Sava*	1

Part 1: Interdisciplinary Approaches in Collective Capacity Building

1.	Science, Truth, Democracy: A Troubled Marriage? *Mircea Dumitru*	15
2.	Capacity Building by Enculturation *Ekkehard Nuissl*	25
3.	Cultural Heritage, Identity and Collective Capacity Building *Sorin Vlad Predescu*	35
4.	Recovering Parsons through Roma's Voices for Constructing European Societal Community *Teresa Sordé, Olga Serradell, Esther Oliver, Emilia Aiello and Garazi López de Aguileta-Jaussi*	45
5.	Distorting the Message of Religious Symbols by Fallacious Reasoning in the Electoral Posters of Political Campaigns *Gheorghe Clitan and Oana Barbu-Kleitsch*	59
6.	Political Communication on Social Media during February 2017 Protests in Romania *Simona Bader*	73
7.	Learning Democracy: Beyond the Traditional Didactics *Katarina Popović, Maja Maksimović and Aleksa Jovanović*	83
8.	Critical Reflection in Contemporary Adult Education: An Essential Element for Personal and Collective Capacity Building *George A. Koulaouzides and Theodore Koutroukis*	99

v

CONTENTS

Part 2: Collective Capacity Building in Higher Education

9. Who Are the Knowledge Producers in Higher Education?
   An Inquiry into the Self-Perceptions of Postdoctoral Researchers
   in Higher Education in Spanish Universities 109
   Georgeta Ion and Marina Tomàs-Folch

10. Nudging Generation Y towards Education for Sustainability 123
    Liliana Donath, Monica Boldea and Ana-Maria Popa

11. Capacity Building in Initial Teacher Education (ITE): Collaboration
    for Collective Capacity Building 137
    Irina Maslo and Mikael Cronhjort

12. Building Collective Capacity for Adult Learning in Distance Education 153
    Maria N. Gravani

13. Nurturing the Well-Being of University Students for Improved
    Capacity Building 165
    *Ioana Darjan, Loredana Al Ghazi, Anca Lustrea, Mihai Predescu and
    Mariana Crasovan*

14. The Normative Value of Health: Epigenetical, Bioethical and
    Theological Approaches to Health Education 185
    Aurora Carmen Bărbat

Index 197

FIGURES AND TABLES

FIGURES

5.1. Poster 1 (Source: https://www.news.ro/alegeri-2016/psd-si-pmp-distribuie-in-arges-calendare-ortodoxe-dar-cu-siglele-de-partid-patriarhia-e-regretabil-ca-s-a-ajuns-atat-de-departe-1922403206002016122016070616) 66

5.2. Poster 2 (Source: http://www.mediafax.ro/politic/pmp-arges-si-a-facut-calendar-religios-cu-adam-si-eva-psd-e-incult-noi-suntem-niste-baieti-subtiri-16018200) 67

6.1. Online posts with #rezist. (Source: Zelist Monitor, https://www.zelist.ro/monitor/) 76

6.2. The impact of #rezist on social networks. (Source: Zelist Monitor, https://www.zelist.ro/monitor/) 77

6.3. The dynamic of online posts. (Source: Zelist Monitor, https://www.zelist.ro/monitor/) 78

6.4. Age distribution of posters. (Source: Zelist Monitor, https://www.zelist.ro/monitor/) 78

6.5. Space distribution of posts. (Source: Zelist Monitor, https://www.zelist.ro/monitor/) 79

10.1. The structure of generations by age groups (based on https://www.worldometers.info/demographics/world-demographics/#age-structure) 126

10.2. Sustainable investments (2016). (Source: http://www.ussif.org) 129

10.3. A multi-stakeholder approach of ESD 133

10.4. Quality of information acquired by students 134

11.1. A multidimensional model of personal capability and collective capacity building (modified from Maslo et al., 2014) 139

11.2. A model of pedagogical leadership of collaborative learning 141

13.1. Phases of developing an organizational strategy 173

13.2. Levels of academic distress, well-being, and well-being dimensions 179

13.3. The relations between levels of academic distress and psychological symptoms 180

14.1. Parameters of health 188

TABLES

4.1. WORKALO analysis table 50

9.1. Sample of respondents 113

vii

FIGURES AND TABLES

10.1. Finite and infinite games (based on Carse, 1986)   128
11.1. Evidence of efficiency of pedagogy of collaboration in practice in self-evaluation rubric of generic competences in the module on cultural diversity   142
11.2. Evidence of efficiency of pedagogy of collaboration in practice in self-evaluation rubric of pedagogical competence in the module on cultural diversity   142
11.3. Evidence of efficiency of pedagogy of collaboration in practice in self-evaluation rubric of transversal competences in the module on cultural diversity   143
13.1. Descriptive statistics for Ryff scale and subscales   177
13.2. Comparative results on CCAPS 34 between study sample and the etalon   178
13.3. Impact of different levels of academic distress on well-being and mental health   179

NOTES ON CONTRIBUTORS

Emilia Aiello (https://orcid.org/0000-0002-0005-6501) holds a PhD in Sociology at Universitat Autonoma de Barcelona (UAB). At present, she is a Post-Doctoral researcher in the Community of Research on Excellence for All (CREA), at the University of Barcelona. She is a research collaborator for the Research Group on Migration and Ethnic Minorities (GEDIME) of the UAB. Her research interests focus on the grassroots levels of organization of the most vulnerable social groups, in order to overcome social inequalities, as well as on the best ways to maximize the social impact of all types of scientific research focusing on topics related to social vulnerability and inequalities. She has collaborated in EU-funded investigations, such as FP6 INCLUD-ED, FP7 IMPACT-EV, H2020 PROTON, and in Spanish RTD investigations, such as DROM-IN (2009–2011), TRANSROMA (2012–2015) and SARTUCUE (2016–2019). Her recent research contributions have been published in *Frontiers in Psychology, International Sociology, Int. J. Environ. Res. Public Health* (IJERPH) and *Qualitative Inquiry*. She was a visiting researcher at Harvard University's Kennedy School of Government (2014) and at the Department of Sociology at Oxford University (2016).

Loredana Al Ghazi, PhD, is a lecturer at the Department of Educational Sciences at the West University of Timisoara (WUT). She has a BA in Psychology, an MEd in Special Education and a PhD in Developmental Psychology. She is a principal supervisor psychologist in Special Education, she has a vast experience in experiential counseling, child development and counseling in special education. She is director of WUT's University Clinic for Therapies and Psycho-pedagogic Counselling. Her key areas of interests include Developmental Psychology, Existential and Positive Counseling, ASD Integrative Interventions and Neuromotor Disabilities.

Simona Bader is a Lecturer of Communication, Mass Media and Public Relations and has been Vice Dean of the Faculty of Political Science, Philosophy and Communication Sciences at the West University of Timisoara (Romania) since October 2018. She received her PhD at the West University of Timisoara in 2014, with a thesis on theatre in the cultural press in Timiș. Her main research interests include communication, journalism, public relations, press survey and continuous education. She has published articles in Romanian and international communication journals (*Applied Social Sciences, Communication Studies, Revista Română de Jurnalism și Comunicare, Journal of Romanian Literary Studies*, etc.) and participated in many international and national conferences. She is the author of the book *Arta spectacolului în presa culturală timișeană*.

NOTES ON CONTRIBUTORS

Aurora Carmen Barbat, MD, The University for Medicine and Pharmacy "Victor Babes", Timişoara, Romania/Dipl. in Caritas Science and Christian Social Work (Albert Ludwig-University, Freiburg i. Br., Germany), is a senior lecturer at the West University of Timisoara, Faculty of Sociology and Psychology, Social Work Department. She has published 3 books, approximately 50 articles and book chapters in scientific (inter)national volumes and journals, covering areas such as social medicine, social work, addictions, coping with illness, religion as coping. She has participated in national and international socio-medical and psycho-spiritual trainings, research programs and conferences, has organized scientific events, and is a member of Romanian and international scientific organizations.

Oana Barbu-Kleitsch, PhD, is a practitioner and a researcher specialized in Brand Communication, Sports Branding and Online PR, with a professional experience of almost 15 years. Her postdoctoral research, "Between Identity and Image: The Production of Meaning in the Relationship between a Sport Brand and Members of Specific Communities", is the first Romanian research study on rugby sports branding. Her main research field and published articles include Symbolic Communication, Advertising Communications and Communication Theory. Currently she is a lecturer at the West University of Timişoara, The Department of Philosophy and Communication Sciences, where she is head of the Advertising Specialization and teaches introductory courses to Advertising, Advertising Discourse Analysis, Advertising Strategies, Advertising and Promotional Strategies, Social Media, Storytelling and Personal Branding.

Monica Boldea, Alma Mater the West University of Timisoara, is a lecturer at the Faculty of Economics and Business Administration, at the Department of Marketing and International Relations. Her main teaching areas are Business English, Intercultural Communication, European Diplomacy. She has a doctorate in the field of Economics and her main research interests are: culture and cultural intelligence, social development, European policies, regional development.

Claudia Borca is a Lecturer PhD at the Department of Educational Sciences, Faculty of Sociology at the West University of Timisoara. She has a BA in Special Education, an MEd in Special Education and Educational Management, and a PhD in Educational Psychology. She became a supervisor psychologist in Special Education in 2010. She is the author and co-author of several books and articles on metacognition, neurodevelopmental disorders, educational inclusion of children with special needs and education. She has developed and conducted training courses for teachers and education specialists in the above-mentioned topics. She has vast experience in the theory and practice of special and inclusive education.

Gheorghe Clitan is Prof Dr Habil and Head of the Philosophy and Communication Studies Department, Faculty of Political Sciences, Philosophy and Communication

Studies at the West University of Timisoara. His main research interests include critical thinking, rhetoric, pragmatics, information theory and advertising analysis. He has published articles in Romanian and international journals, studies in volumes published at international and Romanian publishing houses. He has participated in many national and international conferences. He published a book on pragmatics and postmodernism, he is the author of a monograph on critical thinking and the co-author of a Romanian guideline to help students solve the Law School Admission Tests (LSAT). He is one of nine Romanian experts in LSAT for The National Institute of Magistracy (NIM). His national and international scientific professional affiliations are: the Social-Political Studies Institute of Timisoara, the Institute of Philosophy and Psychology "Constantin Radulescu-Motru" – Romanian Academy, the Romanian Committee for the History and Philosophy of Science and Technology (CRIFST) of the Romanian Academy, the Romanian Society of Philosophy (SRFil), Société Roumaine de Philosophie de Langue Française (SRPLF), the Trainers' Association of Journalism and Communication (AFCOM), and the International Applied Research Studies of Innovations in Communication (IARSIC).

Mariana Crasovan is an Associate Professor at the West University of Timisoara, The Department of Educational Sciences. She received her BA degree and also her PhD in Educational Science at Babes-Bolyai University, Cluj-Napoca. Her areas of interests include continuing professional development, instructional design and curriculum development and community professional learning.

Mikael Cronhjort, PhD, is a lecturer, a researcher and an educational developer at KTH Royal Institute of Technology, Stockholm, Sweden. His background is in engineering physics and he defended his doctoral thesis in theoretical physics, "Models and computer simulations of origins of life and evolution" in 1995. Since then, he has taken a master's degree in education, and he has been teaching mathematics at KTH and mathematics and physics in upper secondary schools in Stockholm. He has been an educational developer at KTH since 2011. Since 2014, he has been programme director of the integrated dual degree programme "Master of Science in Engineering and in Education" at KTH. His research fields are engineering education and teacher education, with a special interest in mathematics education and flipped learning. He has been the secretary of ICMI-Sweden, a sub-department of the National Committee for Mathematics at the Swedish Royal Academy of Science since 2015.

Ioana Darjan, PhD, is a lecturer at the Department of Educational Sciences, Faculty of Sociology at the West University of Timisoara. She has BAs in Psychology and Pedagogy, an MEd in Special Education and a PhD in Psychology. She is a trained psychologist in special education and a Senior LSCI trainer. Her professional, academic and scientific activity is focused on educational and therapeutic approaches to children with emotional and behavioral disorders, speech and language disorders

NOTES ON CONTRIBUTORS

and therapy, positive behavioral management and discipline, trauma and resilience, wellbeing, and cognitive-behavior therapy. She is the author and the co-author of several books and articles on the above-mentioned topics and has developed and conducted trainings for teachers and educational specialists.

Liliana Donath, Alma Mater at the West University of Timisoara, studied Finance and Accounting and completed her doctoral studies in the field of corporate finance. Currently, she holds the position of Full Professor at the Faculty of Economics and Business Administration in Timisoara where she teaches Public Finance, Behavioural Finance and supervises doctoral theses in the field of Finance and Banking. Her research focuses on public expenditure performance, sustainable finance, tax compliance, tax administration, financial stability, and bank supervision.

Mircea Dumitru, PhD Prof, teaches Analytical Philosophy and Philosophical Logic at the University of Bucharest. Mircea Dumitru is a Doctor of Philosophy at Tulane University (New Orleans, Louisiana) with a thesis in mathematical logic focusing on modality and incompleteness. He was awarded a second doctoral degree in philosophy at the University of Bucharest upon defending a thesis in the philosophy of language, concerned with topics of neo-fregeanism and neo-russellianism in the semantics of propositional attitudes and direct reference. He is the author of over 50 articles in specialized journals and book chapters with topics including modal logics, theories of truth, significance, rationality, L. Wittgenstein's philosophy, contemporary logic, realism, essentiality, and relativism. He was re-elected as Rector of the University of Bucharest for a second five-year term (2015–2019). He was Minister of Education from July 2016 to January 2017 and President of the European Society of Analytical Philosophy (2011–2014). In 2014, Professor Dumitru was elected a Corresponding Member of the Romanian Academy. In 2017, he was elected president of the International Institute of Philosophy. He is Fellow of Academia Europaea since 2019.

Maria N. Gravani is an Assistant Professor in Continuing Education/Adult Education at the School of Humanities and Social Sciences of the Open University of Cyprus (OUC). She holds a PhD in Continuing Education (2003) and an MEd degree (1998), both from the Graduate School of Education, University of Bristol, UK, and a B.A. in Classics (Honours) (1997) from the Aristotle University of Thessaloniki, Greece. She is the founder and, since 2013, has become the Academic Coordinator of the Masters and Doctoral Programme in Continuing Education and Lifelong Learning at the OUC. Additionally, since 2016, she has been the Academic Coordinator for the OUC of the Erasmus Mundus International Masters in Adult Education for Social Change (IMAESC) that is delivered in collaboration with the University of Glasgow, the University of Malta and Tallinn University. Her work experience in adult and continuing education has developed in four different countries: the UK, Ireland, Greece & Cyprus. Her research includes adult teaching and learning in different contexts (second chance education, distance education, higher education), adult learning for social change, organization of programmes for adults, professionalization of adult educators, lifelong learning. She supervises doctoral dissertations, has extensively published in peer-reviewed journals, books and conference proceedings (over 400 citations), and presented her work in international conferences. In 2017, she was elected a member of the European Society for the Research in the Education of Adults (ESREA) Steering Committee, and she is an active member of PASCAL and ESREA – ReNadET (Research Network on Adult Educators, Trainers and their Professional Development). She is a member of the Advisory Editorial Board of the *European Journal of Research on the Education and Learning of Adults* (RELA) and she is a permanent reviewer and an occasional one for a number of international journals, including: *Journal of Adult and Continuing Education, International Journal of Lifelong Education, Teaching and Teacher Education, Educational Technology & Society, Adult, Community and Professional Learning.*

Georgeta Ion has a degree in Psychology and Educational Sciences, a Master's degree in management and evaluation in education from the University of Bucharest and a PhD in Educational Sciences from The University of Barcelona. Her research interests include: the study of higher education institutions, the relationship between educational research and educational policy and practices. She has been involved in innovative projects at higher education level and has conducted research on competences-based assessment and research-based education. She has been involved in consultancy activities for the public administration in Romania and for several research and development projects at the European level. Georgeta Ion is currently a Professor at the Department of Applied Pedagogy of the University Autònoma de Barcelona. She acts as convenor for the network on higher education of the European Educational Research Association.

Aleksa Jovanović is a PhD student and Research Assistant at the Department for Pedagogy and Andragogy (Adult Education), Faculty of Philosophy of the University of Belgrade and an assistant editor for the *Journal of Andragogical Studies*. He is also a personal construct psychotherapist.

George A. Koulaouzides studied mathematics and adult education. He teaches the theory and practice of adult education at the Hellenic Open University and the Democritus University of Thrace. He has designed the accredited training program for the instructors of the National Centre for Public Administration in Greece and has a vast experience in the training of trainers. He has contributed to the internationalization of the Greek community interested in adult education. His research interests are learning practices, transformative learning, educational biography, and critical reflection. He has translated three books on adult education, edited journals and several textbooks. His published work counts more than 75 papers in academic journals, edited volumes and conference proceedings.

xiii

NOTES ON CONTRIBUTORS

Theodore Koutroukis is an Assistant Professor at the Democritus University of Thrace. His research interests include Personnel Economics, Employee Relations, Vocational Training, Labour Market and Human Resource Management. He has taught at several Universities and has acquired experience as a regional and national co-ordinator/expert of EU funded projects (ESF, ADAPT, RETEX, NOW, EQUAL, YOUTHSTART, etc.) and as an evaluator of projects funded by the Greek Ministries of Education and Labour. He has published many studies and participated in research projects concerning industrial relationships, labour market, vocational training since 1990. He is a member of the International Industrial Relations Association (1989) and the European Association of Labour Economists (2002) and the Greek Association of Adult Education (2008).

Garazi López de Aguileta-Jaussi (https://orcid.org/0000-0001-7571-3556) is a member of CREA (Community of Research on Excellence for All) at the University of Barcelona. She conducts research in schools with great cultural and ethnical diversity, which implement Dialogic Literary Gatherings, evaluated as very successful educational practices by INCLUD-ED, coordinated by CREA, and the only SSH selected by the European Commission among the 10 success stories in research. Her research focus is on children's development in relation to school-relevant language skills in Dialogic Literary Gatherings, fostering excellent academic results in children from diverse cultural backgrounds. Garazi has recently been granted a scholarship by La Caixa Foundation, one of the most competitive scholarships in Spain, which gives her the opportunity to conduct her PhD in a North American university.

Anca Lustrea, PhD, is an Associate Professor at the West University of Timisoara (WUT), at the Department of Educational Sciences. She has a BA in Psychology, an MEd in Special Education and a PhD in Educational Psychology, with a thesis on the psychology of learning. She became a principal supervisor psychologist in Special Education in 2013. She has extensive experience in the theory and practice of special and inclusive education, mainly in special didactics. She has been a trainer in Adult Education since 2008 and a board member of the Centre for Psycho-Pedagogic Support for Students and a member of the University Clinic for Therapies and Psycho-Pedagogic Counselling of WUT. Her key areas of interests include Special Didactics, Educational Inclusion, Case management in Special Education and the Psychology of deaf impaired children.

Maja Maksimović, PhD, is an Assistant Professor at the Department for Pedagogy and Andragogy (Adult Education), Faculty of Philosophy of the University of Belgrade and a researcher at the Institute for Pedagogy and Andragogy. She has a degree in Andragogy, obtained in Belgrade, Serbia, an MA degree in Counselling Studies defended at the University of Nottingham, UK, and a PhD in Andragogy, at the Faculty of Philosophy, University of Belgrade. She is a deputy editor of *The Adult*

xiv

Education Journal (Andragogical Studies). Her research interests are related to art education, power relations in adult education, feminist epistemology, educational policy, and public pedagogy.

Irina Maslo is Prof Dr Habil Paed. She defended her PhD thesis "Out-school activities for active work-life participation" in 1987 and in 1995 she habilitated due to the international accreditation of her scientific contribution "Individualization of the pedagogical process of school". Since 1997 she has been Full Professor at the University of Latvia during which time period she has created and co-implemented models of Latvian bilingual education (1997–2002). She was director of the Scientific Institute of Pedagogy at the Faculty of Education and Psychology of the University of Latvia (2007–2015) and since 2015 she has been Head of the Scientific Council at the same institute. She is the educational designer, implementer and director (2007–2016) of a master's degree programme on educational practices of diversity, created within the framework agreed between the National Distance Education University (Spain) and the University of Latvia. She has an essential contribution to the doctoral studies program in pedagogy (2010–2011) and the doctoral school "Human capacity and life wide".

Ekkehard Nuissl, Prof Dr Dr h c mult, University of Kaiserslautern (Germany), was qualified as a journalist (1965–1967), then he studied German languages and Social Sciences in Heidelberg and Bremen. In 1974, he received his PhD with an empirical thesis on mass media, in 1987 he was habilitated in Adult Education in Hannover. As Director of the Institute for Empirical Educational Research (AfeB) in Heidelberg (1974–1988) he focused his research on adult education, as director of Hamburg Folk High School (1988–1991) he connected his scientific work to the practical field. In his capacity as director of the German Institute for Adult Education (DIE, 1991–2011), he successfully combined scientific, practical and political interests. His activity in these institutions has been always coupled with his pursuit of an academic career as Full Professor at prestigious universities in Germany (Hanover, Marburg, Duisburg, Essen), as Professor at several international universities (Florence (IT), Torun (PL), Timisoara (RO), New Delhi (IND)) and as lecturer in Bern (CH), Klagenfurt (A), Copenhagen (DK), Heidelberg and Oldenburg (D). Since 2011, Professor Nuissl has been teaching at the University of Kaiserslautern. He is a chair of national and international associations and conferences, consulting governments, and he represented Germany in international contexts. In 2006, he became a member of the International "Hall of Fame" for Adult Education, and since 2016 he has been one of its board members. Since 2016 he is also research fellow of the UNESCO Institute for Lifelong Learning (UIL) in Hamburg. His most recently published books are *Bildung im Raum* (Educational Spaces, 2015), *Lernort Tagung* (Learning in Conferences, 2016), *Keine lange Weile* (Not Tedious, 2016), *Einführung in die Erwachsenenbildung* (Introduction in Adult Education, 2017), Empirical Research in Adult Education (2017), and *Kultur Aneignen* (Acquiring Cultural Identity, 2017).

NOTES ON CONTRIBUTORS

Esther Oliver (https://orcid.org/0000-0002-4801-0131), PhD, is Professor of Sociology at the Department of Sociology of the University of Barcelona (UB). She has been a Ramon y Cajal researcher at the UB, a postdoctoral researcher at the University of Warwick (United Kingdom) from 2006 to 2008, and Visiting Professor at the University of Duisburg-Essen (Germany). Her research interests include social change and gender. Dr. Oliver was the main researcher of the project funded by the Spanish RTD programme, "The mirage of upward mobility and the socialization of gender violence" (2010–2012) and participated in many projects funded by the European Commission, such as IMPACT-EV (FP7, 2014–2017). The contributions resulting from these projects, where she was a coordinator or a member, are published in high ranked journals, such as *Research Evaluation, Teachers College Record, Qualitative Inquiry* and *British Journal of Sociology of Education*, among many others. Dr. Oliver is Deputy Editor of the *International Sociological Association Journal, International Sociology* (JCR-ISI) and a board member of the Research Network 29 on Social Theory of the European Sociological Association.

Ana-Maria Popa, Alma Mater West University of Timisoara, is an aspiring student with a financial background in the field of higher education. Currently, she is an International Corporate Finance MA student at the Faculty of Economics and Business Administration and an International economics student at Universite de Savoie Mont Blanc in France. Her extracurricular interests include: educational issues and stakeholders' participation in the learning system. She is an active member in student associations and she is an event organizer of educational and cultural activities.

Katarina Popović is an Associate Professor at the Department for Pedagogy and Andragogy (Adult Education), Faculty of Philosophy of the University of Belgrade and a researcher at the Institute for Pedagogy and Andragogy. She received her PhD in Aachen, Germany and is a Visiting Professor in adult education and lifelong learning at several universities. Dr Popović is president of the Serbian Adult Education Society and she is a member of The International Adult and Continuing Education Hall of Fame and of other important European and international organizations. She is also the editor in chief of the *Journal of Andragogical Studies* and the author of numerous publications, articles and books in the field of adult education and lifelong learning. Dr Popović is also the Secretary General of ICAE (The International Council for Adult Education) and she has conducted research at the global policy level and within the UN. She is a certified trainer (Swiss) in adult education, with extensive experience in trainings worldwide. For many years, she was vice president of EAEA and project coordinator of German DVV International.

Mihai Predescu, PhD, is an Associate Professor at the Department Educational Sciences, Faculty of Sociology at the West University of Timisoara. He has a BA in Psychology, an MEd in Special Education and a PhD in Psychology. He is a principal psychologist in special education and his professional, academic and scientific activity is focused on special education, educational research, trauma, resilience, wellbeing, and adult education. He is the author and the co-author of several books and articles on the above-mentioned topics and has developed and conducted training programmes for teachers and educational specialists.

Sorin Vlad Predescu, PhD, is a lecturer at the West University of Timisoara, Department of Educational Sciences and Director of Timis County Cultural Directorate. He has a BA in Psychology, an MEd in Special Education and a PhD in Social Psychology. He has a vast experience in community development, adult training and cultural organization management. His key areas of interests include social psychology, cultural education and political psychology. He is the author and the co-author of several books and articles on these topics and has developed and implemented many projects on community development and cultural heritage.

Simona Sava, Prof Dr Habil, has been teaching at the West University of Timisoara since 1997 and in 2009 she became Full Professor. In 2003, she received her PhD from the University of Bucharest, in distance education and in 2015 she habilitated there in the field of adult education. In addition to her academic achievements, she was director of the Romanian Institute of Adult Education (IREA) from 2000 to 2013. Her main research topics are professionalization in adult education, pedagogy of higher education, educational policy and educational management, at national and international levels. She is a member of national and international boards for developing the educational system, such as the European Commission. She is a consultant for The Ministry of Education, The Ministry of Labour, The Ministry of Information and Communication, DG Employment, etc. Her publications include more than 90 studies and articles and she is the author and the co-author and the editor of more than 15 books. She is a member of The International Hall of Fame on Adult and Continuing Education since 2017.

Olga Serradell (https://orcid.org/0000-0003-4077-1400) is a Ramon y Cajal research fellow at the Department of Sociology of the Autonomous University of Barcelona and a member of GEDIME. Currently, she is the general coordinator of the academic grading system at the Faculty of Political Sciences and Sociology in Barcelona. Between 2006 and 2008, she obtained a grant from La Caixa and the French government to develop her postdoctoral research studies as a guest researcher at the CADIS, Centre d'Analyse et d'Intervention Sociologiques from l'École des Hautes Études en Sciences Sociales in Paris. In 2008, she became a Juan de la Cierva researcher at the Department of Sociology of the UAB. In her entire research career, her main contributions have involved educational principles and practices that overcome social inequalities concerning vulnerable cultural groups, such as the Roma population and the Arab-Muslim community. Her research conducted

NOTES ON CONTRIBUTORS

with groups of Arab-Muslim women has helped her consolidate a research line on interconnected topics of gender, citizenship, and migration.

Teresa Sordé (http://orcid.org/0000-0003-0336-3061) holds a doctorate degree from Harvard University and is a Serra Húnter Associate Professor of Sociology at Universitat Autònoma de Barcelona. Her research work focuses on social inclusion and inequalities faced by migrants and ethnic minorities. Dr. Sordé has participated in many research projects funded by the European Commission, such as WORKALO (FP5, 2001–2004), dedicated to Roma labor inclusion, and INCLUD-ED (FP6, 2006–2011), focusing on educational strategies for social cohesion. She has also participated in IMPACT-EV (FP7, 2014–2017), aimed at developing a permanent system of selection, monitoring and evaluation of the various impacts generated by research in Social Sciences and Humanities. Her main research interests focus on Cultural Studies and Education and her publications include *Perspectives on Theory, Methodology and Practice* (Harvard Educational Press, 2004), *Roma Immigrants in Spain: Knocking down the Walls* (Hipatia, 2010), in addition to articles in academic journals like *Qualitative Inquiry, Ethnicities, Journal of Ethnic and Migration Studies, Harvard Educational Review*, and *Journal of Interpersonal Violence*. More recently, she has published in *Nature* and *PLOSONE*. Dr. Sordé is also a member of the board of the EC European Toolkit for Schools, part of the School Education Gateway. In this capacity she has been invited as a keynote speaker at many cultural events, for instance, OSCE Human Dimension Implementation meeting or at the Great Start in Life Conference, organized by the EC in November 2017.

Marina Tomàs-Folch is a primary school teacher, an educational instructor and a Doctor in Philosophy and Education Science at the Universitat Autònoma de Barcelona (UAB). She teaches in the field of Didactics and School Organization at the Department of Applied Pedagogy at Universitat Autònoma de Barcelona. She has run many research projects (I+D) on the university organizational culture and change processes. She has been involved in other projects on leadership, participation, decision making and gender at the University of Barcelona. She has authored several publications, including over ten books and numerous articles, some of which were published in prestigious international journals. She has worked on several occasions for the Catalan educational administration on school autonomy and management.

xviii

SIMONA SAVA

INTRODUCTION

Towards Collective Capacity Building in a Transdisciplinary Perspective

INTRODUCTION

A definition of 'capacity building' includes a broader approach to other two adjacent topics: development and construction of know-how. Today, 'capacity building' is a dominant concept, but previously it had a more limited use, being popular only in organizational development. The United Nations (UN) (1996) was among the first organizations to define this concept, but their focus was on the idea of 'institution building', seen as an asset for sustainable development. In the last century's '90s, there was an increase in the number of more complex development processes, such as national governments, public and private institutions, NGOs and many more. These complex developments showed the need for new concepts, which were able to address the inner functioning of larger entities and the general aim of sustainable changes. 'Capacity' is believed to be the engine of these latest developments, which are regarded as processes of empowering and enriching existing structures and cultures. In this way, 'capacity building' has developed in four main directions: political, social, organizational, and educational.

In 1996, The United Nations defined 'capacity building' as a long-term process of development, continuously run by all types of stakeholders, like ministries, NGOs, professionals, practitioners, and others. Following this definition, the aim of capacity building is "to tackle problems related to policy and methods of development, while considering the potential, limits and needs of the people" and the entities involved (UN, 1996). Thus, capacity building involves all the levels of a society, including individuals, groups, organizations and institutions, the state itself, and the society as a whole. In other words, it is not enough to train individuals and help them develop, but it is necessary to develop and constantly improve the environments where people live and work, and therefore call for a collective involvement.

Since it was first coined, collective capacity building (CCB) has addressed the community's own capability to prove it can advance towards open and effective governance, which creates the required mechanisms involving all the relevant stakeholders that can design and further implement plans and strategies, which ensure social cohesion and human capital (Simmons, Reynolds, & Swinburn, 2011; Kaufmann, 2013; Scully & Diebel, 2015).

© KONINKLIJKE BRILL NV, LEIDEN, 2020 | DOI: 10.1163/9789004422209_001

Approximately 20 years ago, CCB was first conceptualized and since then its main aims have been (UN, 1996; McGinty, 2002; Craig, 2010; Noya, Clarence, Craig, 2009; Miller, 2010; Harris, 2011): "(a) strengthening peoples' capacity to achieve sustainable livelihoods, ensuring the well-being and the quality of life, the needed infrastructure and facilities for easy access to education, health, culture etc.; (b) A cross-sectoral multidisciplinary approach to planning and implementation, touching the economic, environmental, cultural, social etc. dimensions; (c) emphasis on organizational and technological change and innovation, with focus on fostering network building, on enabling the organizations and institutions to proactively identify problems and formulate solutions; (d) emphasis on the need to build social capital (i.e. voluntary forms of social regulation) through experimentation and learning" (McGinty, 2002).

To reach these goals, it is crucial to build capacity in our countries, in national organizations and institutions, in the administrative system, and last but not least, in people. Networking is a very effective way that can bring together distinct organizations, which work on different levels, and it is also a very convincing way to develop synergies and ensure progress, and finally achieve sustainability (Mischen, 2015; Pierre, 2017). It is clear why many concepts and activities promoted through capacity building include the basic elements of networking, partnership, transparency, and participation. At the same time, they are the fundamental assessment criteria used to evaluate the monitoring methods necessary to establish whether CCB occurs (Pryima, Dayong, Ahishenko, Petrushenko, & Vorontsova, 2018; Keller, Lancaster, & Shipp, 2017; Wood, 2016; Wu, Ramesh, & Howlett, 2015).

Our reflection on what is capacity building is similar to the approach followed when we construct capacity building: it is an interactive multifaceted reflection, which considers wider perspectives and seeks the best ways to achieve successful outcomes for all the players involved.

This principle is followed by academic researchers and also by scientists who embrace topics in an interdisciplinary and transdisciplinary manner. In light of this, the contributors to this volume, with their specialities in diverse fields (philosophy, economy, education, sociology, political science, and psychology), have created an engaging dialogue to bring more light on the complex subject of CCB. The volume shows how scientists from Romania, Germany, Spain, Serbia, Greece, Cyprus, and Latvia aim to clarify complex aspects of capacity building. However, their main research interests concern the impact of CCB on learning, communication and development in political systems. While acknowledging the interdisciplinary nature of their own work, they in fact support interdisciplinary and transdisciplinary perspectives when conducting research on capacity building. Only in this way can CCB be thoroughly comprehended, supported in practice, and increased in different social contexts and practical situations. The essence of this volume captures the current presence of CCB across all social sectors; our approach comes to complement the existing literature on CCB (Craig, 2010), in particular the research dedicated to

INTRODUCTION

how it can be identified, understood, enhanced in a diversity of disciplinary fields and sectors (Stringer, 2013).

As it is increasingly evident that the challenges of a knowledge-based society are more resilient to traditional approaches and the new focus is on how to regulate new skills and capacities, the contributions propose more stimulating reflection and dialogue on how CCB can foster progress in some of the most intricate educational, social, cultural, geopolitical and economic issues today. In light of this, the contributions have tried to address the following questions:

- How can we define collaboration in communication and educational theory and practice?
- What are the tools and the rules adopted by CCB in various practical contexts?
- How can practitioner-researchers develop their theoretical perspective on CCB after their thorough investigation of current and complex educational issues and societal challenges?

In fact, the contributors to this book have been selected with a view to bringing together the insights and perspectives of the experts who have analyzed how capacity building can be activated on all the different levels: on the individual level and on the larger level of the community or the whole society. In the end, capacity building calls for collective impact. Their choice to discuss current societal challenges in different fields, in a transdisciplinary and interdisciplinary manner, illustrates how communication, education, interaction, identity, science, professionalization and others are (re)shaped nowadays. In our knowledge society, friendly and vivid ecosystems can be created only through learning (Jarvis, 2014; Wyszynsky, 2017; Kowch, 2018), founded by their own capacity to integrate all the existing resources and synergies, which are increasingly more technologically facilitated. The whole point is to address all the dimensions of our development (OECD, 2019; Longworth, 2017; Dolata & Schrape, 2016) and ensure nobody is left behind.

COLLECTIVE CAPACITY BUILDING

The conceptualization of CCB is a brave attempt in itself, as the various uses of the term indicate that it has become an omnibus concept for almost anything in every disciplinary field and context; it is often associated with adjacent topics that are related, like the one of community development, capability building, and so forth. It is defined too vaguely and it is inclusive of many perspectives, while its conceptual boundaries are rather blurred (Craig, 2010). Another difficulty in defining the term is that CCB has been applied at different levels ranging from organizations, communities, groups to all kinds of inter-institutional enterprises or partnerships, while its impact may vary from one case to another.

However, there is a real need to address the society's problematic challenges, and, in the end, to ensure that enhanced capacity develops in each individual, who becomes in this way an active member in the society, taking advantage of the services available there (McGinty, 2002). In addition to the individual gains, building capacity can improve the general quality of life or foster "inclusive community change processes" (Walzer, Weaver, & McGuire, 2016), and finally it can create social cohesion and personal well-being (Eurofound, 2018). Our volume is concerned with formulating a definition of capacity building with sound theoretical foundations and well-grounded frameworks of action, so that it will hopefully shed more light on recent complex processes which must be addressed more effectively, i.e. through enhanced capacity. In conclusion, this approach to capacity building has sought a range of solutions for building collective capacities, which are illustrated in this volume.

These complex goals require a 'whole-of-government' approach, a multi-level governance and suitable policy capacity, including competencies and capabilities (Wu, Ramesh, Howlett, 2015; Howlett, 2015; Mischen, 2015; Scully & Diebel, 2015; Pierre, 2017; Harris, 2011; Miller, 2010; McGynty 2002). Furthermore, the collected articles in this volume focus on data driven interventions (Keller, Lancaster & Shipp, 2017; Pryima, Dayong, Anishenko, Petrushenko, & Vorontsova, 2018). They develop a common agenda, oriented towards topics of shared management and inclusive processes. They are interested in developing mutually reinforcing activities and constructing the right administrative capacities or agency, and finally ensuring dialogue for continuous communication to reinforce a citizen-centred democratic ethos, etc. (Wood, 2016, Scully & Diebel, 2015). The real challenge is to ensure that capacity building occurs in our society, which means that people are motivated to participate in social actions and produce the desired policy outcomes (Howlett, 2015; Harris, 2011). Indeed, collective capacity building appears to be at the root of such a broad range of processes of inclusive change and collective learning, which help people "play a larger role in shaping their shared future" (Scully & Diebel, 2015).

"The future we want" or "the trends shaping our future" (OECD, 2019) are topics of increased complexity. Therefore, individuals need to develop a multidimensional empowerment model of capacity building (Eger, Miller & Scarles, 2018), which enables them with control over their own destinies and give them abilities to formulate their new ideas, find excellent sources for their aspirations, personal growth and improvement, which finally helps them reach their full potential. The approach to CCB has been developed as a solution through which such a vision can be translated into practice, as opposed to the traditional instrument of top-down social engineering. The aim of this new approach is to assist individuals, groups, communities and organizations to actively enhance their performance and to adapt to new social changes (Miller, 2010; Scully & Diebel, 2010; Simmons, Reynolds, & Swinburn, 2011; Harris, 2011). However, this attempt is not always successful, since civic engagement is currently in decline. In this context, it is interesting how disengaged citizens show little support for technocratic decision-making while others feel completely alienated by these decisions. This can cause misunderstanding in an atmosphere of conflicting opinions. This is why it is often challenging to build

INTRODUCTION

mutual consensus, to support relationships between differing networks, and finally to stimulate and foster divergent collective action and aims (Walzer, Weawer, & McGuire, 2016).

The conceptualization of CCB is very much driven by a number of theories, such as the social exclusion theory (Pearson), the human capital theory, the social cognitive theory, or the new public management theory, etc. These neighbouring theories deepen our understanding of the mechanisms involved in CCB. However, their main mutual effort is to ensure that capacity occurs in the community, while making sure that inclusive and quality education and services are offered for everyone, which finally increases social cohesion and sustainable development; in other words, the formation of "a coherent policy fabric" (McGinty, 2002; Wu, Ramesh, & Howlett, 2015). Above all, CCB is mainly concerned with the stimulation of collective engagement and commitment.

To stimulate collective involvement, to build functional frameworks of action, and to ensure in this way a suitable collective impact, the programs to be designed and implemented should have a solid theoretical and conceptual foundation, with clear goals, well-defined strategies, and final products that can be immediately delivered (Wanzer, Weawern, & McGuire, 2016). For designing such a concept of collective engagement, there is a set of methods available, ranging from organizing general information campaigns to regular community meetings and online forums, where formal representatives are elected, social networks are established, and individuals are all invited to design new strategies and experience co-leading. Other methods use public gatherings and public debates as the common arena of shared aspirations, and other forms of grassroots and community organizing. Such public events are also meant to "amplify the voice of community members" (Raderstrong & Boyea-Robinson, 2016), to increase their awareness, motivation and responsibility. In the end, they are expected to enhance "legitimacy and support, organizational capacity and the public value", generally known as the three dimensions of the "strategic triangle" (Wu, Ramesh, & Howlett, 2015) used by public agencies.

If the aim is to increase the collective impact of our actions and then to evaluate its effects, there are several factors which are generally involved in this process:

- "establishing a common or shared agenda; utilizing measurement, engagement and communication and providing a backbone infrastructure to support the overall approach within community" (Walzer, Weaver, & McGuire, 2016);
- the focus on knowledge building (i.e. "enhance skills, utilize research and development, foster learning"); leadership enacting (i.e. developing "shared directions and influence what happens"); network building and forming partnerships; valuing the capacity of the communities to achieve their own objectives (McGinty, 2002; apud Garlick, 1999);
- building "strategies based on community strengths, opportunities, aspirations and results" (SOAR) or acting based on a "strategic doing process" (Walzer, Weawer, & McGuire, 2016), by means of informing, consulting, involving, collaborating

5

and co-leading, tested as successful approaches to CCB (Raderstrong & Boyea-Robinson, 2016; Dolata & Schrape, 2016; Bryan & Brown, 2015);
- ensuring a feedback-loop, with follow-up activities, so that the whole process can be repeated.

Waltzer and his research team have thoroughly analyzed the collective impact and have drawn the following conclusion: "rather than trying predetermined solutions, groups should be organized to generate emergent solutions through continuous learning process and a shared measurement system". However, we believe that the collective impact can be also reached by performing social actions together on multiple levels (UN, 1996):

- for enabling individuals to clearly understand their roles and function when participating actively in the society, guided by their heightened sense of belonging to a community (see Chapter 4), which later contributes to their personal well-being;
- for fostering reliable interpersonal relationships, based on mutual trust and other interrelationships between entities;
- for addressing "cross-sectoral issues relevant to all parts of society, state, civil society and the private sector".

In the specialized literature, these factors generating social action are believed to create social cohesion and personal well-being (Eurofund, 2018).

Other solutions for enhanced capacity building are the three Cs process "conscientization – at individual level, conciliation – at the collective level, and collaboration – at institutional level" (Ibrahim, 2017), regarded as the most desirable ways of acting, with a potential to promote and sustain grassroots social innovations. The idea behind this process is to promote real social participation and the empowerment of citizens who have control and power over current social changes (Bryan & Brown, 2015; Ibrahim, 2017) (see Chapters 6 and 7), and also the "power to challenge unequal power relations between local communities and other development actors" (Ibrahim, 2017). In this way, collective capacity is built by specialized social services, collaborative partnerships, collective agency or institutional reforms, and by many others. Nevertheless, in order for CCB to be sustainable, individuals need to be supported and empowered to produce positive changes and to reconcile their interests with the community's general goals (Ibrahim, 2017; Wood, 2016).

The failure to integrate all the perspectives described above can lead to "conflict, confrontation, capture and co-optation" (Ibrahim, 2017) (see Chapters 5 and 6), to the manipulation of the masses by the ones in power, to general mistrust (for instance, the mistrust in the power of science, as illustrated in Chapter 1), to forms of alienation or fragility and finally to social exclusion (see Chapter 2). The presentation below aims to illustrate how the chapters in this book explore a variety of theoretical aspects for broadening the scope of CCB. In what follows, we will briefly introduce the contributions to this volume.

INTRODUCTION

CONTENT OF THE BOOK

The inter- and transdisciplinary concepts of this book seek to further our understanding of general social sciences. The comprehensive theme of *Collective Capacity Building* (CCB) resonates with the complexity of our knowledge society. So, it seems appropriate for such complexity to be addressed by the contributors who work with the theory of CCB in particular scientific fields and who are thus able to build multifaceted discussions concerning this theory.

The contributions to this volume are grouped in two main parts. Embracing more general themes, the first part primarily focuses on an interdisciplinary approach to capacity building. The joint project of the philosophers, sociologists, educationalists, cultural experts, and political scientists in this book offers convincing explanations of how CCB can deepen our understanding of many critical societal aspects. This broad range of approaches to CCB shows how our democratic and increasingly more globalized society can profit from applications of CCB theory. Indeed, CCB is able to reshape our society while facing its new challenges and dealing with controversies that arise every day. The real strength of the CCB theory lies in its quality of reshaping the educational field and many other cultural and political institutions and services. In fact, these are education-oriented contributions that help build our knowledge society.

The second part of our volume is dedicated to the application of capacity building in higher education, since, in our opinion, universities are knowledge producers and specialized higher institutions, which are able to discuss social trends critically, offer plausible solutions, and provide conclusive models of building capacity and acting in our knowledge society. While these two parts of our volume address CCB from slightly different research perspectives yielding particular results, they in fact share a common interest in how capacity can be built collectively. It is evident that all the contributors to this volume agree that there is a need for common commitment, for shared aims and mutual efforts for building capacity.

The first part, "Interdisciplinary Approaches to Collective Capacity Building", presents the contributions of researchers from Romania, Germany, Spain, Serbia, and Greece. It begins with the research question investigating whether science, truth and democracy have been dealing with tough times in their 'troubled marriage'. This question becomes even more relevant in times of fake news and undemocratic developments, in quite a number of countries. The Romanian philosopher Mircea Dumitru, the author of this chapter, traces the complicated symptoms of an irrational fear of knowledge, a kind of epistemic irresponsibility, increasingly more pervasive in our society, which is likely to lead very quickly to a growing public mistrust in the authority of science, truth, and facts. In his analysis, Dumitru argues for a defence of the epistemic authority of scientific knowledge against the disturbing noise produced by voicing indiscriminate opinions. He shows ways in which the contemporary scientific establishment can engage in independent, objective, and dispassionate research, with a view to providing objective scientific input necessary

7

S. SAVA

for grounding the recent research developments in our knowledge society and in our capacity building.

In the second chapter, Ekkehard Nuissl (Germany) raises the question whether the cultural background influences the capacity building of stakeholders and actors involved in differing networks. He argues that 'enculturation' should be regarded as an ordinary process, harmoniously integrated in our daily activities that help us develop our general capacities; otherwise, many difficulties and obstacles are likely to appear. He gives practical examples of how enculturation can occur, but they all argue for the need of a more focused reflection on the cultural dimension in any process of capacity building. In addition, he supports the view that 'enculturation' should be an integral part of all kinds of capacity building.

Sorin Predescu (Romania) continues the same line of research, highlighting the fact that the cultural dimension is always necessary for the development of a community and for an increase in its social capital. Predescu's chapter advocates for coherent approaches in educational and cultural policies, so that our cultural heritage becomes a tool, a context, a space for building collective identity, where the community is empowered with the capacity of self-expression. In truth, education plays an important role in raising social responsibility and the capacity of preserving and promoting our cultural heritage. It also mediates knowledge about our cultural heritage and self-identity and helps us form representations of these two concepts.

In the next chapter, the reputed sociologists from CREA, Spain (Teresa Sorde, Olga Serradell, Esther Oliver, and Emilia Aiello) give a concrete example of a community defined by a strong sense of belonging, i.e. the Roma community. They argue that this community manages to define its self-identity in a Europe that has lost its sense of belonging, now struggling with issues of racism, social polarization, increased populism, and intense Euroscepticism. This article sets out to address this recent challenge, by first reviewing the most significant theoretical contributions that have sought ways to change this social dynamic, leading to a stronger sense of belonging to a community. However, the contributors claim that the change may only occur through a closer and direct dialogue with the citizens. Their main argumentation is grounded in T. Parsons' theories and his critical interpretations.

The analyses of this background can give us a better understanding of the main political changes especially taking place in election campaigns or in massive social protests, which are the subject of the following two chapters. The joint interdisciplinary research of the two scholars specialized in political and communication sciences and philosophy aims to analyze two mass social phenomena that have recently taken place in Romania. Their main research focus is the analysis of mass communication in digital media and through posters. Gheorghe Clitan and Oana Barbu-Kleitsch's hermeneutical analyses of the role of electoral advertising show that political advertising in elections develops our general critical thinking, used as a tool for practical argumentation in our everyday life, which also protects us from manipulation.

8

INTRODUCTION

Simona Bader's analysis investigates the way in which digital media has changed the whole paradigm of communication. If nowadays communication is mainly defined by speed, globalism, decentralization, lack of institutional control, addressability and personal use, these recent changes call for a reinforcement of collective capacity, which in fact is our new civic force empowering us and regulating new ways of doing governance. It is a fact that communication is now represented by '*many-to-many* messages', which not only allows many messages to be sent quickly through viral transmission, but also our collective capacity can be quickly activated. In fact, through this newly built capacity, people are now learning the new lessons of democracy and active citizenship.

Another line of research approached by the contributors from Serbia, Katarina Popović, Maja Maksimović, and Aleksa Jovanović, critically reflect on learning about democracy and citizenship in the new, alternative environments which are created through civic activism. This way of learning is always a kind of community-organized activity, which defines the community through a sense of togetherness and as collective action performed by citizens, who learn the values and mechanisms of democracy through active participation and urban activism. Three theoretical approaches are discussed with reference to these learning practices, i.e. public pedagogy, critical theory, and embodied learning.

While in the newer democracies in the South-Eastern Europe, in particular in Romania and Serbia, affirmative solutions are regarded as ways of strengthening them (see also Koulaouzides & Popovic, 2017), the older democracy of Greece poses other problems for George Koulaouzides and Theodore Koutroukis. In the following chapter, they use Mezirow's filter of transformative learning to advocate that individuals need to master their ability of critical reflection, a sine qua non element, to create new meaning making schemes that will allow them to cope with the challenges of the new societal environments. Their chapter describes the recent structures that have changed our everyday living, while their results have an impact on several major areas of social activity, such as the labour market and adult education. In this context, it is important to understand that our capacity for critical reflection needs to be developed and embedded in all forms of adult learning. Only in this way can individuals be assisted to address directly the recent social changes and the demands that the society requires.

The educationalists contributing to the last two chapters in this part of our volume focus on a number of educational solutions which can enable individuals, organizations, and communities to build individual and collective capacities, for a better development and more sustainable learning.

In sum, the contributions in this first part of our volume analyze capacity building in relation to several urgent and problematic issues in our societies. It is essential especially for our democracy to demand a lot of investment in capacity building. Democracy is a political system of governance, which depends extensively on the capacity of the people and the institutions in the state. Building capacity in people and institutions can be achieved in a variety of areas and cultural contexts, in processes of teaching and learning, in the appropriation of symbols and myths in political decisions, in general forms of communication and education, and, in the end, in the reassurance that all individuals are included in the society and equipped with critical reflection for coping with social developments.

The second part of our volume intends to show that the academia has the very important mission to create knowledge and a fine level education. Therefore, the second part of our volume is dedicated to a detailed analysis of how capacity is built and how it becomes active both in research and in the advanced training and specialization of educators and professionals.

In this light, Georgeta Ion and Marina Tomàs-Folch from Spain investigate the topic of knowledge and how it is produced in higher education. It is a fact that universities are expected to conduct research and produce more knowledge. The new knowledge is presented in the latest research results helping the economy grow and restructuring the existing models related to the knowledge in the academia. However, the authors of this chapter point out that there is a tendency of an unfair development model: while researchers are asked to focus almost exclusively on research and knowledge production, they have very few career prospects. The contributors' focus is on models that should be adopted by the university management, so that researchers may produce better knowledge and conduct more intensive research.

In their analysis of the "Nudging Generation Y Towards Education for Sustainability", Liliana Donath, Monica Boldea, and Ana-Maria Popa, the Romanian specialists in economy, conclude that the Y Generation, better known as the millennials, is expected to occupy by the year 2025 more than 75% of the total labour workforce. Following this estimation, their chapter describes the members of this generation, in particular, their expected behaviour on the labour market, and it suggests ways of nurturing this new generation in the academia, so that their interests harmoniously resonate with the latest trends in business. In the contributors' view, this would mean identifying the latest business trends that are able to contribute to the implementation of a general sustainable development model, which should take into account the attitude of the Y Generation. They conclude that, in general, business success is not only a matter of financial gains and economic performance, but also it can be measured by its positive impact on society, by how it supports creativity, improves our life standards, and our capacity building.

The following two chapters analyze a number of educational offers and the ways providers of qualifications can enhance capacity building for better educational experiences and outcomes. The two contributors from Latvia, Irina Maslo, and Sweden, Mikael Cronhjort, are concerned with teacher training provision in pre-service education, while the scholar from Cyprus, Maria Gravani, is interested in the enhanced capacity building in on-line delivery of educational provision for adult learning professionals. The range of approaches to increased capacity building and flexible delivery in education reflects the different educational solutions developed by new technologies that these scholars have found.

INTRODUCTION

The Romanian educationalists' and psychologists' interdisciplinary contributions to this volume engage with the view that the main aim of universities is to facilitate and improve student learning and their self-development, which means that capacity building is required to ensure the premises for better self-development and academic success of university students. While these contributors are concerned with the issue of mental health, they use the relationship between natural sciences and humanities to analyze the concept of health. Carmen Aurora Bărbat (Romania) grounds her analysis in medical and social sciences and theological studies to demonstrate in an integrated way what are the required capacities to address the "Epigenetical, Bioethical, and Theological Approaches to Health Education".

The contributions collected in the latter part of this volume aim to illustrate the complexity of capacities built by professionals in an interdisciplinary manner, to address educational offers in a qualitative manner, to ensure the well-being of students, and to prepare them for the future challenges of the labour market and the society in which they live. The capacity developed in research is meant to produce knowledge, but it occurs with difficulty, as it is not only about building a complex research infrastructure but also about investing in qualified human resources and advertising the research findings. According to the chapters mentioned above, higher education institutions share a common role, which can only be accomplished by building the right type of collective capacity.

However, a smart specialization strategy developed by universities cannot work properly if the knowledge generated by the university is not fully exploited (see Chapter 9) by the political and business environment (Papamichail, Rossiello, & Wield, 2018; Wyszynsky, 2017). It is therefore evident that a closer relationship between universities and local communities needs to be further investigated and improved. The same effort is needed for "community actors to build inter-organizational networking in compliance with their strategic needs" (Papamichail, Rossiello, & Wield, 2018) and efficiently integrate all the dimensions of a (learning) community (Longworth, 2017).

REFERENCES

Bryan, T. K., & Brown, C. H. (2015). The individual, group, organizational, and community outcomes of capacity-building programs in human service nonprofit organizations: Implications for theory and practice. *Human Service Organizations: Management, Leadership & Governance.* doi:10.1080/233 03131.2015.1063555

Craig, G. (2010). Community capacity building: Critiquing the concept in different policy contexts. In S. Kenny & M. Clarke (Eds.), *Challenging capacity building – Comparative perspectives* (pp. 41–66). New York, NY: Palgrave MacMillan.

Dolata, U., & Schrape, J. F. (2016). Masses, crowds, communities, movements: Collective action in the internet age. *Social Movement Studies, 15*(1), 1–18.

Eger, C., Miller, G., & Scarles, C. (2018). Gender and capacity building: A multilayered study on empowerment. *World Development, 106,* 207–219.

Eurofound. (2018). *Social cohesion and well-being in Europe.* Luxembourg: Publications Office of the European Union. doi:10.2806/261816

S. SAVA

Harris, A. (2011). System improvement through collective capacity building. *Journal of Educational administration, 49*(6), 624–636.

Howlett, M. (2015). Policy analytical capacity: The supply and demand for policy analysis in government. *Policy and Society, 34*(3–4), 173–182.

Ibrahim, S. (2017). How to build collective capabilities: The 3C-model for grassroots-led development. *Journal of Human Development and Capabilities.* doi:10.1080/19452829.2016.1270918

Jarvis, P. (2014). *The age of learning, education and knowledge society.* Routledge: London.

Kaufmann, M. (2013). Emergent self-organisation in emergencies: Resilience rationales in interconnected societies. *Resilience, 1*(1), 53–68.

Keller, S., Lancaster, V., & Shipp, S. (2017). Building capacity for data-driven governance: Creating a new foundation for democracy. *Statistics and Public Policy, 4*(1), 1–11.

Koulaouzides, G., & Popovic, K. (Eds.). (2017). *Adult education and lifelong learning in Southeastern Europe. A critical view of policy and practice.* Rotterdam, The Netherlands: Sense Publishers.

Kowch, E. G. (2018). Designing and leading learning ecosystems: Challenges and opportunities. *TechTrends, 62*(2), 132–134.

Longworth, N. (2017). *Learning city dimensions.* Retrieved from https://www.thersa.org/globalassets/pdfs/city-growth-commission/evidence/learning-city-dimensions.pdf

McGinty, S. (2002). *Community capacity building.* Presented at Australian Association for Research in Education Conference, Brisbane. Retrieved from http://www.aare.edu.au/02pap/mcg02476.htm

Miller, C. (2010). Developing capacities and agencies in complex times. In S. Kenny & M. Clarke (Eds.), *Challenging capacity building – Comparative perspectives* (pp. 21–40). New York, NY: Palgrave MacMillan.

Mischen, P. A. (2015). Collaborative network capacity. *Public Management Review, 17*(3), 380–403.

Noya, A., Clarence, E., & Craig, G. (Eds.). (2009). *Community capacity building. Creating a better future together.* Paris: OECD Publishing.

OECD. (2019). *Trends shaping education 2019.* Paris: OECD Publishing.

Papamichail, G., Rosiello, A., & Wield, D. (2018). Capacity building barriers to S3 implementation: An empirical framework for catch-up regions. *Innovation: The European Journal of Social Science Research, 32*(1), 66–84.

Pierre, J. (2017). Multilevel governance as a strategy to build capacity in cities: Evidence from Sweden. *Journal of Urban Affairs, 41*(1), 103–116.

Pryima, S., Dayong, Y., Anishenko, O., Petrushenko, Y., & Vorontsova, A. (2018). Lifelong learning progress monitoring as a tool for local development management. *Managemen, 16*(3), 1–13.

Raderstrong, J., & Boyea-Robinson, T. (2016). The why and how of working with communities through collective impact. *Community Development, 47*(2), 181–193.

Scully, P. L., & Diebel, A. (2015). The essential and inherent democratic capacities of communities. *Community Development, 46*(3), 212–226.

Simmons, A., Reynolds, R. C., & Swinburn, B. (2011). Defining community capacity building: Is it possible? *Preventive Medicine, 52,* 193–199.

Stringer, P. (2013) *Capacity building for school improvement.* Rotterdam, The Netherlands: Sense Publishers.

UN. (1996). *Community capacity-building.* New York, NY: UN Commission on Sustainable Development.

Walzer N., Weaver, L., & McGuire, C. (2016). Collective impact approaches and community development issues. *Community Development, 47*(2), 156–166.

Wood, D. M. (2016). Community indicators and collective impact: Facilitating change. *Community Development, 47*(2), 194–208.

Wu, X., Ramesh, M., & Howlett, M. (2015). Policy capacity: A conceptual framework for understanding policy competences and capabilities. *Policy and Society, 34*(3–4), 165–171.

PART 1

INTERDISCIPLINARY APPROACHES IN COLLECTIVE CAPACITY BUILDING

MIRCEA DUMITRU

1. SCIENCE, TRUTH, DEMOCRACY

A Troubled Marriage?

We have been told that we are about to get into a time period which is less and less concerned with truth and facts. From amongst several tags that are meant to dub our epoch one may choose "post-truth", "alternative facts", "demise of objective truth".[1]

Frankly, to me all these are symptoms of an irrational fear of knowledge, a kind of epistemic irresponsibility, which gets more and more pervasive in our society. This cultural divide, which opens up in front of us, feeds a moral feeling very aptly phrased by someone who said that "in a time of universal deceit telling the truth is a revolutionary act".

Here there are several issues of utmost concern for all of us who are involved in research and teaching: How are we going to frame the conceptual scheme of the relationships between science, truth, and democracy? What is the role that science plays in a democratic society? Is the standard, traditional values of the objective scientific knowledge compatible with the political values of reasonableness, which are supposed to be the norms for democratic political trade-offs? Could the latter norms for democratic transactions ground the ethos of our claims of objective knowledge, which should be subjected to the close scrutiny of facts? How is it possible and feasible to integrate scientific knowledge and the values that give the real bite of that knowledge with democratic values? What is the role that experts and their evidence-based expertise are playing in a context in which the rhetoric of the public discourse emphasizes in an obsessive manner the concept that everybody – be it an expert or a layperson – is entitled to an equal right to voice his or her opinions or beliefs, regardless of whether or not he/she complies with the epistemic norms of rationality and of scientific reasoning? How is the contemporary scientific establishment defending the epistemic authority of scientific knowledge against the noise of voicing indiscriminate opinions? Have we already reached that critical stage of a methodological anarchism, which Paul K. Feyerabend triumphantly encapsulated into the dictum "Anything Goes"? How dangerous is this critical condition of a fast-growing public mistrust in the authority of science, of the truths of facts, and of the objective and impersonal rules of the empirical methods of science?

It is obvious that all those questions raise very difficult and disturbing issues. And they are symptoms for their existing some serious causes of what I wouldn't be shy to call a cultural malaise. Here is an incomplete list of those causes: the continuous erosion, which up to a certain point is legitimate, of a triumphant scientist vision,

© KONINKLIJKE BRILL NV, LEIDEN, 2020 | DOI: 10.1163/9789004422209_002

which in its heyday made the illusory promise that science is a panacea, a remedy for all our social and political troubles; a simple minded and shallow conception about scientific knowledge, which is on the wrong track committing itself to the view that science could be run in a perfect and purified axiological neutrality; a skeptical if not downright eliminativist conception about our not being able to carry out a fertile and intelligible dialogue or even controversy about the values we share and cherish; but in the same time a shallow and caricatured understanding of the mechanics and the processes of democracy, construed as a kind of soft anarchy; and then again a superficial understanding of the dynamics and progress of science and of its cultural and historic background against which the institutions which create and validate scientific knowledge have emerged and of the complex role that science in general plays in our contemporary society.

Science is based on evidence that is intersubjectively tested, thereby being acknowledged and accepted by the community, which is inevitably elitist, of men and women who produce knowledge. Science works with the classic epistemological distinction between *episteme* and *doxa*, whereas political negotiation and transactions or the speech acts which support our political options emphasize the freedom to express opinions, without insisting upon providing pieces of evidence, justifications or upon making use of methods, which are conducive to truth.

Some people, especially those who remain faithful to the goals and ideals of science, will say that science is the apex of the conceptual, technical, and methodological achievements of our species. From the 17th century onwards, the mathematized sciences of nature uncovered essential truths about the world, and helped create that frame of mind in which one can substitute truths of facts for superstitions and prejudices. All this triggered social and political conditions for more and more people being more educated, healthier, living longer and more decent lives, and being more rational and humane. Of course, the biomedical sciences have had their fair share in articulating and speeding up this very complex social and scientific process.

The seminal role that science is expected to play has remained unchanged so far: it should continue the evolution sketched above; it is supposed to engage in free, objective, and dispassionate research, resisting any attempt to distort the facts motivated by a dubious or unjustified moral, political or religious agenda. Of course, today, in agreement with the morals that one can extract from the new philosophy of science, which is informed by a sociological and an historical perspective which presents the institution of science in a more concrete and credible way, endorsing the values and the ideals of science does not boil down anymore to keeping away science from axiology, and to insisting that research should be free of any moral constraint whatsoever. Quite contrary, they should insist on finding out facts and truths, and they should stay away from using immoral methods, which upset human rights and dignity and also the rights of those nonhuman animals whom they interfere with in labs and in some other contexts of our life.

On the other hand, our political, moral, and religious beliefs should not distort either the way we frame and articulate our scientific projects or the assessment of the evidence in favour of the conclusions drawn from the scientific research. One should not censor the questions and the problems raised in the process of research through the ideals or through the fears or the prejudices, which are prevalent at any given time in our society. And we should not be complacent accepting uncritically everything that is convenient and conventional among our peers especially when those widespread beliefs are severely undermined by lack of strong compelling evidence and reasons. The Kantian imperative *"Sapere Aude!"* has the same force now as it has had since Kant pronounced it at the dawn of the European Enlightenment. (One should dare using his or her own mind!) A complete formation of our students, as members who enjoy the full spectrum of rights and obligations in the society, is achieved not only through their training as specialists but also through the development of their critical thinking and attitude, through their constant struggle to get out from their intellectual and moral infancy and to emancipate themselves from a state of tutelage, as Kant himself put it. Deep down, at the very roots of things, we know that from the lesson of modernity, the epistemic values of truth, scientific honesty and deontology are intrinsically intertwined with the moral values of the public good and with the righteousness of our attitudes and deeds. Genuine knowledge does not occur in an ethical vacuum, since the Truth and the Good/Right are two facets of the same human condition: The Truth is for knowledge what the Good/Right is for action. The Truth is the norm of knowledge in the same way as the Right is the norm of action. One cannot turn the back to the truth and pretend, nevertheless, that one can achieve the social and political good.

What I've sketched so far is an *image* of science. There are people who think differently about science. They see another image or model of science. They believe that the image sketched by me before is just a philosophical myth, which shows nothing else than the vested interests of those who hold the political and the epistemic power in a society and strive to inculcate the idea of a completely value-free and value-neutral scientific knowledge. The aim of this myth is not only that of dignifying what is eminent in science but also, more important, that of marginalizing and of debilitating alternative points of view, which are upheld by those who defy and contest the power. Every decision that people make in what concerns what should be object of scientific research, what should receive financing or institutional support etc. should also strictly observe a set of value norms and judgements. These minimalists or even nihilists of the objective view of science are contesting or even rejecting the legitimacy of the objective concept of "evidence" or "proof", which pertain to the hard core of the realist conception about truth and science. They tend to relativize the outcome of scientific research, claiming that the so-called "scientific conclusions" are always filtered through moral, political, and religious values and convictions, lacking therefore any serious claim to universality and objectivity in the strong sense of those concepts. Moreover, according to the same subjectivist and relativist interpretation of science, the whole idea that science delivers truths about

M. DUMITRU

nature is another ingredient of the same Platonic myth of the universal objectivity of science as a natural kind and as an enterprise which undercover brute facts and "carve the world at its joints" (as Platon put it). What are we going to get out of this relativist image of science? For sure, one rough idea, which is argued for by people like Th. Kuhn, P. K. Feyerabed and the like, is that science is like any other human group (team) activity – be it social and/or political: the scientific establishment is a very efficient and powerful propaganda machine, which serves the interests, not always obscure, of the elites and which imposes upon the underprivileged and the marginalized the views, doctrines and wishes of the powerful. From this vantage point, science works through mechanisms and institutions which are pretty similar to the political and religious institutions which always enforce and reinforce their political and symbolic social control over the oppressed and marginalized masses.

(I can't help making here a sort of ironical remark about this seemingly neo-Marxist critique of science. The dogmatic Marxism-Stalinism supported very much a kind of scientism and positivism. The Marxist dogmatists are worshiping science and they think that whatever is not amenable to the methods and solutions of science is not only worthless but also dangerous political wise or social wise. Science pertains to the essence of the Good, and even the building of a socialist-communist class-free society has to be a centralized and planned scientific process theoretically motivated by high political ideals called, how else! *Scientific-socialism*. What is kind of ironic is that this brand of neo-Marxism that is involved in the characterization of science above is criticizing the very objectivist image of science itself, in other words the image that the orthodox Marxism was worshiping some 50–60 years ago.)

But, after all, what did contribute to the advent of this grotesque constructivist and relativist image of science? To begin with, of course, the serious drawbacks of this ideology which has no real argumentative merits. In addition to that, however, and this is more serious, we have got here a weird situation in which a legitimate and successful criticism against positivism and logical empiricism, and specifically against the would-be axiological neutrality advocated for many years by most positivists, from the vantage point of a philosophy of science informed by the new history and sociology of science, turned itself ungroundly into a demolition of the objectivity of scientific contents and truths. It is obvious that in philosophy positivism is extinct today, and in the humanities in general, with the notable exception of law. But the ravages of this kind of Marxist ideology have eroded massively the intellectual authority that science has deservedly enjoyed and undermined its theoretic credentials in the name of an egalitarian and populist conception according to which all beliefs freely expressed have an equal epistemic dignity and value, in a sort of generalized conversation, from which the normative structure of the society is supposed to emerge in a democratic way.

But then, is it the case that the steady and catastrophic erosion of the intellectual and epistemic prestige of science is something intimately connected to the way democracy is organized and works in contemporary society? Should it also be the case that the values of the democracy get in the way of the values and the logic

SCIENCE, TRUTH, DEMOCRACY

of the development of expert knowledge? Are we witnessing an irreducible and ineluctable paradox and an unsolvable antinomy between the objective truth of scientific knowledge, on the one hand, and the plurality of reasonable beliefs that are of the essence of a democratic way of structuring the social and political values of a society, on the other hand?

What we have got so far are two conflicting images of the role and the value of scientific knowledge in our society. I believe that both sets of views are equally wrong and inadequate, but I am inclined to say that the latter image proved to be by far more pernicious than the former due to its ideological, and more generally, political consequences.

Since we reached this point, it is very natural and useful to make my own position crystal clear. I am not an obscurantist or a negationist in what concerns the social importance and the overwhelming benefits that we all have from the science and technology. Contrary wise, in my capacity as logician and analytic philosopher, educated in the spirit of science, I appreciate very much the beauty and the exactitude of scientific knowledge, of its explanations and forecast, and I am amazed and enchanted by the progress of sciences and of their applications.

Even more to this point, my deep belief is that science constitutes an essential dimension of our European cultural identity, along with the Greek philosophy, and historically, the Christian religion. The objective and impartial search for the truth and for the ultimate essence of reality began many centuries ago in Ancient Greece, when science and philosophy were intertwined. This is why I think that embracing scientism, which leads to the cultivation of science to the exclusion of all the other major components of culture, which pursue the knowledge and the understanding of human values, of subjectivity, feelings, emotions and artistic taste, so, again, embracing scientism, would be a very bad cultural decision. And since one of the roots of scientism is this epistemic dream and aspiration of an ultimate objective and impersonal explanation of whatever is apparent and observable, which seems not to leave any room for human values, subjectivity, emotions and artistic taste, then finding out a way of unifying those two worlds, that of science and that of human subjectivity, emotions and values, is yet a grandiose philosophical project, which is very likely the most important one on the agenda for the 21st century.

Many contemporary philosophers are addressing this vexing issue: how can one make room, in a justified or grounded manner, to the human subjectivity within the framework of the objective, and impersonal scientific outlook about the world? The answer is not obvious, since the force and the success of science seem to depend on measurement, objective observation, and experiment, which all seem to require the abandon of any serious work and understanding of human values and subjectivity. I am strongly convinced that until we can get together in a unified conception the objective and the subjective we cannot claim that we have a full understanding of the Universe and of ourselves, as distinct individuals with an exceptional ontological status, within that Universe. Consequently, until then, we won't have a complete understanding of the science either in this world in which we live.

19

So, why is scientism a deeply flawed conception about science and also about its role and relationships with the other spheres of the human creation? Roughly, this is so because there is no scientific substitute for a full-fledged moral education that we can only get through the humanities and the social sciences; and also because the speculative and the theoretic dimensions of studying the humanities and the social sciences cannot be exhausted and substituted either by a study which is exclusively centred on positivistic values or on postmodern deconstructivism which turns the grand narratives of philosophy and of humanities in general into fictions, phantasies, or sheer ideologies.

Is there an alternative view to those two wanting conceptions? Here it is a sketch of a project of mine, which is work in progress.

There is a metaphysical and an epistemological aspect which lies in the background of this project. It has to do with our species being constantly involved in normative or value judgements in each and every aspect of their lives. The American philosopher Philip Kitcher very aptly called this "the *ethical project*" (Kitcher, 2011) *of human beings.* Building knowledge is part of the project. To strike for a balance between science and democracy one needs to figure out the nature and the role of both epistemic norms (truth, reason, adequacy to the facts) and moral norms (the good, the right, the virtues). This process of valuing different political and social contexts stems from human practices which go way back and were key factors for our ancestors' involvement in this ethical project which consolidated the structure of their society. This is a never-ending project which unfolds with each and every generation. Being a political species and our living together and doing things together being a *sine quibus non* for our social being, all these required a capacity for altruism in our ancestors.

> ... To live together in this way, they required a capacity for psychological altruism. That is, they had to be able, on occasion, to respond positively to the perceived wishes and intentions of those around them, to recognize what another band member was attempting to do, and to modify their own plans so as to help the other realize a goal. Despite the perennial popularity of conceiving animals (including human beings) as inevitably egotistic, there is strong evidence for attributing an altruistic capacity of this kind. (Kitcher, 2011)

The main goal of ethical norms and rules from this perspective is to enforce altruism and to consolidate the moral responsibility of individuals and of the groups to which they belong. Therefore, the ethical project has an evolutionary value and it has to do with our survival as a society. Those practices are distilled and articulated through the requirements or the canon of the public reason, which, in its turn, through the action of a kind of virtuous circle, acts as a validating instance of those social practices themselves.

The whole dialectics which is going on here raises an extremely controvertible issue: is there any substantial role for the layperson to play in the process of science

SCIENCE, TRUTH, DEMOCRACY

validation and certification? To this question one may answer in different ways. We can answer negatively, of course. But that will make extremely difficult to get a compatibility solution to the issue of the relationship between democracy and science. Then, one may answer in the affirmative. And this solution comes in degrees. Ideally, the affirmative answer should not end up in an irresponsible and an epistemophobic kind of relativism.

The radical affirmative answer is one of the kind famously put forward – others would say infamously – by philosopher Paul K. Feyerabend (1978). He claims that one should introduce democratic mechanisms into the very processes of science certification. In his own words: "... it would not only be foolish *but downright irresponsible* to accept the judgment of scientists and physicians without further examination. If the matter is important, either to a small group or to society as a whole, *then this judgment must be subjected to the most painstaking scrutiny*. Duly elected committees of laymen must examine whether the theory of evolution is really as well established as biologists want us to believe, whether being established in their sense settles the matter, and whether it should replace other views in schools" (Feyerabend, 1978, p. 96).

It's obvious that this radical solution won't do it. It cannot work either as a *de jure* solution or as a *de facto* solution. And it is quite natural that when scientists, scholars, and philosophers of science emphasize the importance of scientific research being done in an autonomous way, they fear the worst from this kind of "methodological anarchism" advocated by Feyerabend. Their anxiety to the "mob rule" is motivated by their reasonable reaction against the "Anything Goes!" of Paul Feyerabend.

This is why I find very comforting what Ph. Kitcher says in this regard: "Many people, especially scientists, react to a plea for democracy with alarm. Part of the fear stems from suspicions that democratization, even in the guise of well-ordered science, will submit research to the tyranny of ignorance. It is worth repeating that well-ordered science is deliberately designed to overcome this problem, that it imposes stringent cognitive conditions, and that it assigns an important role to the authority of experts. Moreover, scientific autonomy, like that of other agents, covers many spheres of activity, and it is important to understand just which of these might be threatened. Very likely, the image of the autonomous scientist is a residue of the original commitment to private activity, embodied in the 'gentlemen's club' of the early modern period, no longer apt when Science has become central to the public knowledge system ..." (Kitcher, 2001, p. 118).

This is, indeed, a more balanced view. The idea of a *well-ordered science* (which is Kitcher's contribution to this debate) seems more appealing. The advancement of science depends on constant good epistemic and methodological decisions. And it goes without saying that the experts are the most important and effective decision-makers. To this, Kitcher has the following to say: "These important characteristics of responsible decision making, both in balancing our own lives and in joint activities with those about whom we care, are reflected more precisely in the conditions of mutual engagement ..., and those conditions yield my ideal of well-ordered science. A society practicing scientific inquiry is well ordered just in case it assigns priorities to lines of investigations through discussions whose conclusions are those that would be reached through deliberation under mutual engagement and which expose the grounds such deliberation would present. The society is likely yo contain many different views about how the course of inquiry should now proceed; some, maybe most, of these perspectives may be sadly handicapped by ignorance of the state of the various sciences. Given the cognitive requirements on mutual engagement, that must be corrected. So we should suppose that, in an ideal deliberation, representatives of the various points of view come together and, at the first phase of the discussion, gain a clear sense of what has so far been accomplished and of what possibilities it opens up for new investigation. (…) At the end of this explanatory period, all the participants in the deliberation have been *tutored* (…) The assessment of consequences … will sometimes require judgments about the likely outcomes of pursuing various investigations. Here they will need the testimony of expert witness. (…) Conversation may end in one of three states. The best outcome is for deliberators to reach a plan all perceive as best. (…) Second best is for each person to specify a set of plans he/she considers acceptable, and for the intersection of these sets to be nonempty. If there is a unique plan in the intersection, it is chosen; if more than one plan is acceptable to everyone, the choice is made through majority vote. The third option occurs when there is no plan acceptable to all and when the choice is made by majority vote. That is a last resort for expressing the collective will" (Kitcher, 2001, pp. 113–114).

There are many interesting ideas packed in this long quotation which speak for themselves, and which also deserve a close scrutiny. I'll make very few comments. One idea is that when making decisions one has to keep in mind the actual contingent configurations of science and the needs of the people as they are defined and acknowledged by public reasoning and argumentation. The history of the context is an essential part of the complex mechanism which will causally determine the outcomes of our decision making.

What are then the big landmarks and the meta-constraints for this rational and historic process? Here it is a reasonable proposal, which is rather modest in not being too metaphysically loaded, but rather realist and practical. One may find a defence of this proposal in Hilary Putnam's essay "Capabilities and Two Ethical Theories" (Putnam, 2012, pp. 299–311), in which the author articulates a Deweyan position. The Deweyan response combines two crucial components for a balanced relation between science, with its truths uncovered by the experts, and democracy, with its rule-governed processes of decision making and majority vote taking: democracy and fallibilism.

Democracy recommends this attitude as far as the use of certain argumentative practices in building up overlapping consensual majorities is concerned: *one should strike for arguments which are convincing for substantial majorities, such that, one can hope, the procedure will eventually produce "overlapping*

SCIENCE, TRUTH, DEMOCRACY

consensus". Therefore, one way to go is to set up institutional mechanisms in which experts – i.e., academics, scientific researchers, in concert with stakeholders – i.e., NGOs members, policy makers and so on – would act in a manner which is similar to a voting procedure for public policy matters. However, when it comes to very abstruse scientific matters, one wouldn't expect that all the people who are concerned and involved would take a real vote. Nevertheless, "if their policy recommendation is to be acceptable, they must be arrived at by informed discussion that respects 'discourse ethics' and that tries to understand and makes explicit the concerns of all affected. (…) But it is not to be expected that the result will usually be unanimous agreement, among the experts any more than among the voters. (Putnam, 2012, p. 310)

Does this application of a voting procedure mean that necessarily the weighted overlapping consensus that scholars and policy makers "arrived at by informed discussion" is the right one? It is rather obvious that this cannot be the case. And here one needs the second Deweyan component which brings into focus the empiric content of the scientific concepts, ideas, theories and so on. This is the fallibilist stance. Following Putnam, here it is a sketch of this crucial stance.

Fallibilism: "A Deweyan pragmatist does not propose necessary and sufficient conditions for 'right' and 'wrong', 'reasonable', 'well-being', or any other important value concept. What Deweyans possess is the 'democratic faith' that if we discuss things in a democratic manner, if we inquire carefully, if we test our proposals in an experimental spirit, and if we discuss the proposals and their tests thoroughly, then even if our conclusions will not always be right, not always justified, not always even reasonable – we are only humans, after all – still, we will be right, we will be justified, and we will be reasonable more often than if we relied on any foundational philosophical theory, and certainly more often than if we relied on any dogma or any method fixed in advance of inquiry and held immune from revision in the course of inquiry. In sum, what Winston Churchill said about democracy applies to inquiry as well: fallibilistic democratic experimentalism is the worst approach to decision making in the public sphere that has ever been devised – except for those others that have been tried from time to time". (2012, p. 311)

So, to wrap up the whole discussion. How are we going to balance the relationships between science, truth, and democracy? How could we make this complex, and, on occasions, quarrelsome machinery work in a smooth way? Well, as I suggested, what we have got here is a kind of "troubled" marriage, and in such a marriage, we all know too well from our practical wisdom and realist spirit, it is worth pursuing reasonable compromises. More often than not, we know not only that it is worth fighting for such a cause but one can even get eventually the desired result. And in those public reasoning's and debates we need a lot of patience, mutual recognition,

23

M. DUMITRU

and trust. And it does not hurt a bit of love, as well! Which, of course, in our case, here, is "love of wisdom", that is *philosophy*!

NOTE

[1] Philip Kitcher's books *Science, Truth, and Democracy*, Oxford, 2001, and *Science in a Democratic Society*, Prometheus Books, 2011, Kindle Edition, offered me the proper framework against which I could develop in a complementary way, and some time even in a more polemic way, my own thoughts regarding the intricate and tortous relations between science, truth, and the democratic mechanisms of our contemporary society.

REFERENCES

Feyerabend, P. K. (1978). *Science in a Free Society*. London & New York, NY: Verso Books.
Kitcher, P. (2001). *Science, truth, and democracy*. Oxford: Oxford University Press.
Kitcher, P. (2011). *Science in a democratic society* [Kindle ed.]. Prometheus Books.
Putnam, H. (2012). Capabilities and two ethical theories. In H. Putam (Ed.), *Philosophy in an age of science*. Cambridge, MA: Harvard University Press.

EKKEHARD NUISSL

2. CAPACITY BUILDING BY ENCULTURATION

INTRODUCTION

For the last two decades, the so-called 'cultural turn' has been debated extensively in society and in education. The main point is that culture is now playing a more and more important role in all societal issues, so that everything has to be seen from a cultural point of view. On the other hand, in education we can notice a strong trend to measurement, data, and quantities. Nowadays many things are measured and quantified, which shows that there is a need for an evidence-based policy making in the field of education, too.

If we look at one side of the coin, the cultural one, it can be noticed that new aims and topics are now emerging, like the one of intercultural understanding, which is due to the large amount of migration in Europe and around the world. In addition to this type of intercultural exchange, there is also an opposing trend characterizing those national cultures that return to their native land, such as the cases of Hungary and Poland, which emphasizes a number of essential elements that shape our culture: our language, our behaviour patterns and the values that we share. There is also a coincidence showing an extensive use of the concept of competence, in particular the social and personal competences, which are closely linked to the process of 'enculturation', referred to here as cultural socialization.

The other side of the coin shows a great number of surveys, such as PISA[1] for pupils and PIAAC for adults or the annual OECD, 'Education at a Glance'. The fact is that we establish qualification frameworks with exact measurements of competence levels, we count workloads in ECTS points for students and in ECVET points[2] for vocational learners, as academics we count the points we get for articles in reviewed journals, and evaluations with accurate quantifications are carried out in almost all educational institutions, and surely this also happens in other places. In sum, the discussion before on capacity building supports the claim that it focuses more on data, measuring, and evaluations made according to precise criteria and focused interests (Keller, Lancaster & Shipp, 2017).

At the same time, culture becomes increasingly more important and, therefore, we become more aware of culture, including the culture in education, because all these data of quantitative measuring are in danger of producing gaps in the understanding and sense-making of learning. Culture covers everything which is scarcely measured, or probably not measurable at all, given the fact that everything associated with culture involves human skills and competences, creativity, phantasy, curiosity, and

© KONINKLIJKE BRILL NV, LEIDEN, 2020 | DOI: 10.1163/9789004422209_003

E. NUISSL

learning, which are all hard to quantify and, therefore, any ensuing data is difficult to obtain. Regarding the debate on capacity building, this is almost a blind spot, similar to the approaches in organizational and managerial theories, which focus on structures and data rather than on culture itself. However, structures in organizations can be changed in a short time span, but not cultures; there are even doubts whether organizational cultures can be changed intentionally at all (Bleicher, 2004).

Capacity building is relevant in different contexts, for individuals, groups, organizations and communities: "Capacity development is the process by which individuals, organizations, institutions and societies develop abilities to perform functions, solve problems and set and achieve objectives. It needs to be addressed at three inter-related levels: individual, institutional and societal" ... "Specifically, capacity-building encompasses the country's human, scientific, technological, organizational, institutional and resource capabilities. A fundamental goal of capacity-building is to enhance the ability to evaluate and address the crucial questions related to policy choices and modes of implementation among development options, based on an understanding of environment potentials and limits and of needs perceived by the people of the country concerned" (UNDP, 2006, p. 6), and it continues along the same line: "UNDP recognizes that capacity-building is a long-term, continuing process, in which all stakeholders participate (ministries, local authorities, non-governmental organizations and water user groups, professional associations, academics and others)". In all the contexts cited above, the existing culture is as important as the one intended by enculturation. Nevertheless, this chapter's main thesis and major contribution is that capacity building is not possible without enculturation, i.e. culture is an indispensable element of capacity building. In line with my argument, there is one essential question that requires an answer: What is the exact relevance of culture and enculturation in the process of capacity building?

CULTURE AND ENCULTURATION

Culture is one of the versatile terms difficult to define. Etymologically, the term comes from the Latin language: 'coltivare' means shaping nature.[3] This is, at the same time, the dominant approach to the definition of culture, regarded as an opposition to nature, which dates back as early as to Aristoteles's philosophy, in the history of European philosophy. In this sense, culture qualifies all man-made products, whereas nature only exists on its own. However, in retrospect and with our hindsight knowledge, the matter is much more complex. It is Claude Levy-Strauss who already pointed out that the human being lives in two different systems: they are part of the fauna according to the data concerning their birth, biology and psychology, but they are also part of the society in which they live and which is also their own creation (Levy-Strauss, 1958). This approach can be easily recognized in the following sentence: "Man is a body and has a body". For pedagogical reflections, this is a relevant fact: the dualism between nature and culture produces a dilemma, showing only divisions and no connections, and, thus, it can be an obstacle for sustainable and ecological learning (Bahro, 2002, p. 24).

It is primarily in sociology and anthropology where the debate on 'culture' and the many theoretical and empirical research activities widened our understanding and knowledge of this fundamental term. The following scientists and researchers have some outstanding reflections about culture: for instance, Max Weber concludes that "culture is a pattern of symbols and gives meaning to parts of the meaningless infinity", Margaret Mead identifies the elements of post-figurative, con-figurative and pre-figurative as elements and functions of culture, and Talcott Parsons perceives culture as a system developing next to the social, personal and attitude systems. Combined with philosophical and historical contributions, the scientific literature on culture can be hardly examined. In addition, pedagogy as an academic discipline has contributed surprisingly less to this topic. In the end, there is one very general understanding of culture that we all embrace: in fact, culture[4] is the sum total of all human creations and productions. Baecker (2003, p. 33) takes this even further and shows that there is no definition for culture: "If there is a definitive characteristic of the term culture, then it is the opinion that it can't be defined. Who tries anyway proofs only that he is not up to the term".

On the other hand, the term 'culture' is needed as a heuristic instrument, particularly developed in politics that is why many definitions have been given here. One of the most relevant definitions was given by UNESCO when it started the selection procedures for what was to be included on the world 'cultural heritage' list:

> In its widest sense, culture may now be said to be the whole complex of distinctive spiritual, material, intellectual and emotional features that characterize a society or social group. It includes not only the arts and letters, but also modes of life, the fundamental rights of the human being, value systems, traditions and beliefs. (UNESCO, 1982)

However, in the field of pedagogy, we still need to polish a definition of culture. Our understanding is based on the definition given by Fuchs (2012, p. 65): "In its widest sense, culture may now be said to be the whole complex of distinctive spiritual, material, intellectual and emotional features that characterizes a society or social group. It includes not only the arts and letters, but also modes of life, the fundamental rights of the human being, value systems, traditions and beliefs". In this light, culture must not be understood as a static element in our lives or in societies, but as a dynamic, flexible, and changeable complex of distinct features. Culture is produced by human beings, not only by shaping nature, but through a mutual interaction between the individual and the natural forces, while the human body is seen here as an integral part of nature. Culture is therefore a societal and an individual element, which is part of our biography as well as part of our history and heritage for the future. Then, culture is both visible and invisible, both explicit and implicit. This understanding of culture is essential to a further valuable

E. NUISSL

point: we acquire and produce culture; this is a circular process, during which 'culture' regarded as an object undergoes extensive changes (Nuissl & Przybylska, 2017, p. 22).

Enculturation is the process during which culture is acquired partly by learning and partly by socialization. The way to maximize our enculturation and to enjoy its results is by adopting as many human attitudes as possible, behaviours and beliefs. This takes place both in private contexts, such as the learning of foreign languages, the acquisition of new values and beliefs, the development of personal relationships like love and friendship, and in public contexts, such as schools, peer groups, neighbourhoods, and public places. Furthermore, historical facts become part of our heritage by enculturation, in given social and natural environments. Yet, it is the term 'enculturation' that best defines the process through which the individual is able to acquire culture. Socialization is the process of growing in a social environment, where individuals find their place in the society, but, by contrast, enculturation is the process of socialization with the focus on culture, values, attitudes, and personal behaviour, and it is a lifelong process involving constant development.[5] It is evident that it is closely linked to the lifelong process of learning.

Enculturation is not a process that is received, but a mutual interaction between individuals and their cultural environment. Individuals or groups of individuals produce culture in many ways and they contribute to the development of culture, but they also influence and change it over time. It is due to this mutual influence that societies are perceived as living entities, which are stable, on the one hand, but flexible, on the other. One example would be the women's liberation activities that have been able to change the relationship between men and women in many societies, more evidently in the recent decades, or the production of ICT, which has already caused a kind of a social revolution.

This mutual process of production and consumption of culture is an ongoing activity, most of which is not intentional, as the one stated in the following sentences: "I/we want to acquire culture" or "I/want to contribute to the development of culture"; so, most of this process happens informally, in the family, in peer groups, at the work place, in sports activities, while watching TV or playing computer games, or just while surfing the internet. Each portion of consumed culture changes the production of culture in a quantitative way (i.e. when one requires the production of culture, more offers will automatically appear on the market), but also it happens in a qualitative way (for instance, in fashion, music, etc.). In short, culture is permanently produced and acquired. It is a fact that education plays a limited role in this process of enculturation, it is important to be aware of the limits of education and its characteristic role to sharpen our cultural activities.

Above all, it has to be said that education, in particular educational institutions like schools, universities and also adult education at the workplace and in educational institutions, are part of our cultural environment. They belong to the network of institutions, which is like a cultural skeleton embedded in our environment. This means that the path we take in education, exams, training sessions and studies is

CAPACITY BUILDING BY ENCULTURATION

important not only for our own biography, but also for our individual enculturation. This is true for any form the educational system might adopt (open or narrow, diversified or limited, restrictive or flexible, etc.), but also for the teaching and learning taking place in these institutions. Frontal teaching, cognitive learning, competition and performance orientation create other cultural habits than the ones produced in open learning arrangements, collaboration and creativity. The role of education in our cultural acquisitions does not primarily depend on the content. In the broad sense of 'Bildung', education is not an isolated island, but an integral part of our cultural continent (Bruner, 2006) and the subjective filter through which we acquire the objective meaning of culture (Ehrenspeck, 2010).

Education aims to achieve concrete outcomes, it is meant to obtain knowledge, develop competences and skills. On the other hand, culture is not as well-grounded as education, it is in fact ambiguous, it allows and demands for even more ambiguous results. Culture is acquired in three steps: (a) seeing, perceiving, accepting, (b) analyzing, reflecting, classifying, (c) estimating, valuing and judging.

BUILDING 'CULTURAL CAPACITY'

In geopolitics, anthropology, sociology and other disciplines, it is a doubtless fact that the natural environment influences and partly determines the culture of its inhabitants. Nature and people influence each other: the individual grows the surrounding nature, while the nature determines our knowledge, awareness and emotions. Our language and perceptions of the world are closely linked to the nature in which we live, and so are our behaviour, wellbeing and our daily life. For instance, people living in the Northern countries have many words for different types of snow, but people in the Mediterranean areas have only two such words. People in warmer countries are considered to be lazy by the Northern visitors, because they work only in the morning and in the afternoon, they have a long siesta. They have their dinner very late and share their social life outside, for instance this is best encapsulated in the Italian word 'corso'. Again, this is to say that not only do humans shape nature, but nature itself shapes humans. Culture and Nature are nowadays seen in a complex interaction, there is a process of 'culturing' nature and 'naturalizing' culture (Schiemann, 2011). The nature of culturalization can be seen in simple daily activities, such as giving names to the weather (the storm named 'Hanna', etc.), or talking about the 'felt' temperature (instead of the objective one) and integrating animation of animals in movies. The process of 'naturalizing' culture can be seen in our evaluation of culture as something unchangeable (the opposition between our fixed home culture and the migrants' culture) or as something inevitable. However, very little has been discussed in pedagogy about this mutual influence of culture and nature and how it affects us.

The following concluding line is extremely important: culture is the basis of capacity, not only its background. 'Capacity' can't exist without culture. The very existence of culture and its inner character is the determining element of capacity.

29

According to our understanding of the term 'capacity', we know that its cultural dimension is diverse, but, nevertheless, always basic and effective. In the debate on 'capacity building', there are three major subjects relating to its core theme: the capacity of organizations, the capacity of groups, and the capacity of individuals (Ibrahim, 2017).

Cultural Capacity in Organizations

All organizations of any kind do not only have a structure, but also a unique culture. This is true for both bigger and smaller organizations, for enterprises, institutions, networks, also for the state itself. It was Herder who, for the very first time, reclaimed explicitly a national culture, including in it the race of the population, the country and the state, its history and traditions, its religion, its norms and values and, last but not least, its language. According to Herder, this makes the difference between nations and this was seen as the real foundation of our national identity. At his time, there were many little German states, little monarchies, so Herder's approach (1791/1967, XII/8) was meant to bind them together, not as governmental units but by uniting them through a shared cultural identity, while in the end his purpose was to have these states compete with other more centralized states, especially with those in France.

Nevertheless, it is not only the state, but also the society that is shaped by capacity building. The society itself is part of our culture, it is the environment in which individuals live, so in this way, it becomes a sort of social and cultural framework that we all share. The society consists of material and immaterial elements, perceived as a cultural background and a network connecting us. "Culture is", says Niklas Luhmann (2002, p. 58), "the memory of social systems", in which all relevant social elements are preserved. In light of this definition, myths help us achieve the cultural unification of our social systems, but it is a fact that they are hardly translatable into other languages. Our myths and our idioms and proverbs, the symbolic interaction we perform, the hidden rules we own, the ways of communication and interaction are all fundamental cultural elements, on which a unified society is built. Many such elements decorate artistic creations, for instance statues, monuments and sculptures placed in the public space, are part of street names or special name days and memorials, they may appear in music, literature, and art. Pierre Nora (1984) points out that the 'lieux de memoire' (places of memory) are crucial, either in their physical form or in more metaphorical forms created in literature and in the political discourse.

In organizations, there is a difference made between organizational culture and organizational climate. The climate is more related to the mood of the individuals working there, therefore it can change fairly quickly for the better or for the worse. On the other hand, culture consists of social facts like self-esteem, unshared knowledge, behaviour and rules, organizational style, aesthetics and other elements,

CAPACITY BUILDING BY ENCULTURATION

which are the result of a common history of the organization. All this is related to the philosophy, history and the aims of the organization.

The organizational culture has three main dimensions: the basic one, including the relation to its environment and nature, the understanding of our humanity and the nature of our social interaction; the normative one, including the values, preferences and rules of the organization; and the operative one, including the behaviour, symbols, slogans, a particular jargon used by the organization and its traditions (Schein, 2010).

The capacity of organizations depends on the extent to which they can integrate their cultural elements into the process of capacity building. The existing ones have to be acknowledged and valued, or they have to be intentionally transformed (this will be developed in the section below).

Cultural Capacity in Groups

Groups are perceived as a number of people held together without necessarily the validation of a formal framework, without sharing written contracts or fixed rules. Groups are often formed for the purpose of working together or spending leisure time together, but they always share a mutual aim, which is the first building block of their cultural basis. "We can conceptualize a group, in this sense, as a collection of individuals who perceive themselves to be members of the same social category, share some emotional involvement in this common definition of themselves, and achieve some degree of social consensus about the evaluation of their group and of their membership in it" (Tajfel, 1974). This definition is applied to all kinds of groups, from small groups to ethnical groups, serving as a principle for the society as a whole. Sociologists see a group as defined by the mutual social relationships developed between the group members, by their awareness of the amount of coherence and interaction taking place between them. In a well-defined group, the members develop a group identity, a common speech and group cohesion. This cohesion is essential for developing the necessary binding elements that hold a group together, facilitate more interaction between group members, who thus become more familiar one with another and gain trust in each other.

Without these cultural elements, there is no capacity in the group, and so there is no capacity building taking place. These elements could possibly unlock the potentials discussed in the discourse on the learning cities (Valdes-Cotera et al., 2015; UIL, 2017) and in other studies that analyze the process of networking and how it can become successful (Stegbauer & Häußling, 2010).

Cultural Capacity of Individuals

Our individual identity is in fact a cultural identity, which relates to all the elements that form the cultural environment in which we all live. In this sense, our individual personality is unique but shares the particular characteristics of our

31

E. NUISSL

cultural environment: we are shaped by our personal biography and by the cultural phenomena we all share. This combination forming our individual personality is a long-term marker of our human identity, very similar to our own fingerprints.

This individuality has to be understood in the cultural framework in which it has developed. This can be exemplified with the image of a 'cultivated' or 'well educated' person who has learned the right behaviour in society (for instance, the right table manners), has acquired a good taste in fashion and style, etc. Then other more elaborated acquisitions are made; for example, we are able to associate abstract knowledge, master communication, perform fine interaction, be sensitive to social awareness, or show empathy, etc. Finally, we are able to cherish human values, such as trust, friendship, solidarity, and perform sophisticated mental processes, such as reflection and critical thinking, etc. It is the cultural environment that dictates how this pattern of being 'well educated' is formed. In some cultures, values are more important, in others (a good case in point are the Western cultures) behaviour patterns, good tastes in fashion and style are more treasured (Nuissl, 2017).

In current didactic theories and in the latest analyses of learning outcomes, the cultural capacity of individuals is mainly defined as personal and social competences. It also appears in several qualification frameworks,[6] as the competence of planning, evaluating, reflecting and guiding, as examples of the most elaborated competence type. It is a fact that these competences are highly important in developing our individual capacity, since they can be acquired by learning, but also in processes of enculturation (Bryan & Brown, 2015, p. 3).

BUILDING CAPACITY CULTURALLY

It is obvious that we have to reflect on the role and the character of 'enculturation' as they have been presented so far.[7] Having analyzed several examples of cultural education, we can conclude that it can and has to contribute to the acquirement of culture by developing and sharpening our senses. Opening our eyes, allowing all our senses to be involved in the process of cultural learning, raising our reflective capability – this is the challenge. Capacity Building has to enable learners to understand their own way of acquiring culture.

Culture is embedded in life; life is embedded in culture. Culture refers to the whole person, to the whole entity of groups and organizations. Most of cultural learning happens in informal settings, and it is related to biographical and historical approaches. Enculturation is a softer process, but it polishes the learning outcomes obtained in formal, non-formal and informal contexts. It is true that a cultural way of capacity building relies on the power of learning, the power of culture in all kind of 'capacities'. Without reflecting on the cultural dimension, more exactly, without 'enculturation', there will be no sustainable capacity building (Bishop & Glynn, 2003).

There are a number of principles that generate capacity building in a cultural way, which is seen as part of enculturation. One principle is that no one gives orders,

32

CAPACITY BUILDING BY ENCULTURATION

which creates a less oppressive atmosphere. In this sense, capacity building has to be a bottom-up strategy, even if it is initiated by leading authorities. Another principle, but closely related to the first one, aims to integrate all the people involved and transform them into active participants. A third principle is meant to promote transparent interaction and action and reject all types of secret policies. A forth principle acknowledges our different values and accepts differences. Finally, the most important principle is 'trust'. All the people being involved in capacity building have to trust each other and trust the value of their capacity development. Capacity building in its different forms always relies on a shared community, which doesn't mean that everybody knows the same things and does the same things, but it is important that everybody has trust in the other members sharing the same community.

The basis for capacity building, which does not only refer to a general increase in knowledge but also to better teambuilding strategies and organizational development, aims at the development of a mutually-shared culture and the application of the methods that are appropriate for the given task (Heslop, 2010). Each process of capacity building begins with a reflection on the importance of enculturation for the actors involved and on the role of culture for achieving sustainable results.

NOTES

[1] The acronyms PISA and PIAAC are international large-scale studies on competences, with the global participation of about 30 countries.
[2] ECTS and ECVET points are acronyms for measuring workloads in educational contexts in the European Union: European Credit Transfer System (ECTS) and European Credits in Vocational Education and Training (ECVET).
[3] 'Nature' has also a Latin origin: it derives from the verb 'nascere – natus', which means 'be born'.
[4] This can be easily seen in the handbook edited by Elaine Baldwin, Brian Longhurst, Scott McGracken, Miles Osborn and Greg Smith, in 2004 as an 'introduction to cultural sciences'.
[5] In other contexts, the term 'acculturation' is also used, focusing more on the acquirement of a new culture, such as the one migrants or 'social migrants' need to acquire, during their journey in the society, made in a vertical way (the 'nouveau riche' is another popular term to describe these 'social migrants'). The term 'acculturation' is mainly relevant for the life of adults.
[6] In the EQF of the European Union there is one such category, in the German DQR ('Deutscher Qualifikationsrahmen') from 2012, there are two such categories, including, for instance, reflection, self-esteem as personal competences, team-working and leadership as social competences.
[7] The term 'enculturation' is used instead of 'art education', because 'art education' is associated with the higher culture, the mastering of sophisticated performances in all arts disciplines, such as painting, architecture, theatre, or music, etc. But cultural identity is not derived from objects of high culture.

REFERENCES

Baecker, D. (2003). *Wozu Kultur?* Berlin: Kulturverlag Kadmos.
Bahro, R. (2002). Die Idee des Homo integralis. In F. Alt, R. Bahro, & M. Ferst (Eds.), *Wege zur ökologischen Zeitenwende*. Berlin: Edition Zeitsprung.
Baldwin, E., Leonghurst, B., McCracken, S., Ogborn, M., & Smith, G. (Eds.). (2004). *Introducing cultural studies*. Harlow: Pearson Education Limited.
Bishop, R., & Glynn, T. (2003). *Culture counts. Changing power relations in education*. London: Zed Books.

33

E. NUISSL

Bleicher, K. (2004). *Das Konzept integriertes Management*. Frankfurt/New York, NY: Campus Verlag.

Bruner, J. (2006). *The culture of education*. Krakau: Universitätsverlag.

Bryan, T. K., & Brown, H. C. (2015). The individual, group, organizational, and community outcomes of capacity-building programs in human service nonprofit organizations: Implications for theory and practice. *Human Service Organizations: Management, Leadership & Governance, 39*(5), 426–443.

Ehrenspeck, Y. (2010). Philosophische Bildungsforschung. In R. Tippelt & B. Schmidt (Eds.), *Handbuch Bildungsforschung*, Wiesbaden: VS Verlag.

Fuchs, M. (2012). Kulturbegriffe, Kultur der Moderne, kultureller Wandel. In H. Bockhorst & V. I. Reinwand, & W. Zacharias (Eds.), *Handbuch kulturelle Bildung*. München: Kopaed.

Herder, J. G. (1791). *Ideen zur Philosophie der Menschheit*. Frankfurt a.M.: Deutscher Klassiker Verlag. (Reprint: 1967, Sämtliche Werke, 12 Volumes, Hildesheim: Georg Olms)

Heslop, V. R. (2010). *Sustainable capacity: Building institutional capacity for sustainable development*. Retrieved from https://researchspace.auckland.ac.nz/docs/uoa-docs/rights.htm

Ibrahim, S. (2017). How to build collective capabilities: The 3C-model for grassroots-led development. *Journal of Human Development and Capabilities*. doi:10.1080/19452829.2016.1270918

Keller, S., Lancaster, V., & Shipp, S. (2017). Building capacity for data-driven governance: Creating a new foundation for democracy. *Statistics and Public Policy, 4*(1), 1–11.

Levy-Strauss, C. (1958). *Anthropologie structurale*. Paris: Plon.

Luhmann, N. (2002). *Das Erziehungssystem der Gesellschaft*. Frankfurt a.M.: Suhrkamp.

Nora, P. (1984). *Le Lieux de mémoire – Tome 1: La Republique*. Paris: Gallimard.

Nuissl, E. (2017). "Well Educated" – Pedagogical reflections on a sociological term. *Journal of Educational Sciences, 34*(2), 10–20.

Nuissl, E., & Przybylska, E. (2017). *Kultur aneignen. Vom Erlernen kultureller Identität*. Hohengehren: Schneider Verlag.

Schein, E. H. (2010). *Organizational culture and leadership*. New York, NY: Wiley.

Schiemann, G. (2011). Natur – Kultur und ihr Anderes. In F. Jaeger & B. Liebsch (Eds.), *Handbuch der Kulturwissenschaften*. Stuttgart/Weimar: Metzler Verlag.

Stegbauer, C., & Häußling, R. (Ed.). (2010). *Handbuch Netzwerkforschung*. Wiesbaden: VS Verlag.

Tajfel, H. (1974). Social identity and intergroup behaviour. *Social Science Information, 13*, 65–93.

UNESCO Institute for Lifelong Learning (UIL). (2017). *Unlocking the potential of Urban communities. Case studies of sixteen learning cities* (Vol. II). Hamburg: UIL.

UNESCO. (1982). *Mexico City declaration on cultural policies, Mexico City, August 1982*. Retrieved from https://unesdoc.unesco.org/ark:/48223/pf0000054668

United Nations Committee of Experts on Public Administration (UNDP). (2006). *Definitions of basic concepts and terminologies in governance and public administration*. New York, NY: UNDP.

Valdes-Cotera, R., Longworth, N., Lunardon, K., Wang, M., Sunok J., & Crowe, S. (2015). *Unlocking the potential of Urban communities: Case studies of twelve learning cities*. Hamburg: UNESCO Institute for Lifelong Learning.

SORIN VLAD PREDESCU

3. CULTURAL HERITAGE, IDENTITY AND COLLECTIVE CAPACITY BUILDING

INTRODUCTION

Cultural heritage policies are a result of society's perception on which part of the past is considered worthy of preservation for the future. The key term here is perception and there are ample debates on what constitutes and what does not constitute cultural heritage. For a country in which the importance of cultural heritage was almost exclusively linked to a nationalistic view of history, the re-evaluation of the importance of cultural heritage for a democratic society has become, almost exclusively, a community practice. The bottom-up community pressure has reached an important degree of maturity as there are more and more NGOs that focus on the identification, the preservation and the promotion of cultural heritage, as well as the professionalization of jobs connected to cultural heritage actions. Moreover, the responsibility towards cultural heritage has transformed itself from a vague position into an assumed one, a key topic of public debates and political platforms.

CULTURAL HERITAGE AND COMMUNITY

Although the term 'cultural heritage' appears to be self-explanatory, it contains an intrinsic value, beyond the used one (Babic, 2015), acknowledging here of course an older concept attributed to Riegl (Choay, 2014). Admittedly, the oldest form of exploitation of heritage is the economic one, triggered mostly by tourism, which transformed cultural heritage into a product, a resource to be easily introduced in any development strategy. The economic valorization of heritage has become the hegemonic paradigm of public policies; practices such as labelling, museumification, pastiche and transformation of cultural heritage into a background amusement park for mass tourism have increased in occurrence. Beyond this first level of transformations a second one emerged, one related to the cultural and socio-political value of heritage (Graham, Ashworth, & Thurnbridge, 2000) for the communities who live in close proximity to cultural heritage sites and precincts. The modification of historical representations, the empowerment of communities, and the local or national identity construction were made possible through the deliberate usage of heritage as signifier. The manipulation of cultural heritage for political gains has a rather rich history, which needs no further argument. Lowenthal (1996) amply discusses the capacity of the representations of cultural heritage to change history, the

© KONINKLIJKE BRILL NV, LEIDEN, 2020 | DOI: 10.1163/9789004422209_004

present, or to serve partisan causes. Any totalitarian inclined state will use heritage as an argument of national, territorial, civilizational or religious legitimacy. Similarly, Wang (2015) remarks the fact that cultural heritage conservation constitutes a matter of national identity. The manner in which a nation or a state confronts its history usually finds expression in its heritage policies.

In democracies, heritage becomes far less attractive from a political standpoint, the interest towards a certain type of cultural heritage or the occultification of another is no longer reflective of state policy. The very cultural heritage inventories of historical monuments have become less eclectic and diverse. It is in such a context that the community's interest for its own heritage is sparked, a reaction which best characterizes local rather than national identities, shifting from curiosity concerning local heritage towards community organization and construction of local identity. A democratic culture of heritage can be described as accepting the imported heritage as part of the national one and integrating it with the local identity. It is not uncommon in Europe for heritage landmarks to differ from the actual borders; we have Moorish fortresses in Spain, German cities in Poland, France or Romania, Greek fortresses in Russia or signs of lost civilizations. It has almost become a rule that cultural heritage does not illustrate a national story. At the same time, there are very different communities, with distinctive experiences and orientations reflected in the social capital.

SOCIAL CAPITAL AND COMMUNITY HERITAGE

Social capital is not a new concept. The most widely used definition is adapted from Putnam's study (1993): "Social capital is a term describing those elements of social organizations – social networks and the norms of reciprocity and trustworthiness that arise from them – which facilitate cooperation with the aim of obtaining a mutual benefit".

Social capital is even less tangible than human capital and refers to the quality of the relationships among people within a community, the way in which these people do activities together, abide by collective norms, as well as the degree of trust in the social environment as a source of rights and obligations for the community members. Most of the debates regarding social capital focus on the degree of trust and the models of social network that are typical of a certain community. For Putnam (1993), social capital reflects "features of social organization, such as trust, norms, and networks, that can improve the efficiency of society by facilitating coordinated actions". Both Coleman (1990) and Putnam (1993) consider that trust and reciprocity emerge as the result of common activities that can generate social capital.

Earlier researchers emphasize that a balanced form of the five capitals – physical, financial, human, natural and social – are optimal variables for a successful community development (Dasgupta & Serageldin, 2001). Later, Flora (2004) and Karlsson (2005) challenge this claim and explain, by relying on several studies, the transmission-belt-like importance of social capital among the other forms of capital;

social capital thus becomes the foundation stone for research in the community development area (Soulard et al., 2018). At present, the Network View is dominant, and it distinguishes between Bonding Social Capital and Bridging Social Capital (Larsen et al., 2004; Putnam, 1995). Bonding Social Capital refers to the connections that are formed between the members of a community. Bridging Social Capital refers to the social connections linking one network to another, encompassing social and institutional connections between NGOs, organizations, institutions and representatives of the non-governmental area (Hwang & Stewart, 2017). Bonding Social Capital is described as occurring horizontally (Zahra & McGehee, 2013), while Bridging Social Capital is described as having a predominantly vertical dimension.

Although the concept of social capital is intangible, it is obvious that its variables have consequences. It is well-known that functional social networks as well as a high degree of interpersonal trust lead to an efficiency of social relations and the decrease of transaction costs (Portes, 1998), both having direct implications on the social, economic and political behavior. The idea that through the social capital other elements of social life are affected is a recurrent issue.

It does not suffice to say that the level of social capital is high. This level reflects cultural norms transmitted from one generation to another, norms which cannot be explained as logical answers to current circumstances. Such cultural norms are long-lasting: they allow for short-term interventions, but they also reflect a long evolution of the community. At the same time, these norms represent a significant factor in generating economic and political performance. Associative models can be historically traced back to almost a thousand years ago. Social capital growth precedes and generates community development and regeneration.

Perhaps nowhere as in the issues pertaining to cultural capital is there such dispersed responsibility. The laws governing the national cultural heritage share the responsibility of its protection among proprietors, local authorities and central authorities, which makes it difficult for the community to identify the ones to be held responsible for potential damage to the built heritage. In addition to this, there is the spirit of Romania's legislation which, with revolutionary impetus, has given disproportionate rights to proprietors versus the state, in an attempt to mend a symmetrical disproportion in the Communist period. The fact that responsibility for heritage is dispersed leads to a delegitimization of stakeholders, and their legal impossibility to react results in a loss of the state's relevance in the heritage matter, thus generating a need of community action.

Case Study – How Is Community Activated? Mühle House, Timisoara

Transylvania and Banat (historical provinces situated in the central and western parts pf Romania) have a typically Central-European urban heritage, built according to urban plans used in the Hapsburg Empire and later in the Austro-Hungarian Empire. As the majority population in many Transylvanian settlements is now Romanian, historical heritage tends to be considered allogenous, hence not representative for the current inhabitants, which leads to an almost schizoid way of social representation of towns; the Hungarian town versus the (mainly interbellic) Romanian town, the German town versus the Hungarian town, etc. Although the urban communities' relation to their own heritage may be relatively different – the German, Armenian or Jewish heritage being easier to claim than the Hungarian one – the recrudescence of nationalism has repercussions on the perception of the built heritage as well. Heritage is used by the minority population (German or Hungarian) as an argument for prestige and precedence, while the lack of care for this heritage is perceived by national minority groups as disdain towards the minority group's history and identity. On the other hand, the Romanian population feels the need to continue to Romanianize this heritage with quasi-representative buildings and public monument plaques, with the town of Cluj-Napoca in Transylvania as a case in point. During the 1990s, under a local administration with evident nationalist features, Cluj became a large sculpture park with national significance, a sea of tricolour flags and street signs trying to change the urban landscape.

In Timisoara, the capital of the Banat region, the community's awareness of its cultural heritage followed an unusual trajectory, a trajectory explained by the city's urban history. After the Habsburg conquest, the city was built according to Enlightenment principles: multicultural, integrative and democratic. At that time, the Orthodox (Romanian and Serbian), Catholic (German and Hungarian) and Jewish cultural heritage were intentionally put on equal footing, which led to global acceptance of this multifaceted cultural heritage in the community. During the Communist period, the buildings that are part of the city's cultural heritage were completely neglected. In the 1990s, awareness was raised as to their economic value, which led to a small economic dispute, sometimes with ethnic and racial undertones, a dispute that was facilitated by unclear legislation with regards to retrocessions. At the beginning of the current decade, the danger of degradation that heritage buildings were facing became evident. The social capital of these buildings in Timişoara is high by tradition, being underscored by the exceptional character conferred to the city and its architecture by the 1989 revolution. The community's increased awareness of the importance of cultural heritage had two causes: the intentional destruction of a building with high significance for the denizens (the destruction of the Mühle house, which used to belong to an important city florist, the creator of the parks that define Timişoara) and the coming of age of a new generation, graduates of the Faculty of Architecture of the Polytechnic University of Timişoara. The destruction of the Mühle house in 2013 showed the community the danger that threatens the architectural heritage of the city, as well as the inefficiency of the state in dealing with this case, raising the awareness of both amateurs and experts in the field. There were public protests, the picketing of the Mühle house being organized by a series of NGOs and individuals who were discovering cultural heritage as subject to community action. The effect of this was that Timişoara today has the most significant community involvement in relation to architectural heritage. The

CULTURAL HERITAGE, IDENTITY AND COLLECTIVE CAPACITY BUILDING

quantification of community concern for issues of cultural heritage is possible. In the past couple of years, over 30 NGOs that focus on architectural heritage, dozens of TV and radio shows, exhibits, qualification sessions for rehabilitators, social media pages, guided tours, community actions related to cultural heritage have cropped up. Issues related to cultural heritage are undergoing a collaborative phase, in which alliances and partnerships that operate locally and nationally appear. Several contextual factors create a hospitable atmosphere for this type of discourse: an older symbolic confrontation between centre-margin (Timişoara – Bucharest) in which cultural heritage is proof of prestige, increased urban and suburban development, contrasting with incapacity to rehabilitate heritage buildings, and with a higher social capital, as well as pre-existing associative reflexes respectively.

The currency of cultural heritage topics in public discourse has an important educational component as well. If cultural heritage is, naturally, a topic more relevant to experts in the field – Smith describes it as a hegemonic topic of authorized discourse in the field of cultural heritage (2006), which is, inevitably, a minority discourse – in the case of Romania, the relative absence of institutional discourse has democratized and educated community discourse related to cultural heritage. The example of the Mühle house encouraged the protection of local cultural heritage: professional associations of young architects or heritage enthusiasts became organizations dedicated to saving the rural and balneary architectural heritage of the Banat region; wooden churches, stone towers or watermills in Banat benefited from reinforcement and safety assurance actions put into motion by donations; public awareness raising and architectural heritage promotion projects became the focus of Romanian and European documentaries.

In the context of vague legislation and of institutions for the protection of cultural heritage with limited powers, the only option to save and protect cultural heritage is raising awareness within the community, along with developing the ability thereof to understand and act. Empowering local people, who are the true guardians of cultural heritage, ensuring their right to democratically take part in the management of cultural heritage is the only way to preserve it long term in the face of degradation and of the pressure of modernity. This practice first started four decades ago in France where it proved useful, cultural heritage becoming there one of the community's most important concerns. Referring to the same practice, Babic (2015) introduced the concept of Heritage Literacy, similar to that of Citizenship Literacy, which includes it. Heritage Literacy represents the idea of a systematic global lifelong method through which an individual or a group has the guaranteed and inalienable right to participate, benefit from and use cultural heritage as it is defined. Implemented by individuals or communities, it represents an attachment to universal human values and the condition for city development towards common prosperity. Thus, the need for education about cultural heritage becomes essential.

Even though cultural heritage does not feature in the policies of the European Union, it can become an important liaison between member states, as was shown by the success of the European year of cultural heritage, 2018. Architectural heritage is essentially local and rehabilitation policies are perhaps the only ones aimed at local communities. European projects that propose the rehabilitation of cultural heritage are embraced with enthusiasm by communities because it is specifically addressed to them. National and local prestige is reinforced and described by rehabilitated heritage because cultural heritage seems (although it is not always so) community specific. Additionally, the destruction of cultural heritage is seen as an attack on community identifies (Rountree, 2012) and tends to be a risk factor in administrative and economic decisions.

COLLECTIVE CAPACITY BUILDING AND HERITAGE EDUCATION

Collective Capacity Building is a concept strongly connected to educational reform, a concept which has extended from the idea of training teachers for change to the idea of Learning Organization (Mitchell & Sackney, 2000) and, subsequently, to that of Learning Community and Deep Cultural Change. Fullan (2010) suggests that the process called Building Capacity refers to the accumulation of competencies, resources and motivation in the community. Community Learning is thus an educational vision of community which suggests that the success of a community depends of its capacity to learn and use gained knowledge (Harris, 2011). This vision is relatively romantic, but capable of producing change in other areas of community development. Collaboration between institutions, organizations and other members of the community is based on sharing knowledge and representations. Melucci (1996) defines public space as ambivalent because it has a double meaning: that of presentation – of interests – and that of representation, the latter having more deeply entrenched cultural and communal roots.

The public space is represented with a high degree of variety. Its representation becomes more or less varied according the autonomy it has been granted (Melucci, 1996). The public space is defined as a flexible space of representation which can remain open and functional only through a close relationship between collective action and institutional action.

It is essential to have historical and technical knowledge in order to represent cultural heritage. Unlike the educational system that is the subject of numerous reforms, cultural heritage has gone through very few changes of public policies at national or European levels, as it is a rather marginal topic in the public discourse. If most changes in education tend to be top-down, where community capacity building is in fact a mixed form of coping and resilience, when it comes to cultural heritage, the changes follow exactly the opposite direction: bottom-up, while the term of collective capacity building refers to the professionalization of the community actors with reference to cultural heritage. The interest in heritage always begins with a rediscovery of history, with a re-evaluation of our identity, and with an admiration for past achievements. It is a fact that a deep understanding of the subjects related to cultural heritage is the basic condition for developing collective action in this field. Any collective action related to cultural heritage begins with this type of knowledge, which is both a trigger and an indicator of the interest the community has in its heritage. The fact that the press approaches the subject of heritage quite often and then there is a variety of other sources that inform the public about their cultural heritage, and finally the subject becomes more popular in social media is the first step leading to a reformation of local and national policies regarding cultural heritage. Choay (2014, p. 50) discusses three main possibilities for heritage preservation: firstly, education and formation; secondly, the ethical use of our long-lived public legacy, i.e. our cultural heritage; thirdly, our collective participation in the creation of a lively cultural heritage.

In this light, it is essential that we build a coherent strategy for developing our educational capacity related to the topic of cultural heritage. In Romania, there is no coherent approach to education for cultural heritage in the public educational system. As it has been shown above, the topic of cultural heritage is already very much debated at the level of community, but since there is no overall coherent strategy about how it should be approached, the subject can be easily steered towards a politized and anti-democratic approach, thus changing it into a political actor. Such tendencies are already evident, since there is no systemic education as regards heritage, which can lead to a host of differing representations of its value even within the same community that oscillates between sheer ignorance and an acute sense of symbolic hyper-evaluation.

IDENTITY

In the 21st century, the construction of our identity has become increasingly fluid. Geographic, social, and linguistic mobility has eroded the classical factors involved in identity construction: the neighbourhood, the social class, and monolingualism. Our identities are changing at the same speed with which our social roles are changing, although identify is a stable term by definition. Nevertheless, we still feel the need to relate to a natural, anthropic environment, which remains inscribed in the individual's affective memory. The anthropic environment overlaps to a great extent with the environment of cultural heritage, because this type of environment is specific to a particular space.

The current interest in culture and cultural signification is supported by an increasingly more actual debate on collective and individual identity, which encompasses a wide range of subjects in social sciences (Melluci, 1996). Their interest is specifically focused on critical approaches to aspects of continuity and discontinuity regarding the identification and multiplication of identity in its varied forms in our contemporary society (White, 1992; Burke, 1992).

Tangible cultural heritage is concerned with this fascination of reinterpretation and re-signification. More exactly, this is a process of 'pastpresenting' (Macdonald, 2013), during which the past gets the present involved in an active process of remembering and forgetting. Once the signification of cultural heritage has been created, it begins to relate to the needs and aspirations of the present (Smith, 2006), which inevitably takes us back to the definitions of a collective and individual understanding of cultural heritage (Graham, Ashworth, & Tunbridge, 2000). The sense of place is determined both by a conceptual understanding of cultural heritage and a direct contact with the space inhabited by the cultural heritage. Therefore, cultural heritage is not only a constructor of sense and identity but also a supporter for our positioning as a nation, a community and an individual, helping us to find our own cultural, social and geographical place (Smith, 2006, p.49). Chaoy (2014) further supports this point claiming that "standardized products of techno-science, artificially built in the geophysical space of our planet, cannot by any means replace the unreplaceable diversity of cultural heritage [...] to which a wide range of earthly cultures has contributed in time".

The topic of identity gives direction to the community and helps it to relate to itself. Community capacity building is one essential factor defining this identity built around the sense of place and its corresponding environment. The 21st century seems to reopen discussion about historical destines and national ethos, while cultural heritage has an important role to play in supporting our national exceptionalism. As always, the only suitable answer to sheer ignorance is education.

CONCLUSIONS

In this chapter, I have attempted to explain the importance of cultural heritage for the community. In the past years, cultural heritage has turned from a topic preferred by the elite and experts into an object representing the community, from a scientific niche into the educational mainstream, and from a symbolic value into an experiential asset. In addition to the economic value of cultural heritage, it also has an identity value, which contributes to an increase in the social capital of the community and the redefinition of its aims. In the end, the need for serious education about heritage is both generated by the interest in the subject but also by the fact that heritage is a main component of our civic education.

A change in our attitude to cultural heritage follows a number of steps that also take place in processes of community development: informing, experience, representation, and action. For Romania, heritage preservation is essential for its self-definition, since its past remnants show the way in which its future will be shaped. This change is inevitable only if our future challenges are connected to the capacity of our educational system to steer this change and maintain it in its democratic and participative form. The educational system is required to contribute to the constructions of new representations and identities and to increase the capacity of the population to relate to the physical environment in which they live and, in this way, become closer and more faithful to it. At the same time, it is essential that this system should be able to understand and reflect on the subject of cultural heritage, so that it can be part of a democratic discourse rather than become an argument supporting a political identity.

CULTURAL HERITAGE, IDENTITY AND COLLECTIVE CAPACITY BUILDING

REFERENCES

Babic, D. (2015). Social responsible heritage management- empowering citizens to act as heritage managers. *Procedia Social and Behavioral Science, 188*, 27–34.

Burke, P. (1992). We, the people: Popular culture and identity in modern Europe. In S. Lash & J. Friedman (Eds.), *Modernity and identity* (pp. 293–308). Oxford: Blackwell.

Choay, F. (2014). *Patrimoniul la răscruce, antologie de luptă.* Bucureşti: Ozalid.

Coleman, J. S. (1990). *Foundations of social theory.* Cambridge, MA: Harvard University Press.

Dasgupta, P., & Serageldin, I. (2001). *Social capital. Multifaceted perspectives.* Washington, DC: World Bank Publications.

David, L. (1996). *Possessed by the past: The heritage crusade and the spoils of history.* New York, NY: Free Press.

Flora, C. B. (2004). Community dynamics and social capital. *Agroecosystems Analyses*, 93–107.

Fullan, M. (2010). *Motion leadership.* Thousand Oaks, CA: Corwin Press.

Harris, A. (2011). System improvement through collective capacity building. *Journal of Educational Administration, 49*(6), 624–636.

Hwang, D., & Stewart, W. P. (2017). Social capital and collective action in rural tourism. *Journal of Travel Research, 56*(1). 81–93.

Karlsson, S. E. (2005). The social and the cultural capital of a place and their influence on the production of tourism – A theoretical reflection based on an illustrative case study. *Scandinavian Journal of Hospitality and Tourism, 5*(2), 105–115.

Larson, L., Harlan, S. L., Bolin, B., Hackett, E. J., Hope, D., Kirby, A., ... Wolf, S. (2004). Bondig and bridging: Understanding the relationships between social capital and civic action. *Journal of Planning Education and Research, 24*(1), 64–77.

Macdonald, S. (2013). *Memorylands: Heritage and identity in Europe today.* Abingdon: Routledge.

Melucci, A. (1996). *Challenging codes: Collective action in the information age.* Cambridge: Cambridge University Press.

Mitchell, C., & Sackney, L. (2000). *Profound improvement: Building capacity for a learning community.* Lisse: Swets & Zeitlinger.

Portes, A. (1998). Social capital: Its origins and applications in modern sociology. *Annual Review of Sociology, 24*, 1–24.

Putnam, R. D. (1993). *Making democracy work: Civic traditions in modern Italy.* Princeton, NJ: Princeton University Press.

Putnam, R. D. (1995). Bowling alone: America's declining social capital. *Journal of Democracy, 6*, 65–78.

Rountree, K. (2012). Tara, the M3, and the Celtic Tiger: Contesting cultural heritage, identity, and a sacred landscape in Ireland. *Journal of Anthropological Research, 68*(4), 519–544.

Soulard, J., Knollenberg, W., Boley, B. B., Perdue, R. R., & McGehee, N. G. (2018). Social capital and destination strategic planning. *Tourism Management, 69*, 189–200.

Smith, L. (2006). *Uses of heritage.* London: Routledge.

Wang, R. W.-C. (2015). Culture heritage and identity – Some cases in Taiwan on the protection of cultural heritage. *The International Archives of the Photogrammetry, Remote Sensing and Spatial Information Sciences.* Retrieved from https://www.int-arch-photogramm-remote-sens-spatial-inf-sci.net/XL-5-W7/539/2015/isprsarchives-XL-5-W7-539-2015.pdf

White, H. C. (1992). *Identity and control: A structural theory of social action.* Princeton, NJ: Princeton University Press.

Zahra, A., & McGehee, N. G. (2013). Volunteer tourism: A host community capital perspective. *Annals of Tourism Research, 42*, 22–45.

Zhang, R., & Smith, L. (2019). Bonding and dissonance: Rethinking the interrelations among stakeholders in heritage tourism. *Tourism Management, 74*, 2012–2023.

TERESA SORDÉ, OLGA SERRADELL, ESTHER OLIVER,
EMILIA AIELLO AND GARAZI LÓPEZ DE AGUILETA-JAUSSI

4. RECOVERING PARSONS THROUGH ROMA'S VOICES FOR CONSTRUCTING EUROPEAN SOCIETAL COMMUNITY

INTRODUCTION

The crisis of credibility for European institutions, the rise of racism in some European countries and the social and economic crisis of recent years express a weak sense of belonging among the European Community (de Wilde & Trenz, 2012; Outhwaite, 2014; Scalise, 2015). To tackle this challenge, it is necessary to review theoretical contributions that help to understand how it is possible to change this dynamic and to construct a strong sense of belonging to the same community. Scholars in sociology are performing analyses in this regard, opening a fruitful and egalitarian dialogue with citizens to explain these kinds of processes (Burawoy, 2004; Soler-Gallart, 2017). One of these analyses focuses on the Roma community as an ethnic minority that serves as an example of a community characterized by a strong sense of belonging. The analysis that we offer below is an excellent example of collective capacity building because it allows us to reflect on the construction of a sense of belonging, which is linked to aspects that are sufficiently abstract so as to allow the creation of strong links between very diverse people in a framework like the European one.

According to the FRA EU-Minorities and Discrimination Survey (2009), the Roma are one of the most discriminated-against ethnic minorities in Europe. Self-proclaimed as a people without a territory (Sordé, Flecha, & Alexiu, 2013), the Roma are recognized as a transterritorial community spread across countries and nation-states. However, after more than five centuries of living in Europe, discrimination, poverty and social exclusion have led to their being invisible at different societal levels and to the European scientific community (Munté, Serradell, & Sordé, 2011; Clough Marinaro, 2017). Recent data have evidenced that an important percentage of 10–12 million Roma who live in Europe are facing marginalized situations in both rural and urban areas. They have restricted access to high-quality education and poor integration into the labour market, and they also receive lower-quality health care than the non-Roma population (European Commission, 2010; Amador, Flecha, & Sordé, 2018). Drawing from Parsons' concept of the societal community and going beyond it, the main objective of this chapter is to contribute new scientific

© KONINKLIJKE BRILL NV, LEIDEN, 2020 | DOI: 10.1163/9789004422209_005

knowledge regarding Roma's contributions to the construction of the concept of a European Societal Community.

For Talcott Parsons (1969a), the societal community was the integrative subsystem that unified the economic, political and cultural subsystems, setting the common norms under which all members of society could feel identified. From this perspective, democracy requires that all individuals and diverse groups that constitute the societal community respect a common normative frame. Parsons noted the European challenge to build a societal community based on a moral imperative among people of different ethnicities, cultures and religions, in contrast to the United States. He was inspired by the US Civil Rights Movement of the 60s to develop the concept of the societal community and to make such statements in his more recent works. However, there has not yet been a similar consistent theoretical reflection and development that focuses on the Roma in Europe. Jürgen Habermas (1996a) wrote about the communicative turn of the societal community to face the theoretical challenges of European integration, but he did not correctly capture (and did not cite) the potential in Parsons' concept of the societal community; he proposed instead the concept of "constitutional patriotism". This chapter will take the lead in adding to this scientific and theoretical debate by analyzing the Roma contributions studied under the RTD Framework Programme V WORKALO project The Creation of New Occupational Patterns for Cultural Minorities: The Gypsy Case (2001–2004).

To achieve this purpose, the chapter is structured in three main sections. First, a theoretical review has been conducted to reflect on Parsons' concept of the societal community and its possible implications for European society. Second, Roma's contributions to a European Societal Community have been collected and classified in two main parts: barriers faced by the Roma people in the construction of a European Societal Community and the enabling conditions that make such barriers possible. The chapter ends by discussing its main contributions and proposing directions for future research in this field.

THEORETICAL REVIEW

This section is divided into three parts. First, we reveal the contribution of Talcott Parsons regarding the societal community, which was inspired by the US Civil Rights Movement (Parsons, 1969a). Second, we reflect on how, in European academic debates, Parsons' concept has not been fully understood and therefore has not been interpreted as Parsons intended. Finally, this theoretical review ends with an open question about the possibility of taking Roma's contribution into account in constructing a European Societal Community.

Parsons (1969a) developed his concept of the societal community in the 60s and 70s, inspired by the Civil Rights Movement in the US. He mentioned societal community as a subsystem for the first time in *The Social System* (Parsons, 1969b), describing how African Americans had managed to change the understanding of citizenship in the United States and the creation of the American societal community. In Parsons' words, "the concept of citizenship, as used here, refers to full membership in what shall I call the societal community" (Parsons, 1969a, pp. 709–710). This work was notable because Parsons presented his analysis of how African Americans achieved full citizenship by drawing on the essential right to equality, thus becoming full members of the American societal community. Parsons (1977b) treated integration as one of the main problems of modern societies and considered the societal community to be the integrative subsystem that unifies the other (economic, political and cultural) subsystems. In fact, Parsons argued that the societal community is the core of society in which people are associated (Parsons, 1977a). He defined the societal community as follows:

> The core structure of a society I will call the societal community. More specifically at different levels of evolution, it is called tribe, or "the people" or for Classic Greece, polis, or for the modern world, nation. It is the collective structure in which members are united or, in some sense, associated. Its most important property is the kind and level of solidarity – in Durkheim's sense – that characterizes the relations between its members. (Parsons, 1968, p. 182)

Its main function is to establish common rules on the basis of a moral consensus whereby people belonging to a society can feel identified with it. From this perspective, democracy requires that all individuals and cultural groups within a society respect a common regulatory framework (Parsons, 1978). Parsons (1977b) classified the "societal community" as a subsystem because of the importance of its internal organization. The societal community is based on a system of collective rules that govern social cohesion. Referencing Weber (1946), Parsons considered that the societal community forms a system of legitimate order, in other words, a regulatory system that is required to maintain the social order. Habermas (1984) also deepened the concept of the societal community from a communicative perspective. However, he did not consider the latest theoretical contributions of Parsons, and he focused on the conceptualization of "constitutional patriotism" (Habermas, 1996a). Specifically, Habermas misunderstood the analysis of Parson's concept of expressive revolution.

Industrial, democratic and educational revolutions were social processes that separated the economy, policy and culture subsystems from the origins of the societal community in Parsons' contribution. In his book *Action Theory and the Human Condition,* Parsons (1978) exposed how expressive revolution unified the other three subsystems through other new integrative social systems. However, Habermas (1987) thought that this expressive revolution would reproduce patterns similar to those in previous revolutions and lead to another separated system, in contrast to Parsons' idea that expressive revolution would lead to an integrative social system.

Habermas (1996a) stressed the consciousness of belonging to a society that does not condemn part of a set of destination but respects the universal principles of a democratic constitution. According to this analysis, it was no longer possible to create a citizenship based on a country connected to a unique language, origin, culture and territory. Rather, the sense of belonging to a community is linked to principles of coexistence held in common by people from different backgrounds, languages and cultures. He continued to strengthen his argument regarding constitutional patriotism as a solution for Europe by arguing that such a system would prevent the promotion of the type German patriotism that had led to so many atrocities. Thus, he affirmed the necessity of Europeanization and democratization as cohesive elements (Habermas, 1996b). In that reflection, Habermas forgot the effects of German patriotism on vulnerable groups such as Roma. Thus, Roma researchers have recently contributed their own analysis, which includes two main aspects: (1) that Roma people were victims of the Nazi genocide in conjunction with the Jewish people and (2) the shaping of Roma identity is unrelated to a territory but is based on common principles and values (Sordé et al., 2013).

Other conceptualizations of the societal community have considered contributions from different theoretical perspectives: dual, systemic and subjectivist. The dual perspective includes the influence of the system and the action of subjects' analysis in understanding how society is constructed. In this regard, Merton (1975), who combined both perspectives, has had a wide influence on social analyses. On the other hand, Berger (2008), following a systemic overview, contributed to this discussion with his analysis of religion and the existing differences between Europe and the United States. According to him, in Europe, it is more difficult to understand Parsons' concept of the societal community because there are more conflicts caused by the non-recognition of religious diversity and the cliché of secularization as a feature of advanced societies. In the United States, it was possible to better articulate this conflict because religious pluralism has nearly always been respected, which has fostered a more general moral consensus (Berger, Davie, & Fokas, 2008). This statement implies that it is possible to create the conditions required to maintain solidarity as an integrative principle of the societal community, enabling all members of the different groups to be equally involved in the different subsystems.

Despite these remarkable contributions, Parsons provided the most useful insights into the reasons for the difficulty in Europe in developing a shared sense of belonging. He compared the level of development of the societal community in Europe and the United States and, using the example of religion, concluded that the societal community would be easily developed in the United States, whereas in Europe, the lack of religious plurality would be an added difficulty in achieving a common moral ground (Parsons, 1977b). The inclusive component in Parsons' proposal is universal tolerance, which creates a fluid political structure more focused on the interests of groups than on specific issues (religion, ethnicity, etc.).

However, Parsons did not know about the efforts made by several groups to create a common sense of belonging. Roma are an example, because they are not apart from the economy, politics and culture or the societal community. Indeed, they are helping to transform the European societal community, as was observed when the Roma were recognized by the European Parliament (Aiello, Mondéjar, & Pulido, 2013). Roma are one of the most important cultural minorities present across Europe, and their identity is not linked to a specific territory or nation; instead, they share identity values beyond such frontiers. Based on this premise, it is possible to construct a societal community in Europe; taking Roma as example, such a community should be based on an egalitarian dialogue in which all voices are heard and acknowledged. This is how a collectively developed moral frame can be prioritized with other factors, and a system of institutionalized values can be created from the principle of equality of differences (Flecha, 2000).

From this perspective, a societal community is possible that includes all voices, thus strengthening the other three subsystems and the social system. Simply by consolidating the societal community, it is possible to provide a centralized fiduciary system and the norms that are needed for communal validity. Each person could feel the responsibility of loyalty to every individual and at the same time to diverse groups belonging to a common society. Thus, following Parsons' approach, organic solidarity could become a reality (Parsons, 1951). Nevertheless, Parsons also stated that in order to make such a system possible, it is necessary to consider a hierarchy of loyalty and to assure that the cultural legitimacy of normative society has a prominent role.

In short, several implications emerge from the theoretical contributions presented here, particularly those linked to the analysis of multiculturalism and the debates around identities in modern societies. Thus, regarding to the collective capacity building and as will be explained in detail in the following sections, minority cultural contributions could be crucial in fostering a European societal community in which it is possible develop a solid sense of belonging that ensures a plural and cohesive society.

METHOD

The empirical data that will be presented here come from WORKALO, a large-scale research project funded by the Fifth European Framework Programme (Flecha, 2004). WORKALO was conducted using the communicative methodology that is characterized by the involvement of stakeholders and end users in the whole research process on an equal basis, thus breaking the interpretative hierarchy and opening an egalitarian dialogue between researchers and subjects (Munté et al., 2011; Gómez, 2014). The aim of WORKALO was to define innovative strategies for economic and social development oriented toward enhancing social cohesion in Europe. To achieve this aim, the research focused on Roma, a cultural group that has many practices that can contribute to strengthening European social cohesion. Beginning with this aim, two sub objectives were defined: (a) to analyze the exclusionary dimensions related to structural constraints on access to education and employment, (b) to identify transformative dimensions, for instance, those that facilitate the social inclusion of Roma, thus overcoming the inequality systematically suffered by Roma in Europe.

Data Collection

WORKALO researchers conducted exhaustive fieldwork in five countries in Europe (Spain, France, United Kingdom, Portugal and Romania). The results presented in this chapter are selected from all contributions specifically related to the Work Package 6 focused on Roma labour insertion and its repercussions for the shaping of a societal community. The data collection instruments were 44 communicative life stories, 15 communicative discussion groups and 3 communicative observations. The Roma involved were aged between 16 and 55, their education levels were quite different (illiterate, with basic education and with professional and college education) and both men and women were involved.

Following the communicative approach, the guidelines of the data collection instruments were designed based on the review of scientific literature and contributions from WORKALO's Advisory Council. The Advisory Council was in charge of review documents and orientation of the development of the research and its results. To guarantee that this process was properly fulfilled, the WORKALO Advisory Council composition was crucial; thus, Roma involved in associations and who served as representatives of their community were selected. In addition, the research team also include Roma researchers to ensure scientific rigor and the deepening of the knowledge created (Munté et al., 2011).

Data Analysis

The analytical strategy was based on a theoretical background that was created during the research, using a dual (subjects and systems) conception of reality and taking into account the communicative approach (Flecha, Gómez, & Puigvert, 2003). Thus, an analysis table (Table 4.1) was created that included the three subsystems (Economy, Policy and Culture) and the societal community mentioned by Parsons. The table included five elements linked to social structure and related to both the exclusionary and the transformative dimension: gender, ethnicity, social class, age and education level. These five elements could establish a relation between the aforementioned

Table 4.1. WORKALO analysis table

	Economy		Policy		Culture		Societal community	
	Gender (a), Ethnicity (b), Age (c), Social class (d), Education level (e)							
	Subjects	*System*	*Subjects*	*System*	*Subjects*	*System*	*Subjects*	*System*
Exclusionary Components							X	X
Transformative Components							X	X

subsystems and the societal community. In this chapter, we focus on the results for the societal community.

FOR THE CONSTRUCTION OF THE EUROPEAN SOCIETAL COMMUNITY

Roma participants in the fieldwork denounced the stereotypes and prejudices they suffered in the different countries involved in the project. This experience showed the distrust of the Roma based on the values and norms represented by the majority. According to Parsons (1968), a societal community is possible if the subjects feel united or associated with the given social structure. This section analyzes the main barriers identified by Roma that make it difficult for them to feel that they are European citizens (Gómez, 2014). According to the data collected, four barriers were identified: (1) the disintegrative role of institutions, (2) the lack of respect of Roma's human rights, (3) ignorance about Roma and (4) difficulties in coexisting and multicultural cohesion.

The Disintegrative Role of Institutions

The first structural barrier is the disintegrative role of institutions. According to many of the Roma voices heard during the data collection, institutions that belong to economy, policy and cultural systems and that are responsible for guaranteeing equal opportunities are systematically failing to fulfil their purpose. Participants affirmed that the three subsystems are not guaranteeing equal treatment. Prejudices and cultural discrimination are barriers when Roma are looking for jobs, as previous findings have confirmed (Kelley & Evans, 2015). The labour market is not generating the proper conditions to overcome this inequality. Roma interviewees considered that a society that fails to guarantee equal opportunities does not enforce a sense of belonging. Rosa, a young woman with a secondary studies level of education, explained that she felt rejected because of her Roma identity, although she had the same training as her non-Roma colleagues. Manuel, a 50-year-old Roma man with a vocational studies level of education, stated that the fact that he is Roma is perceived by businesspeople as a barrier in the job selection process. He also affirmed that Roma people must constantly prove that they have competences.

Education is another social area in which several barriers are identified with examples of failure in terms of Roma integration. The Roma interviewed said that they felt distrusted in educational institutions because of the segregation they suffered in different European countries. These educational practices include separating Roma from non-Roma children because it is assumed that Roma children do not have the same intellectual competence as the others. One example is explained by Alba, a 24-year-old Roma woman with a secondary studies level of education. Alba shared that training addressed to Roma children was low quality:

Since we were children (Roma children), precisely, we did not receive a higher-quality education; teachers gave us lessons that are not the same as for non-Roma children, and they confused us. They have trained us with a bad educational plan; we don't learn the same lessons as the others do. School is giving Roma children a disastrous education.

Alba reflected about the discriminatory treatment she had received and asked why Roma children are not taught the social and academic competences required in the information society, as Roma are demanding. She described how Roma are prevented from having access to high-quality education, making it very difficult for them to have enriched job opportunities. In fact, Alba's experience evidences how members of the working class are easily labelled "educational failures" by teachers, and our research results show that this label is often used with Roma students. This prejudice serves to justify the fact that some teachers do not implement official curricula for Roma students.

The fact that essential institutions, such as the labour market and the educational system, fail to reinforce social integration provokes a wider estrangement between Roma and non-Roma people because the practice of democratic and egalitarian values has not been effectively achieved. Many times, Roma are asked to make greater efforts to be socially included; such requests are based on the ignorance of these barriers that compose a systematic practice of social exclusion.

Lack of Respect of Roma's Human Rights

According to Sen (1999), those societies in which human rights are a reality become the most advanced ones. The lack of respect of a minority cultural group's Human Rights towards damages not only vulnerable groups but also the social majority. Social inequality leads to a failure of Human Rights and generates social conflict instead of progress. Roma interviewed about daily practices of infringement of Human Rights reported that the conditions for an egalitarian dialogue were not fulfilled. An example of such experiences was narrated by Miguel, a 30-year-old Roma man with a primary level of education and with a temporary job, who explained the discomfort he felt when police did not respect his rights.

This type of inequality is systematic and not exceptional, according to the Roma interviewed; they felt that their Human Rights are damaged every day. Pedro, a 40-year-old university student who is unemployed, affirmed that verbal and nonverbal languages transmit discrimination in daily interactions:

You know, some of us try to hide ourselves to avoid racism, because we feel bad about it. Every time you go out, you feel people glancing, speaking, how they look at you, their distrust .... Sometimes they manage to make you feel less than they are.

Ignorance about Roma and Lack of Recognition of Roma's Historical Exclusion

The interviewed Roma usually highlighted that the rest of society does not know what the Roma's current situation is. They noted that knowledge of Roma culture is based on social prejudices and not on reality or scientific evidence. An example is provided by Ana, a middle-aged Roma woman with no education, who emphasized this idea:

> There is a lack of knowledge about Roma. Our culture is so unknown. The social majority has no knowledge about daily practices that for us are very common ... When they really know, they are amazed about that.

> This ignorance based on prejudices is promulgated by people who have never lived with Roma but possess prejudices based on previous racist interactions. These interactions are found in all subsystems: economy, policy and education. An example is provided by Ruth, a Roma teenager who is a secondary student. Ruth explained that her Colombian friend heard some people denigrating Roma. After becoming friends with Ruth, she realized that those comments were prejudices.

Another contribution identified through our analysis was the lack of institutional recognition of the historical social exclusion suffered by Roma in Europe. Roma demanded the same institutional recognition that Jewish people obtained several decades ago. The Roma interviewed provided information and details about persecution suffered in different European countries. For instance, several Roma women interviewed explained that they had suffered sterilization in European countries, including Sweden, Slovakia, and the Czech Republic, among others (Albert, 2011). Thus, Roma demanded an official recognition from European institutions of their history of social exclusion. If Europe is able to overcome these daily discriminatory practices, then Roma believe it will be possible to build a societal community in that territory.[1] Roma perceive this lack of recognition as being closely connected to their disadvantaged situation. This permanent exclusion makes it difficult to build an egalitarian multicultural relationship that leads to a positive coexistence. For instance, Antonia, a 23-year-old Roma woman with a secondary studies level of education and a temporary job, explained a painful experience suffered by a Roma couple who were rejected for an apartment rental because they were Roma.

> Given such situations, the Roma interviewed wish to claim egalitarian treatment in all systems and to have the opportunity to demonstrate their predisposition to coexist in peace with others. To make it possible to fulfil this desire, they affirmed that it is crucial for non-Roma people to put aside all prejudices and racist attitudes.

T. SORDÉ ET AL.

TRANSFORMATIVE CONDITIONS FOR THE CONSTRUCTION OF A EUROPEAN SOCIETAL COMMUNITY

Among the transformative dimensions identified in the fieldwork, two are crucial for understanding the steps that Roma identified as necessary to move towards a European societal community: 1) the inclusion of Roma voices in defining social norms and 2) institutions' recognition of different cultures, such as the Roma one, and commitment to the European project.

The Inclusion of Roma

Roma claimed the need for European institutions to recognize their culture and to develop more inclusive and effective policies to overcome their social exclusion. In fact, a valuable impact of the WORKALO project was that it obtained the recognition of Roma by the European Parliament by sharing its results with Roma, other stakeholders and Members of the European Parliament (Aiello et al., 2013; Flecha, Soler, & Sordé, 2015). In addition, ten years later, the social inclusion of Roma has become a priority in the European Policy Agenda. This recognition has been useful for investing in policies that generate social changes and facilitate the improvement of Roma's lives. Although the current situation is not yet ideal, there is more specific institutional support that is visibly changing the public discourse about Roma.

In Roma's reality, social inclusion is not understood as a condition that results in loss of identity; instead, they understand social inclusion as an egalitarian participation in all three subsystems (economy, policy and culture) without renouncing their own culture. The data analyzed expressed how the Roma interviewed desired the normalization of the Roma presence. Luis, a 35-year-old Roma man with a basic education, affirmed that he can be Roma without losing his identity because he wants to give sense to his life:

> I don't like to be equal as they [social majority] are. I'm very happy to be Roma. Non-Roma talk about coexistence, and I respect and I can adapt to it, but without losing our identity, isn't it true? I'm a Roma until I die, while my people could remember me.

Thus, Luis noted the fact that he would maintain his identity even when receiving egalitarian treatment. The only path for doing so is to favour the understanding of differences through equality (Flecha, 2000), recognizing the differences between groups as well as agreeing on basic norms for a common coexistence.

Integrative and Effective Role of Institutions: Public Recognition of Roma

Roma people are advancing towards overcoming the discrimination and barriers analyzed in the previous section. In this process, the institutional recognition

54

obtained by bodies such as the European Parliament has a very important role, since it reinforces the collective capacity building of this community. But Roma do not think only of their culture when they claim recognition; they think about other ethnic minorities too. For this purpose, the same claim that Roma formulate for themselves is claimed for all cultures. According to Parsons' analysis, the recognition of the same rights for others as for oneself is an important step in establishing an egalitarian dialogue among citizens who are very different. Furthermore, in order to make such recognition a reality, it should be present in each subsystem. For instance, in education, the curriculum needs to integrate cultural diversity, and the experience of Roma and other ethnic minorities should be present in subjects such as History. Victoria, a 34-year-old Roma woman with a higher education level, explained this necessity:

> Our society is becoming more multicultural and over time will be even more so; we should acquire more knowledge of all cultures. It will be necessary to include more contents about these cultures in our classrooms; we have to know who is living with us …

In fact, when institutions from the three subsystems (economy, policy and culture) carry out their role in an effective manner, the aforementioned distrust radically changes. Thus, European institutions are currently working to guarantee Roma's full access to human rights and monitoring institutions to ensure that none violate their basic rights. Moreover, this process involves Roma inside institutions and includes dialogic strategies (for instance, advisory councils with Roma members) to promote the effectiveness of policy and actions or programmes addressed to Roma (Munté et al., 2011). Therefore, Roma are participating in processes of decision making, which is improving living conditions in their community, and they feel supported, thus recovering their trust in public institutions.

An example of this integrative role of institutions was the creation of the National Advisory Council of Roma in Spain in 2005.[2] Collaboration between civil society and the Spanish Public Administration is officially endorsed in this interministry council. The purpose of this collaboration is to develop social policies based on the promotion of the Roma population. Once historical social exclusion was recognized in all systems, the next step was to institutionalize the collaboration between the Public Administration and Roma in order to design policies to guarantee social inclusion. Of the 40 council members, 20 were members of the government and 20 were from Roma associations.

Even though the situation of Roma has improved since 2004, recent economic crisis is having negative consequences for social cohesion. For example, new racism has grown up, and Roma have been one of the most harmed groups (ENAR, 2013). Roma have demanded a global stance towards addressing racism from the European Parliament. For instance, the case of the expulsion of Roma from France provoked a global Roma mobilization to claim an intervention that would ensure the free movement of Roma as European citizens (Kushen, 2010). Despite these conflicts, the European recognition of Roma in 2005 is achieving policy change and hope because Roma have begun to be considered as interlocutors.

CONCLUSIONS

Roma were not considered to be an example that informed social theory, as African Americans were in the United States. The experience of Roma in building their own identity, not linked to a territory but based on shared values, has not been included in social analyses. However, this way of experiencing identity favours the feeling of belonging to Europe because Roma are present not only in one but in all European countries. Even so, the Roma case would be helpful in advancing theoretical contributions from scholars such as Habermas. Although Habermas read Parsons, he did not read Parsons' last contributions, and his initial response to the concept of societal community was that it was not a plausible approach to European social reality. Later, Habermas advocated promoting a feeling of belonging and loyalty through the support of a European constitution, which for him was a crucial component in understanding the European project. The main disadvantage of this concept is that people cannot be forced to feel connected by a constitution if there has previously been no inclusive recognition of cultural diversity. For these reasons, Habermas' constitutional patriotism failed in Europe too. The aim of this chapter, based on empirical research, is to reveal Parsons' concept of societal community and to identify the conditions that make it possible in Europe.

In doing so, we have identified the exclusionary and transformative dimensions of the societal community in Europe by taking Roma as an illustrative example. Thus, we have recognized common barriers suffered by the Roma interviewed, such as the disintegrative role of public institutions, the persistent violation of Roma's human rights, educational segregation of Roma in elementary school, their exclusion from the labour market and the lack of recognition of Roma culture by the rest of society. In regard to the transformative dimension, the results indicated that it is necessary to ensure the fulfilment of the equality of difference principle within institutions, meaning that each person or group should have access to the same opportunities regardless of their cultural origin. Thus, Roma affirm that when relationships are free of prejudices and differences are promoted and respected, it is possible to create a cohesive community atmosphere and, thus, strengthen the collective capacity building. We argue it is crucial that all cultural minority groups, especially those that are most at risk, have effective access to all fundamental rights. Therefore, we conclude that only by ensuring this fulfilment will it be possible to build a European societal community in which all people feel that they belong.

Dialogues between researchers and Roma interviewed identified other conditions for ensuring that such a societal community is possible. They agreed on Parsons' concept, but they also identified additional conditions. First was the integrative and effective role of institutions; this role included Parsons' perspective (equality and respect towards all minority groups), but there is a further step. It is necessary to include Roma in the core of institutions by hiring Roma workers or establishing an effective dialogue between policy makers and Roma so that they can work together to design priorities and guarantee full access to fundamental rights (housing, education, work, health care). Second was institutional recognition in all European countries. This step was essential for advancing an egalitarian dialogue between Roma and the rest of society because until Roma were recognized, they were always in a weaker position. As was shown in the previous sections, the European Parliament (2005) recognition of Roma played a central role. Third was the recognition of all cultures as a driver of coexistence. This solidarity of Roma with other ethnic minorities is based on their life experience; they know what it means to suffer systematic exclusion, and they desire that nobody experience it anymore. If all minority groups feel recognized, they are closer to feeling that they belong to a common society. Last, and strongly connected with this third element, was Roma's activism to establish an egalitarian relationship with people from different cultures.

All these conditions will favour the constitution of the European societal community. The situation of Roma has improved in recent years in Europe, but newly emerging racist attitudes in some European countries increased during the recession. The European Parliament recognition of Roma has allowed more coherent intervention, but it is necessary to advance further and more deeply in this direction. Next, future research on the societal community in Europe will further the existing analysis and improve our knowledge of Roma practices and successful actions.

NOTES

[1] Roma and the EU. European Commission. Justice. Retrieved from https://ec.europa.eu/info/policies/justice-and-fundamental-rights/combatting-discrimination/roma-and-eu_en (accessed 22 June 2018).

[2] Consejo Estatal del Pueblo Gitano. Retrieved from http://www.msssi.gob.es/ssi/familiasInfancia/PoblacionGitana/ConPuebloGitano.htm (accessed 22 June 2018).

REFERENCES

Aiello, E., Mondéjar, E., & Pulido, M. Á. (2013). Communicative methodology of research and recognition of the Roma people. *International Review of Qualitative Research, 6*(2), 254–265.

Albert, W. (2011). *Forced sterilization and Romani women's resistance in Central Europe* (Different takes). Hampshire: Population and Development Program.

Amador, J., Flecha, R., & Sordé, T. (2018) Drugs and mental health problems among the Roma: Protective factors promoted by the Iglesia Evangélica Filadelfia. *International Journal of Environmental Research and Public Health, 15*(2), 335. doi:10.3390/ijerph15020335

Berger, P. L., Davie, G., & Fokas, E. (2008). *Religious America, secular Europe? A theme and variation.* Hampshire: Ashgate Publishing, Ltd.

Burawoy, M. (2004). Public sociologies: Contradictions, dilemmas, and possibilities. *Social Forces, 82*(4), 1603–1618.

Clough Marinaro, I. (2017). The informal faces of the (neo-)ghetto: State confinement, formalization and multidimensional informalities in Italy's Roma camps. *International Sociology, 32*(4), 545–562.

De Wilde, P., & Trenz, H. J. (2012). Denouncing European integration: Euroscepticism as polity contestation. *European Journal of Social Theory, 15*(4), 537–554.

ENAR. (2013). *Recycling hatred: Racism(s) in Europe today.* Brussels: European Network Against Racism.

T. SORDÉ ET AL.

European Commission. (2010). *The social and economic integration of the Roma in Europe* (COM(2010)133 final). Brussels: European Commission.

European Parliament. (2005). *European Parliament resolution on the situation of Roma in Europe and marking the International Roma Day.* Brussels: European Parliament.

Flecha, R. (2000). *Sharing words. Theory and practice of dialogic learning.* Lanham, MD: Rowman & Littlefield Publishing Group.

Flecha, R., Gómez, J., & Puigvert, L. (2003). *Contemporary sociological theory.* New York, NY: Peter Lang.

Flecha, R. (2004). *WORKALÓ. The creation of new occupational patterns for cultural minorities. The Gypsy case* (RTD project). Fifth Framework Program of Research of the European Commission DG XII, Improving the Socio-economic Knowledge Base. Brussels: European Commission.

Flecha, R., Soler, M., & Sordé, T. (2015). Social impact: Europe must fund social sciences. *Nature, 528*(7581), 193–193.

FRA. (2009). *EU-MIDIS: European Union minorities and discrimination survey.* Brussels: European Commission.

Gómez, A. (2014). New developments in mixed methods with vulnerable groups. *Journal of Mixed Methods Research, 8*(3), 317–320.

Habermas, J. (1984a). *The theory of communicative action, Volume 1: Reason and the rationalization of society.* Boston, MA: Beacon Press.

Habermas, J. (1984b). *The theory of communicative action. V.1. Reason and the rationalization of society.* Boston, MA: Beacon Press.

Habermas, J. (1987). *The theory of communicative action. V.2. Lifeworld and system: A critique of functionalist reason.* Boston, MA: Beacon Press.

Habermas, J. (1996a). *Between facts and norms. Contributions to a discourse theory of law and democracy.* Cambridge, MA: MIT Press.

Habermas, J. (1996b). The European Nation State. Its achievements and its limitations. On the past and future of sovereignty and citizenship. *Ratio Juris, 9*(2), 125–137.

Kelley, J., & Evans, M. D. R. (2015). Prejudice, exclusion, and economic disadvantage: A theory. *Sociological Theory, 33*(3), 201–233.

Kushen, R. (2010). Intolerant Europe: The drive against the Roma. *Global Dialogue, 12*(2), 1–12.

Merton, R. K. (1975). Structural analysis in sociology. In P. M. Blau (Ed.), *Approaches to the study of social structure* (pp. 21–53). New York, NY: Free Press.

Munté, A., Serradell, O., & Sordé, T. (2011). From research to policy: Roma participation through communicative organization. *Qualitative Inquiry, 17*(3), 256–266.

Outhwaite, W. (2014). The future of European democracy. *European Journal of Social Theory, 17*(3), 326–342.

Parsons, T. (1951). *The social system.* New York, NY: The Free Press of Glencoe.

Parsons, T. (1968). Social systems. In D. Sils & R. Merton (Eds.), *International encyclopaedia of social sciences.* New York, NY: Macmillan and Free Press.

Parsons, T. (1969a). Full citizenship for the Negro American? A sociological problem. In T. Parsons & K. Clark (Eds.), *The Negro American* (pp. 709–754). Boston, MA: Houghton Mifflin.

Parsons, T. (1969b). *Politics and social structure.* New York, NY: Free Press.

Parsons, T. (1977a). *Social systems and the evolution of action theory.* New York, NY: Free Press.

Parsons, T. (1977b). *The evolution of societies.* Upper Saddle River, NJ: Prentice-Hall.

Parsons, T. (1978). *Action theory and the human condition.* New York, NY: Free Press.

Scalise, G. (2015). The narrative construction of European Identity. Meanings of Europe 'from below'. *European Societies, 17*(4), 593–614.

Sen, A. (1999). *Development as freedom.* Oxford: Oxford University Press.

Soler-Gallart, M. (2017). *Achieving social impact. Sociology in the public sphere.* New York, NY: Springer.

Sordé, T., Flecha, R., & Alexiu, T. M. (2013). El pueblo gitano. Una identidad global sin territorio, *Scripta Nova, XVII*(427). Retrieved from http://www.ub.edu/geocrit/sn/sn-427/sn-427-3.htm

Weber, M. (1946). The protestant sects and the spirit of capitalism. In M. Weber, H. H. Gerth, & C. Wright Mills (Eds.), *From Max Weber: Essays in sociology* (pp. 302–322). Abington: Routledge.

GHEORGHE CLITAN AND OANA BARBU-KLEITSCH

5. DISTORTING THE MESSAGE OF RELIGIOUS SYMBOLS BY FALLACIOUS REASONING IN THE ELECTORAL POSTERS OF POLITICAL CAMPAIGNS

INTRODUCTION

This chapter tries to present a theoretical framework on the political use of religious symbols in electoral advertising and, starting from a hermeneutical analysis on Romanian electoral posters from 2016, it advances to a critical thinking perspective in which critical thinking is seen as the argumentation practice in everyday life, as a remedy against what is pathological in people's thinking and communication, offering them a cogent (good) reasoning and effective communication formats to support their own points of view (ways of correct thinking), and developing skills that protect and help people against the fallacious (bad) reasoning or manipulations.

Starting from identifying the religious symbols used in political campaign posters found from the 2016 Romanian political campaign, critical analysis of advertising will be used in decoding political posters with critical thinking questions found in *Law School Admission Test* (LSAT). The critical analysis that we propose here will be oriented in three directions: (1) In what consists the critical analysis of the use of religious symbols in electoral posters? (2) Present/propose a model by which we try to show how the religious symbols can be distorted in political posters by fallacious reasoning; (3) The case study, using the proposed model, of the steps by which the religious symbols of the selected political posters of the 2014 and 2016 Romanian political campaign are distorted by the fallacious reasoning embodied in those posters.

THEORETICAL FRAMEWORK

Secularization theory often declares that our society is becoming more and more rational and scientific; hence it is distancing itself more and more from a community based on religious beliefs, symbols and religious values. In this context, Hibbard (2010), Stark and Iannaccone (1997) and others underline that secularization is falsely credited with the so-called "defeat" of religious influence. To the contrary, they argue that religion is facing a maybe undesired upturn in recent times where various secular discourses (such as the political discourse) build their emotional grounding on nationalistic or religious symbols, or even both (Babu-Kleitsch, 2015, p. 1).

Furthermore, advertising is one of the major sources of symbolic signification highly used in nowadays political campaigns. This shift from the PR discourse to the advertising discourse in politics can be linked to the more powerful symbolic content provided by advertising messages. Targeting a specific group of people that may be vulnerable to such messages, the relationship between politics and religion is attributed to the way in which the first one embodies religious dimensions in its persuasive mechanisms (Sheffield, 2006).

The point of view we support in this study is that the incorporation of religious elements into the electoral discourse of posters used in political campaigns does not take place by constructing explicit, rational or emotional convincing messages. They occur by conveying tacit messages using different types of symbols, including religious ones, but whose initial meanings are distorted. The distortion of the initial meanings of the symbols used in political campaigns seems to be a public, ideological business if it is reduced to their explicit reinterpretation from the perspective of a political orientation. But it also becomes a private, personal business of tacit assumption in the public space of political, religious, epistemic or other beliefs.

We will not deal with the social, political, economic and cultural mechanisms highlighted from the perspective of the secularization theory, as they are well known and much discussed in the literature. We will discuss the ordinary man's mechanisms of reasoning of his daily life, which lead him to assume some political beliefs, and to make decisions on the granting of the electoral vote, on the basis of rational and emotional evidence. Rationality of the ordinary man takes the form of arguments, that is to say, of some rows of statements from which some, called premises, express the necessary grounds and evidence for the logical derivation of conclusions. (Cavender & Kahane, 2010) When derivation is both necessary and sufficient, it is valid, and its premises are credible (guaranteed), including all the relevant information (the entire available evidence), we have good reasoning (*cogent*). When one of the three conditions (validity, credibility, relevance) is not met, we are dealing with false (*fallacious*) reasoning.

This is the kind of rationale that can be used by the ordinary man in making the right decisions (for example, granting the electoral vote), in solving current problems of everyday life, or in performing the actions in which he manifests his behaviour. When judging, on one hand, man exercises some of his/her thinking skills looking for good reasons for decision making, that is, sufficient and necessary reasons for solving problems or conducting activities that define his/her behaviour. On the other hand, he mobilizes the other part of his thinking skills to eliminate what is fallacious in his own judgment and in the rationale of others. In other words, it identifies and removes reasoning that is based on problematic premises, lack of evidence or insufficient evidence, on invalid inferences.

In this way, critical thinking can become a remedy against what is pathological in people's thinking and communication, providing them with correct judgments and effective communication formats to support their own points of view, as well as self-defence tools in front of points view promoted in order to manipulate them. As a practice of reasoning and/or reasoning in everyday life, as a way of solving daily problems, as a possible alternative debate centred on conclusive foundations, critical thinking involves three types of attitudes underlying the common man:

- to accept or to support a point of view, a position or another; to justify an opinion or belief, an action based only on grounds/evidence/arguments (material-substantive or logical), convincing/rationally guaranteed, not emotional;
- to reject only knowingly (i.e. grounded, reasoned, argued: rationally, not emotionally) the views, positions, opinions or beliefs, the actions of one person or another;
- to abstain (through convincing reasoning: rational, non-emotional) in relation to a point of view, a position, an opinion or belief, or an action.

CRITICAL ANALYSIS OF ADVERT

The first papers in which the concept of "critical thinking" is mentioned, is Edward Glaser's *an Experiment in the Development of Critical Thinking* (1941). Critical thinking skills have been evaluated by specially constructed tests since the beginning of its systematic investigation, such as that of Glaser's test (*Watson-Glaser Critical Thinking Appraisal*). This tests are seen, over time, not only as a way of assessing the critical thinking skills, but also as real life situations modelling, where thinking is used.[1]

The analysis model used in this study starts from the suggestions of one of the tests on this list (LSAT – *Law School Admission Test*) and it has been developed from these suggestions in several papers already published by the authors of this study. It gives an account of what we called in our research the "critical analysis of advertising" and essentially consists of typing the relevant questions and answers to them about:

- the rationing mode/reasoning (logical-argumentative analysis of the advertisement);
- the message sent/meaning (comprehensive analysis of the advertisement);
- the information communicated/data (information analysis of the advertisement).

The LSAT test consists of three types of items that evaluate skills (*Logical Reasoning* skills, *Reading Comprehension* skills and *Analytical Reasoning* skills) in the form of questions with multiple answers (*The Official LSAT Handbook*, 2010, pp. 2–4). LSAT test items include not just multiple questions and answers (five answer variants, one of which is the correct answer), but also problem formulations (short and concise – for logical thinking, longer and more complex – in the case of comprehensive thinking, requirements or conditions – in the case of analytical thinking). In essence, problem formulations (questions and response variants in the structure of an item) are only partial formalizations modelling of the concrete situations that trigger the critical thinking skills assessed by that item.

In doing so, critical thinking tests provide – practically – models of assessment of the skills involved in the construction and analysis of the public discourse. Starting from the LSAT item type, we can formulate sets of questions whose possible answers give the form of discourse analysis corresponding to the three components of critical thinking: Logical-Reasoning Analysis (for Logical Reasoning), Comprehensive Analysis (for Reading Comprehension), and Information Analysis (for Analytical Reasoning). Together, exemplifying the analysis of advertising as a public discourse, these three forms of analysis give shape to the already mentioned critical analysis of the advertisement (Barbu & Clitan, 2012; Clitan, 2012, 2013a, 2013b, 2015, 2017):

- logical-argumentative analysis: focused on the practice of logical thinking skills, contains sets of questions about the mental patterns by which every person argues for or against in a discourse: the explanation of what is essential; making an inference; identifying a constructive argument (explicit or tacit); identifying a similar argumentation structure; identifying a reasoning error; identifying similar reasoning errors; identifying assumptions or assumptions in an argument; use of additional evidence; the explanation of an event, including the resolution of a conflicting or seemingly paradoxical state;
- comprehensive analysis: focusing on the exercise of comprehensive thinking skills, contains sets of questions about mental patterns by which every person understands the meaning of the expressions he uses in a certain context: identifying the points of view expressed in a discourse; clarifying the meaning of the expressions or the purpose in which a discursive reference is made; argumentative structuring of information in speech; Linking the views/information used in a speech; identifying and capturing discursive attitudes; expanding the informational content of the discourse; identifying the analogies and principles of a discourse; formulating the purpose of the discourse;
- information analysis: focused on the practice of analytical thinking skills, contains sets of questions about the mental patterns of structuring and linking information in speech: identifying a basic information structure; the possible use of the given information ("could" type); the mandatory use of the given information ("must" type); the possible use of new information ("could" type); Mandatory use of new information ("must" type).

How important can these analyses get into the normal life, thinking, behaviour, or activity of the human being? Their reflexive character gives them a special kind of "objectivity" that takes into account the social dimension of human thinking in everyday life. It is not about objectivity, in the traditional sense of the word (the correspondence of thoughts with facts), but of a psychosocial sense. From a psychological point of view, being objective is the ability to return to your own way of thinking and critically examine it. Critical examination of this kind is, in fact, a

DISTORTING THE MESSAGE OF RELIGIOUS SYMBOLS

"process of self-direction and self-correction" of thinking, according to the correct standards and methods of reasoning (Kelley, 1994, pp. 6–7).

The social aspect of objectivity directs thinking from logic (coherent or non-contradictory presentation of ideas) and psychological (critical examination of decisions taken), towards communication (evaluation of the argumentative character of the discourse). Communicative objectivity does not imply neutrality, non-partisanship or indifference, but impartiality in the appreciation of one's own discursive arguments, and of others (Clitan, 2003, p. 62). Thus conceived, objectivity is an attitude that you adopt towards the arguments of others, not just to your own.

This kind of objectivity ensures not only the impartiality in the evaluation of the discursive proposals in the analyzed poster, but also in the use of one's own capacities for discursive grounding of the decision (granting of the electoral vote). Thus, critical thinking offers – through the reflexive analyses that involve them – both weapons of "intellectual self-defence" against non-rational, emotional persuasion, based on predominantly psycho-social discursive interventions (excitation, seduction, manipulation, propaganda, indoctrination etc.), but also "strategies to maintain a critical attitude towards the media", and its discursive interventions (mass media advertisements, often non-rational means of political discourse, editorial policies and practices aimed at a commercial profit rather than a communicational one, etc.) (Baillargeon, 2011).

Self-defence and critical attitude are necessary because, in their everyday lives, people do not formulate and substantiate their claims on sufficient premises, they do not always explain their premises and the conclusions they reach. In other words, they do not think and do not always argue in premises and conclusions, i.e. rational, and if they do so, they use elliptical arguments (by omitting, underlying or confusing some premises and conclusions), or exemplifications, enumerations and illustrations as forms of argumentation. Many have problems to divide between premises and conclusions (in spite of words or states indicating the premises or conclusions that any discourse contains), to distinguish the arguments between them, or to identify argumentative structures in the discourse (the argumentative chain), or the rational steps to follow for the efficiency of an activity (reaching its purpose).

The new media maintains or even amplifies this state of things, the "like" on Facebook becomes – for example – the most convenient and used form of grounding or argumentation (Babu-Kleitsch, 2015, p. 2), "spam" is perhaps the most difficult way to avoid advertising, posters and advertisements are the most striking and costly means of communication; talk shows, music on YouTube, unrestrained broadcasts and mobile phones are competing as the most successful and effective means of communication, etc. Relaxations of the critical spirit, the loss of rationality, the convenience or laziness of thought, are just a few of the effects that manifest in the daily life plan of the contemporary man. Indeed, these are ways of infesting with non-rational, emotional practices, of his critical thinking, turning his normal thinking into a pathological thinking, prone to manipulation. The fall of thought into pathology takes place, for example, when false, invalid or fallacious arguments

G. CLITAN & O. BARBU-KLEITSCH

(such as the sophisms, for example) are substituted for the valid, cogent, and based on a similar logical form or structure (McInerney, 1992, pp. 15–19).

In this context, it is not surprising that advertising in political campaigns often appeals to such means and to such a distorted form of thinking. And here, as in other situations of everyday life, critical thinking can provide tools and strategies for self-defence. One of the strategies is to find the methods and tools that allow us to decide – in any problem – between opposing or competing points of view, that is to say, we choose only the ones rationally founded, not emotionally or in another form (e.g.: verbal or physical violence, material or spiritual constraints, which have material advantages or moral comfort). Evaluating the arguments in support of a point of view, in all their aspects, is the rational decision-making path between several points of view. Supporting a point of view can be done either on the basis of very strong grounds (the premises provide grounds to support the truth or the false conclusion), either on the basis of pros and cons, prejudices or rhetorical tricks (the premises support the truth or falsity of the conclusion by merely asserting it, without giving a reason to support them, that is, simply by setting out ungrounded or ungrounded claims) (Warburton, 1999).

As a consequence of the previous considerations, it is appreciated that in one case, and in another, the foundation or lack of foundation can be deductive (the way of thinking that is based on an inference from general to particular, consisting in deriving the conclusion from premises by customization) or inductive (the way of thinking that is based on an inference from the particular to the general, consisting in the derivation by generalization of the conclusion from the premises). In both ways of thinking (rationing or argumentation), the inference relation shows how "an argument produces grounds for concluding a conclusion". In their standard manifestation, deductive arguments especially contain premises that can be clearly distinguished by the conclusion by words such as "so", "therefore" (concluding) or "because", "consequently", "as" (indications of premises), which is not happening in everyday life (here, the indicating words have a merely guidance role, since they do not indicate precisely that the conclusions would follow the prerequisites, that they might precede them).

Moreover, inductive arguments have a number of peculiarities that affect the relationship between premises and conclusions. One of them would be that the conclusion contains information that is not found in the premises, which makes the premises to support the conclusion without guaranteeing it (since, usually, the grounds given by the premises to support the conclusion are based on observation and assumptions or unacceptable generalizations). Thus, although they may indicate with high probability and certainty what information is true, the inductive arguments never bring convincing and certainty to the truth of the information in the premise or conclusion. In addition, they do not preserve the truth of this information, as do the deductive arguments. The latter, by the quality of their valid structure or form (to preserve the truth of the statements they contain in the form of premises and conclusions), guarantees the truth of the conclusions based on the truth of the

64

premises (this valid form or structure makes it impossible for all premises to be true, and the conclusion false, imposing that if all the premises are true, then the conclusion must be true). Therefore, only deductive arguments may be valid or invalid. Invalid deductive arguments are also called "formal errors" (their structure or form does not preserve the truth), and any other type of wrong or uncertain argument, different from formal error, is called "informal error" (can be perfectly valid from the point of view of the form or structure of argumentation, but without preserving the truth from the premises to the conclusions).

The critical analysis of how the message of the electoral posters is distorted aims, in one of its dimensions, to identify formal and informal errors in the arguments they contain. This dimension is the first of the three to which the critical analysis of the use of religious symbols in political campaigns refers and which we present schematically as follows:

- the argumentative dimension: the reasoning of the electoral posters in which religious symbols appear (the logical thinking problems raised by the arguments of the posters that use religious symbols in the political campaigns) ← the logical-argumentative analysis of the posters that use religion symbols in political campaigns;
- the comprehensive dimension: that of the messages transmitted by the use of religious symbols in the posters of the political campaigns (the complex thinking problems raised by the symbolic communication of the use of religious symbols in the posters of the political campaigns) ← the comprehensive analysis of the significance of the religious symbols in the posters used in the political campaigns;
- the informational dimension: that of the information used in political campaigns using posters with religious symbols (the analytical thinking problems raised by the foundation on religious symbols of the arguments in the posters of the political campaigns) ← the information analysis of the religious symbols used in the posters of the political campaigns.

CRITICAL ANALYSIS OF A CAMPAIGN POSTER

In what consists the critical analysis of the use of religious symbols in political campaigns? Before we make an applied response to the selected posters in the political campaign for the 2016 parliamentary elections in Romania, we will briefly present the model and the steps we will follow in this analysis. The model consists of:

- formulating/selecting type-questions or sub-types of questions for circumscribing or explaining the issue of religious symbols used in a political campaign
- developing/identifying relevant responses to circumscribed or explicit problematic situations as question-questions or by sub-types of questions about how to use religious symbols in a political campaign

- establishing/grounding how to solve the respective problematic situation or the answer chosen as solutions to the problems identified in the use of religious symbols in a political campaign.

The steps we will follow in the analysis are:

- rephrasing the reasoning in a clear, understandable, unambiguous natural language;
- identifying the type or sub-type of questions that we need to ask in relation to such reasoning;
- questioning the content of the reasoning analyzed by customizing the type or sub – type questions to the analyzed reasoning;
- analyzing pertinent answers to particularizing questions;
- highlighting the erroneous reasoning structure and the error of argumentation.

The first step of the critical analysis of the distortion of the message by misleading reasoning consists in inspecting or scanning the elements, representations and religious symbols in the structure of the electoral poster in question. This step is necessary to identify possible units of meaning that can act as a premise and conclusion. It also has the role of rephrasing the main reasoning from the poster in a clear, understandable, unambiguous natural language that indicates how the premises provide grounds for supporting the conclusion. The posters we are going to analyze from here are shown in Figures 5.1 and 5.2.

A poster is defined as any piece of printed paper designed to be attached to a wall or vertical surface, being both noticeable and informative. In advertising and promotion, the modern poster was introduced around 1840, when printing industry made mass production possible (Eskilson, 2012). As Max Gallo states:

Figure 5.1. Poster 1 (Source: https://www.news.ro/alegeri-2016/psd-si-pmp-distribuie-in-arges-calendare-ortodoxe-dar-cu-siglele-de-partid-patriarhia-e-regretabil-ca-s-a-ajuns-atat-de-departe-1922403206002016122016070616)

DISTORTING THE MESSAGE OF RELIGIOUS SYMBOLS

Figure 5.2. Poster 2 (Source: http://www.mediafax.ro/politic/pmp-arges-si-a-facut-calendar-religios-cu-adam-si-eva-psd-e-incult-noi-suntem-niste-baieti-subtiri-16018200)

For over two hundred years, posters have been displayed in public places all over the world. Visually striking, they have been designed to attract the attention of passers-by, making us aware of a political viewpoint, enticing us to attend specific events, or encouraging us to purchase a particular product or service. (2002)

The wall calendars we selected for analysis can be considered posters because: they promote a religious orientation/option, they present, in an informatory manner, the days of the year and the holidays associated with them, they were used for the purpose of popularizing a political party that ran for the election. Also, the graphical elements used to create the calendar contain a strong symbolic message (references to particular religious' figures or events) that can influence the beliefs of the targeted audience.

The relationship between religion and politics dates back to the oldest times, and the strategies of influencing the audience used by one for the benefit of the other have been and are subject to research. Advertising means make it possible today to promote both politics and religion, and posters are just one of the media used. For the association of politics with religion, the influencing technique used in the above posters aim to cluster the symbols (both political and religious) on a single surface, centred to one-another, and present them to the personal beliefs of the audience. However, the association between the two set of symbols (the religious symbol-political symbol) is highlighted in both cases with some differences we will refer to. The influencing mechanism used can be summed up in the following: If the audience is sensitive to some symbols depicted in the poster, their interest may be captured by them. At this point, their judgment may be influenced, and their reasoning may become fallacious. In this sense, the degree of trust or acceptance of a symbol, as part of a set of personal beliefs, makes the association between the political symbol and the religious symbol sometimes dangerous.

As we can see in Poster1, the association between political and religious is accomplished by symmetrically disposing of two major symbols of the two ideologies. First, at the top of the poster, the name and religious affiliation of the poster calendar is made clear: An Orthodox Calendar for the year 2017. The calendar also depicts a strong religious icon, the icon of the Virgin Mary, a central symbol of the Christian church, that is placed top-central. Under the icon, the logo of the political party who printed and distributed the poster calendars is placed. The large size of the logo is striking as it is positioned centrally and at the same size as the religious symbol. Furthermore, the red colour of the logo enhances its importance in the poster construction and furthermore draws attention to the political symbol (both the name of the calendar and the logo are depicted in red colour). The association with religion is supported also by the placement of a political logo in the middle of a calendar containing the Orthodox religion holidays, while the text message at the base of the poster emphasizes this association: *PSD Arges wishes you a Happy New Year!*

In the second poster, the association between politics and religion is subtler, the religious reference being indirectly transmitted through a painting picture. Here, the icon – a recognized religious and ritual symbol (Beckwith, 1979) – was replaced with an aesthetically representation of the religious myth, without regard to the rules of religious painting or dogma. However, the story of Adam and Eve represented as informational content in the painting is clearly communicated by the image: a man and a woman are represented sharing an apple, they are naked, the woman hands the apple to the man, and the background reveals a garden. All these detail an obvious reference to the biblical story of the First Man. To apparently distract the attention from the symbols of a particular religion, the title of the calendar differs from the one in the first analyzed poster. Here we are dealing with a "Calendar of Holidays of the Year 2017", although the holidays marked in are all Orthodox. Below the picture a text was placed, with information about the significance of number 7. The information seems to be taken from numerology, but again the symbol of number 7 has known many symbolic references in many faiths. The political party logo, which also contains the apple symbol, is placed centrally at the bottom of the calendar along with the party's number on the ballot. As happened in Poster1, also in this case, the logo is very large, having the same size as the image, and is placed symmetrically with it in order to create a visual interrelation. The connection between the apple represented in the painting and the apple symbol from the political party's logo underlines the association between the religious/spiritual/mythical and political elements represented on the same canvas. PMP political party also seals the link between all elements by placing their name on the poster calendar and wishing the same thing as the other political party: *PMP Arges wishes you a Happy New Year!*

As can be seen from the point of view of the informational content, the two posters communicate with different means similar information: Both associate political symbols (logo, political party name, graphic elements) with religious symbols (graphic elements, calendar content, representation in the form the icon/picture of some religious figures/moments known by the ordinary man, numbers of special significance). In both posters, the connection between the political element and the religious element are emphasized by a symmetrical, central, large-scale arrangement of symbols on the same surface so as to attract the attention of the viewer.

Returning to the first step proposed for our critical analysis, we will try to take into analysis Poster 1. Reformulated in premise and conclusion, the information content of Poster 1 takes the form of an argument:

Vote the PSD for the unconditional defence of the ancestral faith enlisted in the Orthodox calendar! Those who choose the PSD to defend the ancestral faith of Orthodoxy inscribed in the calendar do so because the defence of Orthodoxy by parties other than the PSD is very unlikely, if not impossible.

The second step is to identify the type or sub-type of questions that we have to ask about such an argument. Since it is obvious that within it we are dealing with a fallacious rationality, it is appropriate to ask two sets of questions about the wrong structures or the mistakes (arguments) of argumentation:

- questions to identify incorrect reasoning structures;
- questions about error source in argumentation.

Particularization of these sets of standard questions is the five step of the analysis. As with the analysis model, for greater intelligibility, we will synthesize the next steps of the critical analysis we are proposing. The particular questions by which we question the content of the reasoning under consideration are:

I. Questions to identify incorrect reasoning structures:
   1. How can the advertisement argument be reformulated into a similar reasoning structure?
   2. On what form of wrong grounding is the argument in the advertisement based on?
   3. What is the groundless conclusion that leads us to the erroneous grounding of the argument in the advertisement?
   4. Why are the proofs of the advertisement argument inconclusive?
   5. What is the wrong structure of reasoning in the advertisement argument (explicit or tacit)?

II. Questions about error source in argumentation:
   1. What is the unfounded support on which the ad's conclusion is based?
   2. What is the inconclusive proof on which the unfounded claim in the advertisement is based?
   3. What other evidence make the main proof of the advertisement inconclusive?
   4. What other evidence would be conclusive to support the ad's conclusion?
   5. What is the error in the ad's argumentation?

The fourth step is to analyze the pertinent answers to the questions in step 3. Before doing so, it is necessary to specify: after formulating the answers, due to space economy, we will not return to their coupling with the theoretical considerations from the first part of the study (the validity of reasoning, the truth of statements, the errors of argumentation), the reader can do this alone, even as a critical thinking exercise or analysis.

Analysis of answers to type I questions:

1. The correct answer to question I (1) is: how the reasoning in the PSD electoral poster was reformulated.
2. The correct answer to question I (2): the foundation is wrong because it starts from the false premise that in all situations it is better to choose to do something than doing nothing.
3. The correct answer to question I (3): the argument concludes inconclusively, starting from the premise assumed, that it is better to do a certain thing than to do anything else.
4. The correct answer to question I (4): the evidence in the argument of the advertisement is inconclusive because it does not serve as a basis for the grounding of the vote required from the public.
5. The correct answer to question I (5): the wrong reasoning structure can be rendered by a conditional statement of the form: *If it is better to do a certain thing than do nothing, then doing that is better than doing anything else.*

Analysis of answers to type II questions:

1. The correct answer to question II (1): the support on which we are recommended to vote PSD as the defender of the ancestral belief is that PSD is preferable to all other parties defending the ancestral faith enshrined in the orthodox calendar.
2. The correct answer to question II (2): this advocacy is based, however, on the fact that PSD voters would most likely be the only authentic defenders of the ancestral faith of Orthodoxy entered in the calendar.
3. The correct answer to Question II (3): Evidence suggesting that PSD voters would be the only defenders of Orthodoxy since only the PSD assumes the Orthodox calendar electoral is inconclusive because there may be voters who do not vote for PSD but other parties that defend or not Orthodoxy, assuming or not the orthodox calendar in the electoral campaign.
4. The correct answer to question II (4): a public who is very likely a defiant defender of the ancestral faith of Orthodoxy.
5. The correct answer to question II (5): since the proof does nothing to show that PSD would most likely be the only and most fervent defender of Orthodoxy, the conclusion of the electoral poster that, once voted, PSD would defend more Orthodoxy than other parties – Vote PSD for defending the ancestral faith registered in the Orthodox calendar! – is unfounded.

As we have already mentioned, we will draw to a close this study by presenting the fifth step of the critical analysis that we propose, by concluding – both the formal erroneous reasoning structure, as well as the informal error of argumentation in the analyzed poster:

1. The erroneous reasoning structure is reproduced by the answer I (5): If it is better to do a certain thing than do nothing, then doing that is better than doing anything else.
2. The error of argumentation is expressed by the answer to question II (3) (Evidence suggesting that PSD voters are the only defenders of Orthodoxy, since only PSD electorally assumes the Orthodox calendar, is inconclusive because there may be voters who do not voted PSD, but other parties that defend or not Orthodoxy, assuming or not the Orthodox calendar in the electoral campaign) along with the answer to question II (4) (… a public who is very likely a defiant defender of the ancestral faith of Orthodoxy).

CONCLUSION

Our study is an explanatory example but critical thinking analysis has recently become a strong point of interest for academics and researchers as it implies functional communication and problem-solving abilities as well as a commitment to overcome persuasive narratives and *sociocentrism*. As we have shown, the social aspect of objectivity conducts thinking from logic (coherent or non-contradictory presentation of ideas) and psychological (critical examination of decisions taken), towards communication (evaluation of the argumentative character of the discourse). Furthermore, communicative objectivity does not imply neutrality or indifference, but impartiality in the appreciation of one's own discursive arguments, and of others. Thus, conceived, critical thinking objectivity is an attitude that you adopt towards the arguments of others, not just to your own. In this sense, we believe that the critical thinking model for analyzing a political campaign poster presented in this chapter can become a valuable research and educational asset. From decoding problems in class assignments to facing moral or social situations, the standardized critical analysis we proposed in this chapter can be used as a pedagogical tool for overcoming misleading persuasion or manipulative associations to our beliefs, like the one between politics and religion.

NOTE

[1] An annotated list of the best known critical thinking tests has been elaborated by Robert H. Ennis, and the latest version can be consulted at http://www.criticalthinking.net/TestListRevised11-27-09.pdf

REFERENCES

Babu-Kleitsch, O. (2015). Advertising, social media and use of religious symbols. In *SMART 2015. Social media in academia* (pp. 1–5) Bologna: Editografica Publishing House.

G. CLITAN & O. BARBU-KLEITSCH

Baillargeon, N. (2011). *Mic curs de autoaparare intelectuala*. Bucureşti: Editura Paralela 45.

Barbu, O., & Clitan, G. (2012). Critical Analysis of Information in the Advertising Discourse. Case study: the advertising poster. In Ş. Bratosin, C. Bryon-Portet, & M. A. Tudor (Eds.), *Epistémologie de la communication: bilan et perspectives*. Proceedings of the ESSACHES - Technopolis International Workshop, 2nd edition, Toulouse, 2011. Iaşi: Editura Institutul European.

Beckwith, J. (1979). *Early Christian and Byzantine art*. Yale: Penguin History of Art.

Cavender, N. M., & Kahane, H. (2010). *Logic and contemporary rhetoric. The use of reason in everyday life*. Whadswhort: Cengage Learning.

Clitan, G. (2003). *Gândire critică. Micromonografie*. Timişoara: Editura Eurobit.

Clitan, G. (2012). Critical reasoning in analysis advert. In I. Boldea (Ed.), *Communication, context, interdisciplinarity. Studies and Articles* (Vol. 2). The Proceedings of the Communication, Context, Interdisciplinarity Congress. Târgu-Mureş: Editura Universităţii "Petru Maior".

Clitan, G. (2013a). Critical analysis of advertising (A model: Informational analysis). In G. Rata, G. Clitan, & P. Runcan (Eds.), *Applied social sciences – Communication studies*. Newcastle: Cambridge Scholars Publishing.

Clitan, G. (2013b). L'analyse du langage dans l'approche critique de la publicité. In Ş. Bratosin & M. A. Tudor (Eds.), *Communication du symbolique et symbolique de la communication dans les sociétés modernes et postmodernes*. Iaşi: Editura Institutul European.

Clitan, G. (2014). About how can operate Unfounded Belief in Advert. In *Espace public et communication de la foi*. Proceedings of the 2nd International COMSYMBOL IARSIC-ESSACHESS Conference, 2–3 July 2014. Beziers, France, Montpellier: Editions IARSIC.

Clitan, G. (2015). Les effets rhétoriques du discours publicitaire sur le citoyen. Une approche critique. In J.-M. Counet (Ed.), *La citoyenneté*, Proceedings of the XXIV Congress of the Association of Societies of Philosophy of French language (ASPLF), Louvain-la-Neuve/Brussels, August 21–25, 2012. Series: Bibliothèque Philosophique de Louvain, 93. Louvain-la-Neuve/Brussels: Peeters Publisher.

Clitan, G. (2017). Gandirea critica – o geografie mentală a omului de rand. In E. Taraburka (Ed.), *Geografii mentale: timpuri şi spaţii ale memoriei europene*, Proceedings of the International Scientific Conference. Chişinău, Republica Moldova, 27–28 May 2016. Chişinău: CEP USM.

Eskilson, S. (2012). *Graphic design: A new history*. London: Yale University Press.

Gallo, M., & Quintavalle, A. C. (2001). The poster in history. New York, NY: W. W. Norton & Company.

Hibbard, S. W. (2010). *Religious politics and secular states*. Baltimore, MD: Johns Hopkins University Press.

Kelley, D. (1993). *The art of reasoning*. New York, NY/London: W. W. Norton & Company.

Iannaccone, R., L., Finke, R., & Stark, R. (1997). Deregulating religion: The economics of church and state. *Economic Inquiry, 15*, 350–364.

Law School Admission Council. (2010). *The official LSAT handbook*. Newtown, PA.

McInerneay, K. P. (1992). *Introducere in filosofie*. Bucureşti: Editura Lider.

Sheffield, T. (2006). *The religious dimension of advertising*. New York, NY: Palgrave.

Warburton, N. (1999). *Cum sa gandim corect şi eficient*. Bucuresti: Editura Trei.

SIMONA BADER

6. POLITICAL COMMUNICATION ON SOCIAL MEDIA DURING FEBRUARY 2017 PROTESTS IN ROMANIA

INTRODUCTION

The presence of digital communication in day by day life led to a modification in the whole paradigm of communication characterized by speed, globalism, decentralization, lack of institutional control, addressability and personal use. Social media are non-institutional media of communication in which the traditional *one-to-many* messages are replaced by shares or *many-to-many* messages, which creates the possibility of fast spreading and viral transmission. For this reason, social media messages, even evanescent, have an enormous potential of penetration and impact on an interested public. The object of the present chapter is an analysis of the activity and outcomes on social media during the protests in February 2017, Romania. We took as item to pursue the main hashtag shared during these events, *#rezist*. The analysis show that the largest distribution of this hashtag was mainly on Facebook, followed by Twitter and press posts. The number of shares had three peaks in all digital media which followed the intensity of events and street protests.

Third millennium was already named the digital millennium. The traditional means of communication (mass-media, TV, street posters) lost their impact and the digital revolution which began at the end of 80's is in full development and affects all sectors of social and personal life. Most of social protests from 2000 till today used extensively social media for mobilization and as a form of activism. While in normal times social media messages tend to be shared among "group of friends" or "followers" limited by certain personal interests, when political disputes raised the interest of a large portion of population, social media can spread fast messages and give rise to radicalization of opinions and action, as shown during Arab spring or Ukraine Euromaidan or in other protests.

Nowadays, the influence that both traditional press and new media (Internet, online press, social networks, blogs) have is more powerful than ever in shaping public opinion. People watch, read, listen, discuss and react, sometimes identify with the opinion or with the tendency of a certain media channel, or of a journalist (Bader, 2012). When through these channels they receive messages that coincide with their opinions, or by contrary, disagree upon a certain issue, they can act spontaneously, creating group social behaviours.

© KONINKLIJKE BRILL NV, LEIDEN, 2020 | DOI: 10.1163/9789004422209_007

One of the theories to explain massive mobilization during the protests is the *threshold theory* (Granovetter, 1973) which states that individuals with a high threshold of sensitivity are easier mobilized by messages. Digital media might be instruments of sensitization by repetition and multiplication of messages which influence the threshold and can lead to larger movements, either virtual (in digital realm) or actual (street protests). Traditional social mobilization implies dedication, effort and logistic, while in *e-mobilization* the means are easy to use with practical no effort and logistical simplicity. E-mobilization (Bennett, 1999; Rheingold, 2003) refers to the way new technologies were used in political and social motions which led to powerful protests in different parts of the world. Nowadays many-to-many political communication is a specific way in social media with some particular forms, i.e. *clicktivism*. According to Halupka, clicktivism is a legitimate political act (Halupka, 2014). Clicktivists use sophisticated email marketing softwares that brags of its "extensive tracking" including "opens, clicks, actions, sign-ups, unsubscribes, bounces and referrals, in total and by source" (White, 2010). But clicktivists are to blame for alienating a generation of would-be activists with their ineffectual campaigns that resemble marketing, as White claims. *Smart Mobs* is another concept extensively applied to some protests, i.e. in Philippine 2001, Ukraine 2004 and Romania 2017 in which mobilization was done by all means (messages, tweets, and posts) by smartphones. This variety of e-mobilization was defined as organized spontaneity (Chadwick, 2006), a combination between decentralization and collective coordination in which the spontaneity of a crowd is somehow coordinated by fast spreading messages on phones. As Bylieva & All shows, "the general meaning of the 'smart mob' is a social group with undefined boundaries of membership, which acts are coordinated in time with specific goals, having previously agreed the actions with the help of the Information and Communication Technologies" (Bylieva et al., 2018). Jurgenson define the kind of new mobilization for social, political changes as *augmented revolution* (Jurgenson, 2012) with many examples, from Philippine protests to Arab spring. Social media and mobile phones allow protests occurring both on and offline to be far more participatory than ever before. But, as Comunello et al. shows, social media should not be considered as isolated from other media, nor online mediated activity as isolated from offline activism (Comunello et al., 2012). According to Gerbaudo, social media is used as part of a project of re-appropriation of public space, which involves the assembling of different groups around "occupied" places such as Cairo's Tahrir Square (Gerbaudo, 2012). Shirky believes in the organizing power of Internet (Shirky, 2008), but Gladwell argues that it is simply a form of organizing which favours the weak-tie connections over the strong-tie connections (Gladwell, 2010, 2011). Social virtual networks led to a mix of media networks, social networks and real networks generated by groups of interests. Granovetter theory states that weak-connections (remote acquaintances) act as bridges among groups and is important for distribution of new information inside social networks. Strong connections are presumably located inside groups among those who have many common friends and share more or less the same interests in different fields (Granovetter, 1973). Social networks online generated secondary groups different from the traditional groups which are the virtual communities and groups aggregated by individual interests without need for spatial proximity or membership of different categories as age, profession etc. The most important factor in online social groups is the content generated by user because without this content they will be empty spaces. This presumes the disponibility of users to debate a subject, proposed by themselves or by others, and to spread and share opinions and information.

Social media have both technological and space qualities used to support the social networks and expand by eMobilization, smart mobs and social movements. Social movements are described by Charles Tilly as campaigns with a clear long-term objective" to right a wrong" that has been inflected on a well specified population and consists of multiple means – ended actions aiming to correct suffering by symbolic, cumulative and indirect actions (Tilly, 1998). Etling et al. make a difference among flash mobs, smart mobs and social movements: last one is longer motions and have well-defined objectives and aim for ending an injustice or persuading authorities to enact laws or modify a state of things (Etling et al., 2010). There are many examples of cellphone-enabled smart mobs in almost all street protests after 2000 (Seattle, Philippine, Venezuela, Ukraine, etc.). Social media are not simple or neutral tools, but may become a powerful instrument to form and shape social movements (Lim, 2012). Because of technological possibilities, large number of connected people create individually or together contents and information and become producer as well as consumers (Momoc, 2004). Internet creates the possibility" to post, at minimum costs, messages and images which can be seen instantaneously by global audiences" (Lupia & Sin, 2003).

The present chapter aims to analyze the way in which social media (Facebook, Twitter, Instagram) reacted during the most massive street protests in the last 28 years in Romania. The analysis of protests reflected in online space comprises the entire domain of internet socializing possibilities, but in the present work we will focus only on social networks activity during the protests period.

A governmental emergency decree emitted at night in complete lack of transparency activated both social media and e-mobilization in Romania because it was interpreted as encouraging corruption, one of the most sensitive items in Romanian society.

The analysis below is focused mainly on the social networks activity during this month of protests and even it used objective tools of observation, it does not reflect all the emotional resources and reasons which led to the expansion of protests. In another work, we considered the same subject from a journalistic point of view (Bader, 2017) but a global analysis should consider all social, cultural and conjectural aspects in their peculiarities in terms of space and time.

METHODOLOGY

We used quantitative and qualitative methods of Internet survey appealing to specialized institution (Zelist Monitor) by following a specific hashtag (e.g. #*rezist*), most frequently used during protests. We followed quantitative web activity indicators as number of apparitions in all aspects of Internet media during one month (1–28 February). Demographic indicators (sex, age) and space indicators were used in analysis. Another topic was the day by day dynamic of posts in all social networks and new media. The analysis results are presented in form of tables and graphics. For qualitative analysis we choose two most shared images and made a socio-semiotic analysis comprehending the form, content and symbolism.

RESULTS

During street protests period 1–28 February 2017, the most used hashtag in social media which showed the connection of posts and messages to the events was "#*rezist*". Hundreds of thousands of posts on social media, images, articles, videos or simple comments were marked with this hashtag, creating a new social tendency online as the focus of awareness increased, showing that the emissors/receivers belong to the group against corruption and the governmental edict. By far, posts of greatest shares and impact were made on Facebook, Twitter and Instagram. The outcome was massive e-mobilization and street protests counting more than half million people.

During the period, the expression #*rezist* appeared 35329 times in Romanian online media as is shown in Figure 6.1.

Most of posts and shares were on Facebook – 14439 (40.9%) and on Twitter – 7660 posts (21.7%). The difference between these two social networks is explained by the fact that in Romania the network space is mostly occupied by Facebook

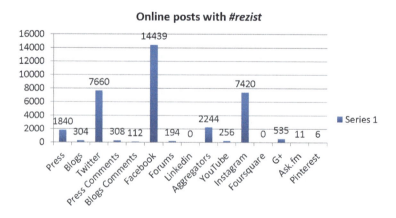

Figure 6.1. Online posts with #rezist. (Source: Zelist Monitor, https://www.zelist.ro/monitor/)

(9,600,000 accounts, represented 80% from the total space), while Twitter is used only by 8.4% by people who use Internet. Close to the percentage of Twitter but only for images, under the same hashtag, was Instagram (21%). Even the posts for professional (online press) and non-professional (blogs) journalism was significantly less important (5.2%, respectively 0.9%), their impact was significant (Bader, 2017).

The impact factor represents reaction of both simple viewers and shares related with the mentioned hashtag: *#rezist* was most visible on Facebook (71.9%), followed by Twitter (8.8%) and by online press (8.7%) (see Figure 6.2).

The online dynamics related with the analyzed hashtag was not linear but differs according to some "heating periods" both on Internet, and the street. We can observe three periods of maximum activity: the first on 5–6 February, the second in on 12–13 February, the third on 26–27 February. These periods are correlated with political communication (declaration of Govern) and the intensity of street manifestation, the last one in 27 February. In Figure 6.3 it can be seen that Facebook, Twitter and Instagram were by far the most viewed in comparison with online press and other social networks.

The demographic distribution of posters was 55.6% men and 44.4% women, most of them with ages from 30–34 years (25.9%), followed by 55–59 (22%) and 35–39 (17%) (see Figure 6.4). This shows a majority of posts made by middle aged people, from 30–39 (almost 43%), people supposal active which are interested to have a healthy social climate in Romania for themselves and their children. In some cities there were organized by online methods so-called "children protests", generally in the afternoon (not in the evening as usual) by parents coming with the children on the street.

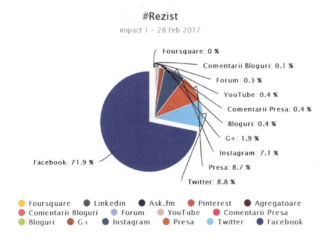

Figure 6.2. The impact of #rezist on social networks. (Source: Zelist Monitor, https://www.zelist.ro/monitor/)

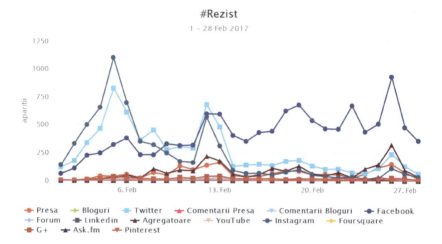

Figure 6.3. The dynamic of online posts. (Source: Zelist Monitor, https://www.zelist.ro/monitor/)

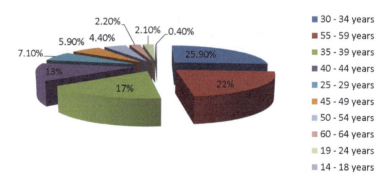

Figure 6.4. Age distribution of posters. (Source: Zelist Monitor, https://www.zelist.ro/monitor/)

The space distribution shows that most posts were in Bucharest (66.6%) where were the largest street protests too, followed by Transylvania (14.5%) and Moldova (4.3%) (see Figure 6.5).

For the qualitative analyses we used the two most shared online images. The first represents the lightning of phone lanterns at the same hour in all big cities of Romania (Bucharest, Timisoara, Cluj, Brasov, Iasi).[1] The coordination of this act was made mainly through social networks and has a symbolic value: because the edict was emitted during night (in *dark*) protesters brought *light* in solidarity.

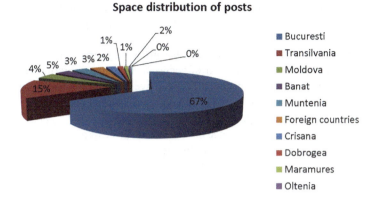

Figure 6.5. Space distribution of posts. (Source: Zelist Monitor, https://www.zelist.ro/monitor/)

The second symbolic image we considered was the depiction of Romanian flag by clothes and small individual coloured banners of participants.[2] This was a highly organized motion and was completely coordinated on Facebook in respect of colours and place. Symbolically it represents the adherence of participants to national values and a kind of "Romania is in the streets, not in political corruption".

It is impossible to evaluate the exact number of posts and shares of these and similar images because they were almost everywhere, under different names, angles, hashtags, social networks, in all groups in online and offline press, Romanian and abroad. The number of participants in Bucharest was approx. 500,000 people and probably most of them made pictures and shared them. The impact of these images was symbolically intense and had one of the greatest impact and viewership of an image in Romania (some millions views). Both these images differ from the usual negative banners or images in a protest oriented *anti*-something. They are not negative as in most protests, but *positive* actions, affirmations of symbolic values as light, transparency, care for nation's future, in contrast with what was perceived as their antinomies: darkness, obscurity, corruption. These two symbolic acts coincide with the two peaks on social networks activity shown in Figure 6.3.

DISCUSSIONS

We consider three main premises of this social phenomenon supported by social media. The first one is a state of lack of trust and susceptibility, not just in government, but in the morality of political class which raised the threshold of sensitivity. Protests were not politically or ideologically oriented, but related to morality. The second characteristic is the velocity and efficiency of communication through viral social media which mobilized hundreds of thousands of people to get out in the street. The third characteristic was the creativity, even humour, in using images as symbols

S. BADER

especially two impressive forms of manifestation art, e.g. lighting of all phone's lanterns at the same time and designing a huge national flag by using colored papers and clothes.

A legitimate question is if these manifestations were simple protests or a social movement. If we follow the definition of social movements as motions to "right a wrong" in a wide sense, we can consider these events both as protests and social movements as they had a definite moral aim and they aimed to correct such a moral infliction (restoration of corruption).

Our analyses show a clear coherence between street protests and Internet dynamics reflecting parallelism between street and Internet motions.

CONCLUSIONS

1. Romanian protests in February 2017 were reflected and potentized by social networks, mainly by Facebook which is the most used channel of communication in Romania.
2. Monitoring the most frequent hashtag showed a larger audience and implication as usual because social networks realized a focus of public awareness with social consequences.
3. All modern concepts of digital communications (eMobilization, SmartMobs, social movements) were distinguished during these protests which show their necessity as operational tools in analyzing the protests in digital era.

ACKNOWLEDGEMENTS

All graphics and analytic tools in the present chapter were disposed by courtesy of Zelist Monitor, to whom I express my gratitude. Thanks also to Gheorghe Jurj who provided valuable support and review of the present work.

NOTES

[1] See https://www.hotnews.ro/stiri-esential-21588649-moment-memorabil-piata-victoriei-toti-protestatarii-aprins-lanternele-telefoanelor.htm
[2] See https://www.digi24.ro/stiri/actualitate/justitie/legea-gratierii/protestatarii-din-piata-victoriei-anunta-un-nou-eveniment-operatiunea-steagul-ue-si-revolutia-luminii-674870

REFERENCES

Bader, S. (2012). The impact of new media on the public. The protests in Romania, January 2012. *Revista Romana de Jurnalism și Comunicare- Romanian Journal of Journalism and Communication, VII*(3–4), 35–46.

Bader, S. (2017). An analysis of online media during February 2017 protests in Romania. *Digitalne Medijske Tehnologije I Društveno-Obrazovne Promene, 7,* 19–30.

Bennett, D., & Fielding, P. (1999). *The net effect: How Cyberadvocacy is changing the political landscape.* Merrifield, VA: E-advocates Press.

POLITICAL COMMUNICATION ON SOCIAL MEDIA

Bylieva, D. S., Lobatyuk, V. V., & Rubtsova, A. V. (2018). Evolution of smart mob: From flash mob to smart city element. *European Proceedings of Social and Behavioural Sciences, 35.* doi:10.15405/epsbs.2018.02.26

Chadwick, A. (2006). *Internet politics: States, citizens, and new communication technologies.* Oxford: Oxford University Press.

Comunello, F., & Anzera, G. (2012). Will the revolution be tweeted? A conceptual framework for understanding the social media and the Arab spring. *Islam and Christian–Muslim Relations, 23*(4), 453–470.

Etling, B., Faris, R., & Palfrey, J. (2010). Political change in the digital age: The fragility and promise of online organizing. *SAIS Review of International Affairs, 30*(2), 37–49.

Gerbaudo, P. (2012). *Tweets and the streets: Social media and contemporary activism.* Retrieved from http://dl.acm.org/citation.cfm?id=2462754

Gladwell, M. (2010). Small change – Why the revolution will not be tweeted. *The New Yorker.* Retrieved from http://www.newyorker.com/reporting/2010/10/04/101004fa_fact_gladwell?currentPage=all

Gladwell, M., & Shirky, C. (2011). From innovation to revolution: Do social media make protests possible? *Foreign Affairs, 90*(2), 153–154.

Granovetter, M. (1973). The strenght of weeak ties. *American Journal of Sociology, 78*(6), 1360–1380.

Halupka, M. (2014). Clicktivism: A systematic heuristic. *Policy and Internet, 6*(2), 115–132. https://doi.org/10.1002/1944-2866.POI355

Jurgenson, N. (2012). When atoms meet bits: Social media, the mobile web and augmented revolution. *Future Internet, 4*, 83–91.

Lym, M. (2012). Clicks, cabs, and coffee houses: Social media and oppositional movements in Egypt, 2004–2011. *Journal of Communication, 62*(2), 231–248.

Lupia, A., & Sin, G. (2003). Which public goods are endangered? How evolving communication technologies affect the logic of collective action. *Public Choice, 117*, 315–331.

Momoc, A. (2014). *Comunicarea 2.0.* Iaşi: Editura Adenium.

Rheingold, H. (2003). *Smart mobs: The next social revolution.* Cambridge: Perseus Publishing.

Shirky, C. (2008). *Here comes everybody.* Great Britain: Penguin Group. Retrieved from https://uniteyouthdublin.files.wordpress.com/2015/01/here_comes_everybody_power_of_organizing_without_organizations.pdf

Tilly, C. (1998). Social movements and (all sorts of) other political interactions – Local, national, and international – including identities. *Theory and Society, 27*, 453–480.

White, M. (2010). Clicktivism is ruining leftist activism. *The Guardian.* Retrieved from https://www.theguardian.com/commentisfree/2010/aug/12/clicktivism-ruining-leftist-activism

KATARINA POPOVIĆ, MAJA MAKSIMOVIĆ AND
ALEKSA JOVANOVIĆ

7. LEARNING DEMOCRACY

Beyond the Traditional Didactics

INTRODUCTION

The discussions in Europe about the challenges and problems in developing a knowledge-based society usually refer to the development of skills and competencies, and focus on the question how to enable access to education for majority of people. Knowledge society is almost automatically associated with the communication via digital technology and participation in technology rich environment, and with education that provides individuals with the necessary vocational, transversal and soft skills.

There are enough data that support this approach – PIAAC results, EUROSTAT data on participation in adult education, youth unemployment, etc.

But the bigger picture that includes multiple data from various sources reveal the crises of the 'project Europe' and crises of the main values it is based on – democracy, antifascism, interculturalism, peace, inclusion, etc. The neoliberal stream of the global development lead to somewhat reductive understanding of education and adult education, which is perceived mainly as the tool for economic development. Broad areas where adult education historically played an important role, and could contribute today, remain outside of its scope after adult education was replaced by the concept of lifelong learning. For instance, the EAEA outlines

> ... four main issues that adult education has to deal with: the economic crisis, the crisis of European cohesion and identity, the ethical crisis and the personal crisis. (EAEA, 2015)

As much as PIAAC results were a kind of the shock and "wake up call" for adult education in Europe, Brexit, crises in Greece, migrant crises, right-wing populism, deterioration of democracy in several European countries – these should be the wake-up calls for adult education and the reminder of the importance of civic education, education for democracy and citizenship.

Some countries in Eastern Europe face multiple challenges in the context of regressive political tendencies. Since democracies in the region don't have the continuity and the tradition, they are still fragile and affected by ideological and political regression – there are strong authoritarian tendencies, nationalism is still a

© KONINKLIJKE BRILL NV, LEIDEN, 2020 | DOI: 10.1163/9789004422209_008

powerful force and political weapon, and civil society (although it plays an important role in the society) is hardly seen as the social partner. Sometimes it faces sever repression, or "it tends to be incomplete and 'dissident' in nature ... In another, less severely authoritarian set of post-communist countries, civil society is treated less harshly, but must cope with tangles of restrictions" (Ekiert, Kubik, 2014).

Some countries even experience a worrisome drift toward authoritarianism and have a long way to go to achieve consolidated democracies.

For adult education this means an urgent need to rethink traditional teaching and learning practices – to rethink concepts, content and methods, ways of work, in order to be able to meet this challenge. Unfortunately, even European countries with rooted, consolidated democracies experiences turbulences of the similar kind and don't have the solution for the growing threats to democratic governance structure and practices, and to democratic civic awareness. "People the world over are rejecting the legitimacy of liberal democracy, hardening themselves against 'enemies', retreating to the security of their tribe, and placing faith in populist leaders" (Kennedy, 2014).

LEARNING ABOUT DEMOCRACY AND CITIZENSHIP

Traditional understanding of education for democracy and democratic citizenship is clearly defined by Council of Europe:

> education for democratic citizenship" means education, training, awareness-raising, information, practices and activities which aim, by equipping learners with knowledge, skills and understanding and developing their attitudes and behaviour, to empower them to exercise and defend their democratic rights and responsibilities in society, to value diversity and to play an active part in democratic life, with a view to the promotion and protection of democracy and the rule of law. (Council of Europe, 2010)

Closely connected with this is human rights education, which is often perceived as the integral part of the education activities aiming at development or consolidation of basic democratic values and pillars of democratic societies.

> 'Human rights education' means education, training, awareness raising, information, practices and activities which aim, by equipping learners with knowledge, skills and understanding and developing their attitudes and behaviour, to empower learners to contribute to the building and defence of a universal culture of human rights in society, with a view to the promotion and protection of human rights and fundamental freedoms. (Council of Europe, 2010)

The definitions are based on traditional understanding of education and teaching where the learners should be "equipped with knowledge, skills and attitudes", and although "skills" are indicating the competency-based approach, it remains in the usual frame of "teaching and instructing", with different teaching strategies to transmit information and to develop competencies. Many of such programmes do include activities of participants, development of critical reflection, various actions and interactions, but the far-reaching impact of this approach remains questionable, as well as its power to develop values and behaviour of citizens that could be resistant to the regressive tendencies in European societies. Learning about democracy was mostly teaching about democracy, emerging dominantly in formal and non-formal education settings, leaving out most of the powerful informal factors (such as media).

In 2015, as the reaction to the terrorist attacks in France and Denmark, European ministers renewed the focus on education for democratic citizenship and reaffirmed the commitment to the main values of European societies. Still, in spite of emerging new issues and problems at the political realm of Europe,

> there was a tendency of 'tiredness' with this kind of topics in Europe, and a feeling that the society is saturated with this content. The financial crises, migrant and refugee crises, terrorist attacks and others problems raised new awareness of the urgent need for new approaches and new topics in the field of civic education and related areas. (Popović & Despotović, 2018)

These new topics and problems raised plenty of discussions, but did not manage to penetrate the curricula and the traditional spaces for teaching and learning. Additional problem is the fact that majority of the countries in Europe are democracies – democratic in form but not necessarily in substance: they have adopted rhetorical acceptance of liberal democracy, practise elections and multi-party system, but institutions might be hollow, weak and ineffective; media freedom very limited, and illiberal or even authoritarian traits very strong. The fulfilment of only formal criteria of democracy hinders engagement and investments in further programmes of education for democratic citizenship, and enables the full dominance of vocational education programmes instead.

Henry Giroux is very critical about the traditional ways of teaching democracy and the "skills concept" for this purpose:

> Democratic societies need educated citizens who are steeped in more than the skills of argumentation. And it is precisely this democratic project that affirms the critical function of education and refuses to narrow its goals and aspirations to methodological considerations. This is what makes critical pedagogy different from training. And it is precisely the failure to connect learning to its democratic functions and goals that provides rationales for pedagogical approaches which strip the meaning of what it means to be educated from its critical and democratic possibilities. (Giroux, 2004)

In his view, both critical education and the promise of global democracy face a crisis of enormous proportions, reflected in tensions between democratic values and market values, between dialogic engagement and rigid authoritarianism. This requires challenging the way ideology and practice of neo-liberalism, as a form of cultural politics, shape the education by devaluing the meaning of the social contract,

K. POPOVIĆ ET AL.

education, and citizenship and by defining higher education primarily as a financial investment and learning as a form of training for the workforce (Giroux, 2004).

EMERGENCE OF NEW DEMOCRATIC INITIATIVES

Serbia is an example of post-communist country, a society in transition, with plenty of ups and downs in its democratic development after the fall dawn of communist regime and one-party system. The authoritarian leader, demonized opposition and civil society, state control over the majority of media, institutions and over the public spaces, the lack of rule of law, corruption and fear as means of ruling – these factors are serious threat to all activities that aim, directly or indirectly, towards increasing the democratic potential of citizens. At the same time, neoliberal discourses are dominating all governmental policies, reducing workers' and civic rights for the sake of increased profit of private companies, investors and semi-legal entrepreneurships.

Serbia has significant tradition in organizing civil society movements in '90s (against war, against regime) and its civic protest played the most important role in overthrowing the authoritarian regime. The famous organization "Otpor" (Resistance) organized in 1996/97 and in 2000 hundreds of non-violent, creative events in the public spaces – on the streets, squares, in the parks. The success of the protests led to massive trainings for non-violent resistance in other countries, conducted by Serbian activists (Popović & Miller, 2015), including some of the countries that initiated "colourful revolutions" and Arab spring later on. "Learning democracy by doing" was exemplary carried out.

Some of this spirit and creativity could be seen in the recent civic actions organized in the public spaces in Belgrade: civic protest against the non-democratic measures of the government, cultural and sport activities, "occupation" of the public spaces for educational and cultural activities and many others. To mention only a few of them:

"Don't Drown Belgrade!" is civic movement against the (mis)use of public spaces, when they are dismantled or destroyed not only without consultation with experts and citizens, but also in illegal way, so that they could be used for commercial buildings, shopping malls etc. The movement organizes protests and other collective actions (marching through the streets of Belgrade, public interventions, blocking the traffic, workshops, exhibitions and public lectures and discussions, collection and dissemination of information on urban developments – BIRN, 2016) in order to express the protest against gentrification, "investors urbanism", domination of private interest and to request more civic participation in urban planning.

Main actions are around Savamala, the downtown Belgrade neighbourhood – the centre of a dispute between residents on one side, who would prefer to build park and green areas, and business owners and the government on the other, who started to build giant-size large complex called Belgrade Waterfront, with residential and office buildings, the largest shopping mall in the Balkans, and a skyscraper and shopping malls following the architectural model of

United Arab Emirate, where the main investor is coming from. (Popović, Maksimović, & Jovanović, 2018)

The movement has a political aim, which is clearly democratic one: fight for the participatory decision-making, involvement of citizens in the making and implementation of the public policy, building sense of people's priorities and contribution to formation of responsive and accountable state. Some of the actions are focused on anti-corruption measures, the others against right-wing and nationalist politics, action and groups, and for the human, civic, minority and migrant's rights, inclusion and participation.

Other initiatives and actions do not have such explicit political character, but they claim the citizens' right to use the spaces that were traditionally controlled by the state or where the state offered services to the citizens.

Self-organized cultural initiatives have emerged as a response and counter balance to top down urban development in Belgrade. Cultural and art inclusive socio-spatial interventions have reinforced horizontal decision making based on the needs of local communities ... Those places, islands within the city dominated by the market needs turn into spaces of social welfare and knowledge exchange. Thus, self-organized initiatives not only that they map existing issues and needs of local communities, but at the same time they function as providers and respond quickly to the identified problems. (Popović, Maksimović, & Jovanović, 2018)

"Occupying" unused spaces for cultural and learning activities has both symbolic character ("to free" the space, to claim the right, to elude the authorities, etc.) and pragmatic one: to win as citizen, to get a space of one's own – group, movement, community, the one that can be used for cultural and learning activities beyond the realm of the state control. One of the examples is the "Occupation of the cinema Zvezda" – an abandoned cinema in Belgrade, "occupied" since November 2014 by young artists who didn't allow cinema to be turned to a restaurant, supermarket or casino in the hasty process of Serbian privatization (Johnson, 2016). Opposing unscrupulous investors, they cleaned and equipped the cinema and started to screen alternative movies, a film repertoire that is not determined by commercial interest and market policy. Their aim is also to enable exchange among film makers from other countries, especially from the neighbouring countries.

Similarly, the project ACTOPOLIS as transnational and interdisciplinary working process (Lab) connects artists from Athens, Belgrade, Bucharest, Ankara, Madrid, Oberhausen, Sarajevo and Zagreb. ACTOPOLIS is designed as a transnational laboratory for art as urban practice, which explores possible answers and action alternatives to the question: how can urban space be expanded and sustained as a common area of society (ACTOPOLIS, 2016)? By establishing a critical space for the reflection of present-day civil society and its challenges, the project raises civic awareness and critical discussions, but also support exchange and cooperation among people from different countries. In the region of former Yugoslavia, which was involved in a bloody war not so much time ago, and is still plagued by nationalism, this is an integral element of all efforts towards democratization of the country.

To round the spectrum of diverse activities, sport should be added as an area traditionally gripped by nationalism, xenophobia and even racisms. The groups and initiatives like "442 crew" – the part of the global "Bridge the gap" movement, consists of "Belgrade Urban Running Team" from Serbia and "Zagreb runners" from Croatia, represent exactly the opposite (442, 2014–2017). It aims not only to raise awareness about the importance of sport and recreation, but even more to cross and question the national borders and to fight against nationalism and xenophobia. The main idea is a bridge that connects people – the different hoods, cultures, and sights. Bridgerunner is about conquering new parts of the city, bridging the gaps between areas, people, cultures, etc.

> In November 2016, 16 runners (eight from Belgrade and eight from Zagreb) ran from Belgrade to Zagreb to complete a course of 442 km in a relay run … The idea of running from Belgrade to Zagreb was born one year earlier, when the border between Serbia and Croatia was closed for motor vehicles for several days due to migrant crisis (September 2014). Members of 442 crew from Zagreb and Belgrade decided to run through theirs borders crossings, to meet for "shake-out run" in "no man's land". Using the kilometre – distance between capital of Belgrade and Croatia, they coined the slogan: "Two cities, two nations, two running crews UNITED in one family, one crew – 442 crew! Belgrade Urban Running Team and Zagreb runners". (Popović, Maksimović, & Jovanović, 2018)

COLLECTIVE CAPACITY BUILDING

The examples from Belgrade urban activism could be hardly seen as "capacity building" in traditional sense, as depicted in one of the widely used definitions, given by OECD and ILO:

> Means by which skills, experience, technical and management capacity are developed within an organizational structure (contractors, consultants or contracting agencies) – often through the provision of technical assistance, short/long-term training, and specialist inputs (e.g., computer systems). The process may involve the development of human, material and financial resources. (OECD, 2002)

This approach sees capacity building as individual, institutional and sectoral process, and usually insists on systematic and integrated approach on developing governmental, organizational and individual competences and capabilities. But within the UN system, the term "capacity development" is more used, since it underlines the fact that it builds on something which already exists and improves it, and doesn't start from the scratch.

UNDP sees capacity development as the process through which individuals, organizations and societies obtain, strengthen and maintain the capabilities to set and achieve their own development objectives over time. An essential ingredient in the UNDP capacity development approach is transformation. For an activity to meet the standard of capacity development as practiced and promoted by UNDP, it must bring about transformation that is generated and sustained over time from within. Transformation of this kind goes beyond performing tasks; instead, it is more a matter of changing mindsets and attitudes. (UNDP, 2009)

The difference might look small at first glance, but it indicates the crucial distinction between paradigms two approaches are based on: capacity building is clearly competency-based concept imported from human capital theory and very much focused on individual needs and outcomes. But capacity development concept which aims the transformation for individuals, community and society and goes beyond the training and teaching, can include even social initiatives and movements.

The "collective" character of the Belgrade civic initiatives consists of much more than sum of the participating actors, and overcomes the "individual – group" dichotomy. The "collective" is the origin of the initiative, the needs, interests and goals, but it brings also the dynamic of transformation and the act of creation through the interaction with Others.

Without losing the right of the person to freedom and to self-realization and self-determination, the "togetherness" of the civic action enables new kind of learning. In "Inoperative Communities" Nancy describes (1991) the modern destruction of the communities which leaves atomized individuals and communication without communities. "Community is what takes place always through others and for others. It is not the space of the egos-subjects and substances that are at bottom immortal-but of the I's, who are always others (or else are nothing)" (Nancy, 1991). In this context, the individual needs are social, but they are fulfilled through commodity consumption, while real social needs are in fact frustrated by the expansion of commodity "needs" (O'Connor, 1984). Similarly, in his concept of bio politics, Foucault recognizes the atomization of a collectively for the purpose of governance and productivity and describes the development of techniques that operated in and on the individual body as apparatuses of discipline: "that discipline tries to rule a multiplicity of men to the extent that their multiplicity can and must be dissolved into individual bodies that can be kept under surveillance, trained, used, and ... punished" (Foucault, 1976). Thus, the "togetherness", "community" and "collective" became clearly political in a broader sense, in the context of post-communist transition society in Eastern Europe. Not allowing the "atomization", the civic, cultural and sport actions in Belgrade escape not the legal framework, but the subtle mechanisms of governance control, and oppose the exercise of authoritarian and commercial power. The described civic actions are "bringing back" real social and communal needs which are not "corrupted" by commercial ways of satisfying.

The process of achieving the common goal supports the unfolding of new identity layers through new relations and interactions; at the same time, it has enormous power in strengthening civic awareness, autonomy and agency of people involved, and their mobilization potential. So, "collective" capacity building is more than group activity – it's empowering the individuals and the community through common action and social mobilization, enabling them to make the free choices and to transform the choices or decisions into the actions. Bartle (2007) puts empowerment clearly into the political and administrative environment and insists on capacity development that would enable community to go beyond formal permission and support self-help improvement and actions towards self-reliance. That's why occupying the cinemas, running across the state boarder, blocking the traffic and camping on the public squares has such a learning potential – there is no curricula and no teaching room that could make such an effect on individual agency, common self-reliance and social mobilization, which are the preconditions for active citizens in truly democratic societies.

The centralized and authoritarian political system, even when matching some of the formal criteria of democratic political system, caused that the potential ability of individuals and communities to shape their life-worlds and cultural spaces evaporated as they become integrated into rationalized systems and procedures (Placa & Knight, 2017). Thinking, and even acting out-of-the-box, daring to do so, takes people out of the system's attempt to atomize the communities and reduce them to depowered bodies/subjects with individual interest. Therefore, learning is here not perceived as an individual act of improvement of knowledge and skills, but as a collective process produced trough common action, participation and agency. Participation is relational, it concerns continuous creation of relations and opening up for new modes of existence and shared living to emerge. Learning is not an individual striving for achievement and success, but has the elements of struggling for the common well-being, which is created through rationality and participation in the world that is constantly emerging through the joint engagement … the political, shared and processual experience that emerge from, and generate further participation … Symbolic liberation, symbolic 'taking over' of parts of the city, symbolic street-trials against politicians and corruption – they should serve, as a powerful collective action, to transcend the passivity of individuals and to give the meaning and the power to the collective actions for the common well-being. They are a collective effort for the betterment of social and physical environment in the urban area – thus is human agency exercised by liberated group of citizens that is mirrored by 'inner' liberation from fear, objectification and loneliness of individuals exposed to broad range of consumerist choice, but reduced to adaptation in his/her own life (Popović, Maksimović, & Jovanović, 2018).

It shouldn't be a surprise that sport initiatives such as "442" are playing similar role: They show that sport has importance beyond health, but significant emancipatory potential. Placing sport and physical activities into the context of philosophical, critical reflection of the reality via interdisciplinary social research was already done by Max Horkheimer and Frankfurt School at the Institute for Social Research. Horckheimer included sport in the complex of social factors that should be studied multidisciplinary and brought into the critical perspective (Schroer, 2017), and Habermas emphasized the role of clubs in the political development. "442" and Bridgrunners are the modern version of sport clubs of that time and they clearly have the civic – political character, including elements like peace, intercultural tolerance, openness, inclusion – crossing the boarders of a closed mind, closed state and closed communities.

The "old" didactic principle of "learning by doing" gets new meaning; civic actions are autonomous, self-organized and self-performed, and self-organization can be seen as the daily production of a non-profit climate of self-empowerment. Non-institutional individuals and groups who work in a self-empowered way are self-organized subjects who take the responsibility for shaping their own community. So, it's not only about learning democracy (its values, rules, mechanisms and limits), it's about doing democracy.

PUBLIC PEDAGOGY AND NEW LEARNING ENVIRONMENTS

Another novelty of civic initiatives and social movements refers to the place where they occur. New learning environments were accepted as an idea and approach in adult education since the time of European Memorandum of Lifelong Learning, that recommended adult educators to go "out" and reach potential participants wherever that reside and work (European Commission, 2000). Furthermore, the concept of life-wide learning includes all learning sites – private sphere, leisure spaces, and workplace. But still – "occupying" public spaces (streets, roads, squares, public buildings), unused buildings and architectural complexes, turning them to learning spaces – this has an additional dimension, which goes beyond the flexibility and diversity of learning sites. Important is an empirical effort to transform the places into the stage of experiment, exploration and learning; further on, it is about the participation in collaborative actions as a socio-political process of place making that challenges conflicted realities of public places and disturbs the grid of existing power relations and positions. Place making through civic initiatives instead of place-marketing (making urban areas attractive place for new investments, new inhabitants and visitors) challenges the post-communist neoliberal practices and depower the authoritarian regime. Dead and unused tissue of the city has lost its original purpose and became polyvalent space that allows new ideas and functions to arise from collective actions of artists and citizens. Unused buildings become spaces of transition and transformation, that actualize only as we embody them and assign the "liberating" content and practice (subversive movies, courageous paintings or photographs, politically loaded music, dissemination of information with political importance).

In his concept of "public space" Habermas (1989) describes a space of institutions and practices between the private interests of people in everyday life and at home or workplace, and the realm of state power with arbitrary and sometimes aggressive forms of power and domination. Exceeding the boundaries of the state power in a transparent, visible ways (at the public spaces) is an act of deconstructing the power structures and mechanisms, and at the same time, it is production of the new reality, the creation of space and architecture of the city which tends to define movements and actions of citizens.

Beyond the traditional understanding of non-formal and informal learning, space-occupying and place making is learning act *per se*, which unfolds within the new framework, whose boundaries are defined by the common interest, surpassing the state interventions. Habermas attributes freedom of political and economic control to the modern public spaces, and Nemeth describes different understanding of "publicness" of the public spaces, from Warren's opinion that they serve repression and control of mass citizen political mobilization in cities, until Lefebvre's statement that public space ideally promotes active citizenship by encouraging exchange and dialogue, and expression of opposing viewpoints (Németh, 2012). The movement "Don't drawn Belgrade" is paradigmatic – it invites the dialogue about the necessity of the dialogue about the public affairs; it asks, questions, reflects, analyses, discusses, it encourages and empowers.

"Architecture becomes pedagogical, and pedagogy becomes architectural" (Ellsworth, 2005), and both become political, at individual and social level, shaping thus a new human right perspective of the well-being in the urban context. The new learning sites are not fixed, imposed, pre-arranged and structured. It is not only about alternative learnings sites, it is about new political realities, whose content and method is learning. "Education and learning in the public spaces are predominantly marked by their character outside of formal structures, state control, accessibility to citizens (putting aside the differences between 'real' public spaces, semi-private and hybrid public spaces" (Nissen, 2008). They are captured within the concept of public pedagogy: "In addition to schools, public pedagogy is now regarded as one of the crucial and influential sites for teaching and learning" (Sandlin, Schultz, & Burdick, 2010).

Biesta (2012) accentuated the importance of the interest of "publicness" as the main characteristic of public pedagogy. He suggests that public pedagogy is "a specific form of doing educational 'work', in which pedagogy 'operates' in a public way". "This form of pedagogy links the Educational and the Political and locates both in the public sphere, supporting the conceptualization of civic activism as the modern learning form" (Popović, Maksimović, & Jovanović, 2018). Activism is among the five primary categories of extant public pedagogy research found by Sandlin, O'Malley, and Burdick (2011): (a) citizenship within and beyond schools, (b) popular culture and everyday life, (c) informal institutions and public spaces, (d) dominant cultural discourses, and e) public intellectualism and social activism. Some authors like Giroux takes another view on public pedagogy, focusing on de-educating character of mass-media, on corporate-driven public spheres, commercialized and commodified public spaces where neoliberal ideology is reproduced and reinforced, critical democracy is replaced by democracy of goods available to those with purchasing power. But he invites:

> ... to preserve and revitalize those institutional spaces, forums, and public spheres that support and defend critical education, help students come to terms with their own power as individual and social agents, and reclaim those non-market values such as caring, community, trust, conviction, and courage that are vital to a substantive democracy. (Giroux, 2005)

Civic, cultural and sportive initiatives in Belgrade are doing exactly that – opposing the neoliberal ideology in its attempt to (mis)uses public spaces for commercial purposes, rejecting the "mass mediated simulacrum", confronting the mainstream of building competitive, self-interested individuals. Good example is sport sphere, where "sporting spectacles and industries are public pedagogies bolstering patriotic, nationalistic, racist, and neoliberal ideologies" (Sandlin, O'Malley, & Burdick, 2011). Running teams from Belgrade and Zagreb create bridges, connect different nations, and establish bounds that are grounded on the set of values beyond nation, patria and race. The subversive character for the mainstream ideology is more than obvious: while state is using sport to boost nationalism and xenophobia, two sport club from the hostile countries (hostile in the main ideological discourse) unite and run across the state border to demonstrate and strengthen friendship, inclusion and the spirit of humanism. This is the kind of public pedagogy as the politics of resistance, where critical theory of educational struggle (Giroux, 2003) can make a case.

ACTIVE, HOLISTIC AND EMBODIED LEARNING

The definitions of skills and competencies usually mention the combination of "certain amount" of knowledge plus performing capability plus some kind of behaviour or attitude, trying to cover all aspects of human learning, but they are still reductive by nature and limited to the development of cognitive and manual skills, with addition of soft and/or transversal skills. While all-encompassing learning, that engages learners intellectually, physically, socially and emotionally, is needed for the sustainable results of educational efforts, some of these aspects are often neglected.

> Part of the problem with psychological approaches to learning is that they are disconnected from the integral role embodiment plays in how I perceive myself, other persons and other things in the world. In this sense, it is argued that a central tenet of any educational learning involves being taught to perceive, come to know ourselves and the world around us ... What makes this account of embodied learning educationally significant is that the whole person is treated as a whole being, permitting the person to experience him or herself as a holistic and synthesized acting, feeling, thinking being-in-the-world, rather

than as separate physical and mental qualities which bear no relation to each other. (Stolz, 2014)

Even the social learning is usually limited to the formal or superficial interaction within the group, whereby the education goal is situated in the realm of individualism and competitiveness, social interaction is not grounded in the concept, goal or content of teaching and learning. Thus, using group, team and social activities in teaching might represent helpful didactic approach but it doesn't add the collective character (understood as new "togetherness") to the educational process.

Most of all, out-of-the-box initiatives and self-organized activities are missing from the common ways of teaching. Although learning theories support clearly the idea of self-activity of learner as the most promising approach for memorizing the content, for changing behaviour or developing the values, it happens seldom, except short-term, superficial and not meaningfully enough for the learner. Indeed, this requires not only resources, time and energy, but liberal institutional framework and flexible concept of learning, which can include elements of transformative learning.

Civic activities in the urban areas of Belgrade are exemplary for the comprehensive approach which includes all these elements.

Embodied learning refers not only to physical activity of participants, but also to physical crossing the boundaries, which underlines its symbolic, political meaning; to feel the power of bodies able to block the streets or square that symbolize authoritarian control, to feel connection with the Others and participate in common physical act through which something new is created. Bodies are liberated through the "liberation" of public spaces, buildings, where they can enter the realm of free participation, where they can Be.

Embodied learning relies on the "body's knowledge", which is of utmost importance for adult education. Embodied learning thus challenges dominant paradigm of how knowledge is constructed and shared, as well as its "location". By involving "body" in the educational process, these actions:

- recognize the need to feel "at home" when being in our bodies, because of the culture that traditionally banned it from education;
- include and use "body's knowledge" which otherwise take part in the process, but not-recognized, silenced or oppressed; they give it epistemological rational;
- increase the "ownership" feeling among the participant about the ongoing action and learning results, that belong to the "whole" person;
- enables engagement, literally; empowers people directly, giving them the chance to feel, exercise and control that power in the context of social goals;
- use the bodies as symbolic mean for creating and sending broader messages in a dynamic and strong way.

"Possibility for learning depends upon the existence of selves in motion" (Ellsworth, 2005). Opportunity for learning would be recognition of the greed and intentional abandonment of the demarcated positions, collective creation and entering into amorphous space in which can emerge what is not yet, thinking that invites what is yet untaught. Through the activity of place making new connections and ways of becoming emerge trough the interaction of bodies and space and the invention of new forms. These corporeal practices and interventions of communities destabilize the established norms of place and potentially lead to new possibilities of engagement and care.

Active learning is included in these activities by default; as a matter of fact, they emanate from the agency, from self-organized actions and engagement. Marching through the long streets of Belgrade, performing cultural activities, running kilometres – "these pedagogies, signal an epistemological and pedagogical shift toward appreciating bodies as agents of knowledge production and creativity as cultural capital" (Garret, 2016). Increasing motivation, enhancing creativity, enabling results – it would be difficult to find "a better recipe" for learning.

Active learning is underlined by the public spaces where activities are conducted, such as streets, which can "be conceived as a space where new forms of the social and the political can be made, rather than a space for enacting ritualized routines. With some conceptual stretching, we might say that politically, 'street and square' are marked differently from 'boulevardand piazza': The first signals action and the second, rituals" (Sassen, 2011).

The runners from Belgrade and Zagreb, Crew 442, formulate this call for "active move" on their Facebook page:

> Connected by life on the run, mutual support and a hope for better times … we founded Belgrade Urban Running Team sometime in June of 2014 with the idea to encourage our fellow citizens to get out of their beds and offices and live an active life, on the go. Also, we feel that everyone is obliged to do something good for the community they live in and make it a better place. (442 crew, 2017)

Strong emotional involvement crowns the epistemological multiplicity of these actions: "… each student is placed in the centre of the educational process, while disinterestedness is transformed into active participation and emotional neutrality into cooperation" (Smyrnaiou, 2018).

BEYOND TRADITIONAL DIDACTICS

Political, cultural and sport activities and initiatives of citizens confirm some of the main didactic principles formulate long time ago, but without a long history of implementation either because of its demanding character, or because of institutional, conceptual or individual limits and constrains. On the other hand, the whole approach has additional qualities which make it substantially different and innovative.

Especially for the field of political, civic and democratic education, these approaches proved to be moving, inspiring, mobilizing and efficient. They do depend a lot on the framework conditions – they are inspired by them and limited by them; conditions are the framework, but also the content.

K. POPOVIĆ ET AL.

The main differences these initiatives show compared to the traditional ways of learning about democracy:

- they are self-organized and bottom-up initiated;
- the topics are emerging from the real life and actual problems;
- "collective/common" is more than "in the group";
- learning and doing (activism) are the same process;
- public spaces are used as new learning sites; they are not given, but created;
- they include embodied learning;
- creativity is one of the crucial factors for the success;
- attitudes and values are included in every stage of the activities; even more – they are the *spiritus movens* of the activities.

New didactic realities, new pedagogical and andragogical practices, new learning environments, and above all – new possibility to help develop critical, open-minded, democratic citizens – all this requires educators to rethink their role, their concept and practices. Broader understanding of teaching and learning, new learning sites, redefined role of a teacher, questions about the content, power and participation in education, the role of formal education – all these questions remain a challenge for the further conceptualization and theorization of new practices. And most of all – how do we deal with the success if it happens, or how to develop further if it doesn't?

REFERENCES

ACTOPOLIS. (2017). *The art of action*. Goethe Institute. Retrieved from http://blog.goethe.de/actopolis/

Bartle, P. (2003). Enabling community empowerment. Political and administrative factors affecting self reliance. *Community Empowerment Collective*. Retrieved from http://cec.vcn.bc.ca/cmp/modules/en-en.htm

Biesta, G. (2012). Becoming public: Public pedagogy, citizenship and the public sphere. *Social & Cultural Geography, 13*, 683–697.

BIRN. (2016). *Serbia waterfront activists stage protest concert*. Retrieved from http://www.balkaninsight.com/en/article/belgrade-s-activists-to-stage-protest-concert-10-19-2016

Council of Europe. (2010). *Council of Europe charter on education for democratic citizenship and human rights education*. Strasbourg: Council of Europe Publishing.

EAEA. (2014). *EAEA statement on adult education in times of crisis*. Retrieved from https://eaea.org/wp-content/uploads/2018/01/2014_eaea-statement_adult-education-in-times-of-crisis.pdf

Ekiert, G., & Kubik, J. (2014). Myths and realities of civil society. *Journal of Democracy, 25*(1), 46–58.

Ellsworth, E. A. (2005). *Places of learning: Media, architecture, pedagogy*. New York, NY: Routledge Palmer.

European Commission. (2000). *A 'memorandum' on lifelong learning*. Commission of the European Communities, Brussels, 30.10.2000, SEC(2000) 1832.

Foucault, M. (1997). The birth of biopolitics. In P. Rabinow (Ed.), *Ethics, subjectivity, and truth. The essential works of Michel Foucault* (pp. 73–79). New York, NY: New Press.

Garrett, R. (2016). Creative and embodied learning as critical pedagogy. Australian Association for Research in Education. Retrieved from https://www.aare.edu.au/publications-database.php/10748/creative-and-embodied-learning-as-critical-pedagogy

Giroux, H. A. (2003). Public pedagogy and the politics of resistance: Notes on a critical theory of educational struggle. *Educational Philosophy and Theory, 35*(1), 5–16.

LEARNING DEMOCRACY

Giroux, H. A. (2004). Public pedagogy and the politics of neo-liberalism: Making the political more pedagogical. *Policy Futures in Education, 2*(3–4), 494–503.

Habermas, J. (1989). *The structural transformation of the public sphere: An inquiry into a category of bourgeois society.* Cambridge, MA: MIT Press.

Johnson, G. (2016). Film buffs stage a sit-in, 15 months and counting, to save a Belgrade cinema. *Los Angeles Times.* Retrieved from http://www.latimes.com/world/europe/la-fg-serbia-cinema-20160304-story.html

Kennedy, M. (2017). Brexit, the rise of Trump, Colombia's rejection of Peace: It's all related. *Medium.* Retrieved from https://medium.com/@mkennedy721/brexitthe-rise-of-trump-colombias-rejection-of-peace-it-s-all-related-8bdb601dd673

La Placa, V., & Knight, A. (2017). The emergence of wellbeing in late modern capitalism: Theory, research and policy responses. *International Journal of Social Science Studies, 5*, 1–11.

Nancy, J.-L. (1991). *The inoperative community.* Minneapolis, MN/Oxford: Minnesota Press.

Németh, J. (2012). Controlling the commons: How public is public space? *Urban Affairs Review, XX*(X), 1–25.

O'Connor, J. (1984). *Accumulation crisis.* New York, NY: Basil Blackwell.

OECD. (2002). *Glossary of statistical terms.* Retrieved from https://stats.oecd.org/glossary/

Popović, K., & Despotović, M. (2018). From education for democratic citizenship to the global citizenship education – On the necessity for a paradigm shift. *Andragogical Studies, 1*, 29–45.

Popović, K., Maksimović, M., & Jovanović, A. (2018). Towards new learning environments – Collective civic actions as learning interventions in post-Communist Belgrade. *European Journal of Education, 53*(3), 365–376.

Popović, S., & Miler, M. (2015). *Mustra za revoluciju.* Beograd: Albion Books.

Sandlin, J. A., O'Malley, M. P., & Burdick, J. (2011). Mapping the complexity of public pedagogy scholarship: 1894–2010. *Review of Educational Research, 81*(3), 338–375.

Sandlin, J. A., Schultz, B. D., & Burdick, J. (2010). *Handbook of public pedagogy.* New York, NY: Routledge.

Sassen, S. (2011). The global street: Making the political. *Globalizations, 8*(5), 573–579.

Schroer, M. (2017). *Soziologische Theorien: Von den Klassikern bis zur Gegenwart.* Leiden: Wilhelm Fink Verlag, UTB.

Smyrnaiou, Z., Sotiriou, M., Georgakopoulou, E., & Papadopoulou, O. (2017). *Connecting embodied learning in educational practice to the realisation of science educational scenarios through performing arts.* Retrieved from https://eclass.uoa.gr/modules/document/file.php/PPP394/Embodied%20learning.pdf

Stolz, S. A. (2015). Embodied learning. *Educational Philosophy and Theory, 47*(5), 474–487.

UNDP. (2009). *Capacity development: A UNDP primer.* New York, NY: United Nations Development Programme.

GEORGE A. KOULAOUZIDES AND THEODORE KOUTROUKIS

8. CRITICAL REFLECTION IN CONTEMPORARY ADULT EDUCATION

An Essential Element for Personal and Collective Capacity Building

INTRODUCTION

Continuing education, recurrent education, further education, human resource development, community or popular education, extension education, and lifelong education are some of the terms that are used in the literature to describe or even to define the framework that serves one of the most fundamental needs of adulthood, the existential need to learn. From the very moment, we enter life we find ourselves in a social situation, a relation with others, and we keep on learning to be able to cope with the demands of our collective environment (Jarvis, 2009). Learning is our natural response to every single divergence of our biographical paradigm with the social reality. And in most cases when our experiences and our meaning making mechanisms are conflicting with the fluctuating conditions of our life, engaging in instrumental or communicative learning process is adequate to create new equilibriums that allow individuals to live in harmony within their social environments.

However, there are changes in our life which are beyond our control and the new conditions that are produced because of these changes need a different kind of learning which demands the development of skills that allow the renegotiation and redefinition of the very basic foundations of our value system: our frame of reference (Mezirow, 1991). This kind of learning has been defined with many different terms (i.a. transformative, emancipatory and expansive) which however inherently contain the same connotation that of the deep transformation of a person's meaning making processes. This kind of transformation has as a prerequisite the development of critical reflection skills (Brookfield, 2011).

Our intention in this chapter is to briefly describe the structures that have changed and continue to modify our everyday living, their consequences in major areas of social activity like the labour market and adult education and to illuminate the process of critical reflection as a *sine qua non* element of all adult learning practices which aim to assist adult learners to create new meaning making schemes that will allow them to correspond to the demands of contemporary societal environments.

© KONINKLIJKE BRILL NV, LEIDEN, 2020 | DOI: 10.1163/9789004422209_009

G. A. KOULAOUZIDES & T. KOUTROUKIS

THE ERA OF GLOBALIZATION AND THE PROJECT OF NEO-LIBERALISM

It is widely recognized that globalization reshaped the international economic, political and social contexts of the modern world (i.e. Crane, Kawashima, & Kawasaki, 2016; Dale, 2007; Guscina, 2006). The contemporary tendency of increased global flows of culture, ideas, technology, innovation, money, and productive resources have become vital to our advanced societies. And although all these characteristics of the globalization phenomenon seem positive and progressive, several negative effects have been diffused especially on national policies (Drezner, 2001; Jarvis, 2007). For some these effects reflected an institutionalized political rationality trap rather than a liberation force driven by economic internationalization (Dolvik, 1999; Prokou, 2007). Globalization fosters among other things company relocation, lower-cost production, flexible specialization, capital transfer, rapid communication and information as well as new patterns of work flexibility (Dølvik, 1999; Lashgarara, Mehdi Mirdamadi, & Farajollah Hosseini, 2009). Moreover, globalization is interrelated with the rise of the service economy and this had as a result the recognition of the significance of social skills to the extent that the latter are now considered by far more important than what was traditionally understood as significant working and living skills (Koutroukis, 2007; Prokou, 2005).

Globalization has created a new form of capitalism which is better known as advanced or postmodern capitalism. This new form of capitalism conceives knowledge and learning in a rather framed understanding that restricts human development. More specifically, learning is conceived as a production-oriented process which is mainly directed by the intense global competition of various research and development departments of transnational corporations. The learning process is not recognized as an essential function for life itself but as a preparatory stage for ensuring and maintaining a position in the world of labour. Therefore, adult education has been substituted by an ambiguous and ill-defined process of lifelong learning within the framework of a person's working life. In other words, citizens learn to become producers, rather than well-educated and critically thinking citizens:

> This is the central idea of lifelong education, recurrent education, permanent education, and other formulations that have become prominent in the discourse of the field. Gone are the days of the 30-year career in the same company, and thankfully so, say the proponents of globalization. This argument maintains that if one is willing to be flexible in continuously upgrading one's skills in a just-in-time fashion, in other words to move with and at the rapid pace of the changing job market, one can enjoy the fruits of globalization. This is the position of mainstream human resource development within the field of adult education. (Brookfield & Holst, 2011, p. 131)

On the other hand, the neoliberal project has dominated the world after the collapse of the post-war Keynesian social/democratic paradigm (Finnegan, 2008). Neoliberalism became the principal ideology of capital-logic globalization, which

CRITICAL REFLECTION IN CONTEMPORARY ADULT EDUCATION

has supported the shift towards the marketization and the privatization processes in almost every aspect of social life (Duggan, 2012). Consequently, the market has become the dominant pillar in western societies and a commodification of social goods and services, including adult education and training has been fostered (Lynch, 2006). At the same time the state has gradually abandoned or reduced its distributive and social role. The social doctrine of neo-liberalism must be conceived as a powerful form of political hegemony. Neo-liberalism not only promotes a perception of human beings as self-interested and calculating individuals, but it promotes a restrictive version of citizenship (Torres, 2002). In that direction, the aim of this atypical ideological oppression project is to educate people to accept inequality, adopt the concept of private interest and abandon social dialogue procedures on social and economic issues (Finnegan, 2008).

Advanced capitalism recognizes knowledge and learning in a different way. The research and development departments of the transnational and detached from society co-operations have metamorphosed the definition of knowledge from a meaning-making processes to a "know-how" process that is adjusted to the needs of the globalized model of production. Adult education is transformed to a barren production-oriented vocational training procedure (Prokou, 2007).

LABOR FORCE & ADULT EDUCATION: NOVEL IDENTITIES

In the aforementioned context labour force is called to adopt to several sorts of flexible, adaptable and precarious forms of work. The economies created by advanced capitalism, known as knowledge economies demand a labour force with high skills, able to correspond to the rapid technological advancements (Brown, & Lauder, 2001). Thus, these economies generously fund the upgrading skills to improve the employability of the working class, and thus to maintain a specialized and well-trained workforce that serves as a competitive advantage. Following that orientation, the state adult education strategies emphasize the workers' need to participate in continuous learning processes to maintain the country's position in the global ranking of economic performance (Prokou, 2005). Investments in human capital is seen as significant, only if it serves growth and productivity. More and more we are witnessing national and international public funding to become re-orientated from the area of popular/liberal adult education to vocational training provisions. That shift has transformed adult education to work-related training, and several educational organizations have been challenged to become significant providers of such training services (Milana, 2012).

The marketization of learning supported by the ideology of neo-liberalism, and the concept of lifelong learning, seeks to implement the fundamental principles of free market approach and the commodification of goods and services in adult education and continuing vocational training (Fejes & Olesen, 2016). Lifelong learning indicates a focus on work and, specifically, on the employees' flexible preparation to upgrade their business-like knowledge and skills and to adapt themselves in the

101

G. A. KOULAOUZIDES & T. KOUTROUKIS

new working conditions and interchange easily among workplaces or enterprises (Jarvis, 2007). In that neo-liberalistic labour market regime, every individual is responsible to be employable in a transnational competitive working environment. Individualized is also the responsibility to participate in lifelong learning activities, whereas the state and the employers gradually abandon their responsibilities in the field educational policy (Finnegan, 2016).

To follow this trend increasingly more people, spend time and money in various individualized (i.e. isolated learner in front of a tablet or a laptop) and individualistic (i.e. learner which pursue just his own interests and/or satisfaction) learning activities (Milana, 2012). However, it is noteworthy that the more educated employees who hold privileged jobs are more likely to participate in advanced training programs than the low-skilled workers (Prokou, 2005; Lynch, 2006). As it was pointed by Jarvis (2007) learning during the working life is shifted to a more utilitarian model and future employees learn for the sake of production rather than to be citizens of an open participatory society where citizens are able to challenge the externally imposed frames of political, social and economic reference. This is not surprising since the neo-liberal project fosters the maximization of individual choice, the regulatory role of the free market forces, a coordinated attack on collective social actors (i.e. trade unions) and the weakening of social solidarity (Finnegan, 2016). In this context "… while vocational skills are still necessary, we need to consider training people in the organizational, mobilizing and advocacy skills that help them to create a society in which the needs of people are put before the needs of profit" (Brookfield & Holst, 2011, p. 140). However, these new skills may not be cultivated in a frame of reference that remains unchallenged and unquestioned by the recipients of its assumptions. Therefore, there is a need to resituate and redefine the core cognitive process that may assist adults to move towards this direction: the process of critical reflection.

CRITICAL REFLECTION RESITUATED AND REDEFINED

Critical reflection as a learning process is discussed by several authors in the literature of adult education. However, the most coherent and practical conception of critical reflection may be found within the critical approach of adult education (Freire, 1973; Brookfield & Holst, 2011). According to this approach critical reflection is a process that aims to direct a learner through a careful, insightful and in-depth examination journey of the assumptions on which rests the perception of reality. More specifically, Brookfield (1988) suggests that a mental exercise may be characterized as a critical reflection process when it includes four important activities: (a) assumption analysis, (b) contextual awareness, (c) imaginative speculation and (d) reflective scepticism. This process of critical reflection is leading to challenging the validity of the prior assumptions of a person's frame of reference or in other words of the conceptual toolbox that a person uses to interpret the world and her/his relations with the self and the others. This course of cognitive action is the core of the process of transformative

CRITICAL REFLECTION IN CONTEMPORARY ADULT EDUCATION

learning (Mezirow, 1991). The question here is what exactly these activities mean for adult educators who are called to facilitate different programs and courses within the socio-political context that was described in the sections above? In what way should we revisit the concept of critical reflection to resituate it in an era which is overwhelmed by the consequences of advanced capitalism, neoliberalism and globalization? We will attempt to answer these questions by providing our opinion for each of these dimensions of critical reflection.

Assumption analysis: is the activity that has as its purpose to is question a person's taken for granted assumptions and their resulting cultural practices in connection to everyday life. In the case of the neoliberal project several assumptions have been recorded as norms that are taken for granted in the societies of the so-called developed countries (i.e. Portes, 1997; Cahill, 2014; Hall, Massey, & Rustin, 2013). The following are some indicative examples of neoliberal assumptions that have a great impact on a person's everyday life: (a) *Economic growth is the main road to prosperity*: this assumption which more or less dominates the political rhetoric all over the world implies that growth produced by capital is the only way to generate new wealth. The implication of this assumption is that people are willing to accept welfare cuts and adopt and reproduce the subsequent distorted view that public education, public health and the environment are tolerable sacrifices for the sake of capital investment and (b) *Human values can be monetarily calculated.* The implication of this assumption is related to a social incoherence point of view that supports the idea that every human value (e.g. trust, love, dignity, peace) including moral values may become a commodity. Adult educators committed in fostering critical reflection must seek for such assumptions within the frame of reference of their learners. The analytic exposure of these assumptions is the opening decisive stage in a transformative learning process.

Contextual awareness: activities that aim to facilitate contextual awareness include to our opinion a process of political conscientization, that is the awareness of the dynamics of political coercion that are lying underneath our meaning making assumptions (Freire, 2005). The recognition of the vital role of the neoliberalism principles and capitalism ethics in the development of our patterns of thought and behaviour are not simple complimentary actions to the recognition of our assumptions. The realization of these dynamics is the foundation stone for the development of new learning that may lead to the creation of other social structures and political agendas (Brookfield & Holst, 2011). From this contextual awareness processes the role of mass media must be exposed. Global media via well-designed and carefully veiled processed of promoting certain social patterns of behaviour, support the foundations of neoliberalism through the creation of new ethics that sustain the assumptions of advanced capitalism (McChesney, 2001; Hesmondhalgh & Toynbee, 2008).

Imaginative speculation: This is one of the most crucial dimensions of critical learning process in our era. Given that both Freire (1970) and Mezirow (1991) have recognized in their work that the distorted assumptions confine adult development through the entrapment within dysfunctional meaning making schemes which are

103

G. A. KOULAOUZIDES & T. KOUTROUKIS

the product of specific ideologies, the stage of imaginative speculation is the element of critical reflection that opens the gates of transformation. Imaginative speculation is about giving adult learners the opportunity to develop and practice alternative views for personal and collective progress beyond the dominion of the neoliberal paradigm. However, we argue that this process should not remain inside the walls of a classroom or any other educational setting. Imaginative speculation has to become a process continuously informed by the analysis of real situations of social struggle. Brookfield and Holst (2011) consider this kind of activity a part of what they define as radical teaching:

> Radical teaching can certainly happen in formal classrooms or in formal ways in fields, factories or cyberspace, but it is always shaped by a particular struggle. Sometimes the teaching will focus on very specific situations, at other times on understanding the historical context and line of march within which highly particular situations need to be understood. Sometimes the teaching will help people learn the specific organizational skills of mobilizing a neighbourhood, setting up committees, establishing food banks, or creating alternative media. But teaching situated in struggle also introduces theory and helps people learn how to analyse experience critically and collaboratively. (Brown & Lauder, 2001, pp. 120–121)

This kind of teaching evolves imaginative speculation by presenting with the best possible manner that the dominant ideologies may not only be challenged in theory but in real life situations.

Reflective scepticism: reflective scepticism is the final activity of a comprehensive critical reflection process. Within the framework we have defined this activity assists the adult learner to reject the narrative of globalization and thus diminish the established values inherently situated to the neoliberal project. Adult learners after being exposed through the process of imaginative speculation to alternative social structure should make one more step forward. And because this final step is important and crucial it has to be guided by the facilitating agents of their learning, i.e. adult educators. At this point adult learners have to engage in a dialectical and deep examination of every belief system adherent to the neoliberalist project to realize that its claim which promises solutions to every single human problem through the globalization process is just one more perceptual deception that aims only in establishing habitual behaviours and deep-rooted social structures that serve the interest of the advanced capitalism.

EPILOGUE

Our world has changed in many ways. The global population has increased with an unprecedented rhythm and more and more people are living in large cities while the internet has transformed almost every aspect of our lives, from the way we meet people, we communicate and express our opinions to how we shop or entertain

CRITICAL REFLECTION IN CONTEMPORARY ADULT EDUCATION

ourselves. Social media have become an influential feature of our life and climate change is becoming a miserable reality for many areas of our planet while numerous social issues related to migration and the rights of certain social groups are finding their way into the public eye. In such a complex and globalized world, the interests of advanced capitalism are served in a cruel and inhumane manner through the domination of a neoliberal paradigm that methodically through technology and media has managed to impose specific meaning making schemes that accept and diffuse authoritarianism and social oppression. In such a unbearable social environments we support to revisit and resituate the notion of critical reflection as a core component of adult education programmes to create the conditions for a social transformation based on the principles of social democracy, solidarity and a commitment to policies that may control inequality, oppression of underprivileged groups and poverty.

REFERENCES

Brookfield, S. D., & Holst, J. D. (2011). *Radicalizing learning: Adult education for a just world*. San Francisco, CA: Jossey-Bass.

Brown, P., & Lauder, H. (2001). Education, globalization and economic development. In A. Bolder, W. R. Heinz, & G. Kutscha (Eds.), *Deregulierung der Arbeit – Pluralisierung der Bildung? Jahrbuch Bildung und Arbeit* (Vol 1999/2000). VS Verlag für Sozialwissenschaften, Wiesbaden.

Cahill, D. (2014). *The end of Laissez-Faire? On the durability of embedded neoliberalism*. Cheltenham Glos: Edward Elgar Publishing.

Crane, D., Kawashima, N., & Kawasaki, K. I. (2016). Culture and globalization theoretical models and emerging trends. In *Global culture* (pp. 11–36). London: Routledge.

Dale, R. (2007). Specifying globalization effects on national policy: A focus on the mechanisms. In *Education, globalisation and new times* (pp. 80–98). London: Routledge.

Dølvik, J. E. (1999). *The globalisation challenge: Convergence or divergence of national labour market institutions?* Oslo: Fafo Paper.

Drezner, D. W. (2001). Globalization and policy convergence. *International Studies Review, 3*(1), 53–78.

Duggan, L. (2012). *The twilight of equality? Neoliberalism, cultural politics, and the attack on democracy*. Boston, MA: Beacon Press.

Fejes, A., & Salling Olesen, H. (2016). Editorial: Marketization and commodification of adult education. *European Journal of Research on the Education and Learning of Adults, 7*(2), 146–150.

Finnegan, F. (2008). Neo-liberalism, Irish society and adult education. *The Adult Learner: The Irish Journal of Adult and Community Education*, 54–73.

Finnegan, F. (2016). The future is unwritten: Democratic adult education against and beyond neoliberalism. *Adult Learner: The Irish Journal of Adult and Community Education*, 46–58.

Freire, P. (1970). *Pedagogy of the oppressed*. New York, NY: Herder & Herder.

Freire, P. (2005). *Education for critical consciousness*. New York, NY: Continuum International Publishing Group.

Guscina, A. (2006). *Effects of globalization on labour's share in national income*. International Monetary Fund.

Hall, S., Massey, D., & Rustin, M. (2013). After neoliberalism: Analysing the present. *Soundings, 53*(53), 8–22.

Hesmondhalgh, D., & Toynbee, J. (Eds.). (2008). *The media and social theory*. London: Routledge.

Jarvis, P. (2007). *Globalization, lifelong learning and the learning society: Sociological perspectives*. Oxon: Routledge.

Koutroukis, T. (2007). Developments in the level and structure of employment and their impact on industrial relations in the service sector of the developed countries: A literature review. *The Cyprus Journal of Science and Technology, 5*(3), 21–26.

105

G. A. KOULAOUZIDES & T. KOUTROUKIS

Lashgarara, F., Mehdi Mirdamadi, S., & Farajollah Hosseini, S. J. (2009, July 6–8). Globalization and adult education. In *Proceedings of the International Conference on education and new learning technologies (EDULEARN09)*. Barcelona, Spain.

Lynch, K. (2006). Neo-liberalism and marketisation: The implications for higher education. *European Educational Research Journal, 5*(1), 1–17.

McChesney, R. W. (2001). Global media, neoliberalism, and imperialism. *Monthly Review, 52*(10), 1.

Mezirow, J. (1991). *Transformative dimensions of adult learning*. San Francisco, CA: Jossey-Bass.

Milana, M. (2012). Political globalization and the shift from adult education to lifelong learning. *European Journal for Research on the Education and Learning of Adults, 3*(2), 103–117.

Portes, A. (1997). Neoliberalism and the sociology of development: Emerging trends and unanticipated facts. *Population and Development Review*, 229–259.

Prokou, E. (2005). Globalization, knowledge society of and lifelong learning: Trends to the policies of continuous vocational training in Europe. In D. Vergidis & E. Prokou (Eds.), *Planning, management and evaluation of adult education programs* (Vol. 1, pp. 129–165). Patras: Hellenic Open University. [in Greek]

Prokou, E. (2007). The "governmental strategy" in lifelong education in Europe and Greece. *Social Cohesion and Development, 2*(2), 179–192. [in Greek]

Torres, C. A. (2002). Globalization, education, and citizenship: Solidarity versus markets? *American Educational Research Journal, 39*(2), 363–378.

PART 2

COLLECTIVE CAPACITY BUILDING IN HIGHER EDUCATION

GEORGETA ION AND MARINA TOMÀS-FOLCH

9. WHO ARE THE KNOWLEDGE PRODUCERS IN HIGHER EDUCATION?

An Inquiry into the Self-Perceptions of Postdoctoral Researchers in Higher Education in Spanish Universities

INTRODUCTION

The conception of a knowledge-based society significantly transforms the models of production and organization of contemporary societies (Hazelkorn, 2005; Felt, 2007) with consequences at all levels, including the university. Knowledge is converted in the base for economic development (Dale, 2005) under the concept of "knowledge economy" (Lucas, 2009, p. 11) and influences the models of its production at university level. To respond to this demand, higher education institutions are organized to respond to the needs of the economy, in terms of scientific and economic innovation, which poses some concern on the change towards a university system that is more competitive and market-oriented. These reforms centre on the alignment of the university and knowledge or information society that has significantly transformed the production models at a social level and altered the organization of contemporary societies (Hazelkorn, 2005; Felt, 2007). To address societal demands, universities began to intensify their research activity, making the production of knowledge a priority (Etzkowitz et al., 2008). This trend has consequences university models and on the researchers as knowledge producers.

In their effort to adapt to market demands, universities intensify their research dimension, which extends beyond the individual contribution and in which scholars are expected to push their ideas to application and eventually to the market. This phase of research intensification is characterized by the creation of a stimulating organizational culture to attract and retain high-level professionals and students. This step enhances the volume of research, the percentage of doctoral qualified staff and the quantity and quality of scientific publications (Slaughter & Leslie, 1997).

Postdoctoral researchers and scholars (PDR&S) represents an increasingly important group, because their high level of expertise (e.g., O'Grady & Beam 2011), contribute to the knowledge production and social and economic growth (Hayrinen-Alestalo & Peltola, 2006). At the same time, they represents a group with high levels of productivity (Lucas, 2009) and are source of research and innovation in academia due to their career prospects and potential in building future research intensive

© KONINKLIJKE BRILL NV, LEIDEN, 2020 | DOI: 10.1163/9789004422209_010

careers (Davis, 2009; Mitchell et al., 2013). In addition, PDR&S became in the last decade's active actors in knowledge mobilization and transfer through the creation of professional networks between academia and society/industry (Horta 2009; Ion & Castro, 2017).

However, in spite of PDR&S role in academia, their academic work and trajectories are still characterized by uncertainty and vulnerability. The recent studies analyze their role in the production of knowledge especially from a quantitative perspective (Van Balen, Van Arensbergen, Van der Weijden, & Van den Besselaar, 2012; van der Weijden, Teelken, & de Boer, Drost, 2015; Felisberti & Sear, 2014, among others) in terms of impact of their production and contribution to the knowledge production. This situation leads us to consider the need for research in depth in PDR&S research activity form a qualitative in depth perspective, bringing new knowledge on who they are (the literature demonstrate that postdocs are weakly embedded and not recognized as a separate staff category in most of European universities (Lucas, 2009). This added to the poor policies for postdocs management and professional development measures (Fitzenberger & Schulze, 2013, among others) leads to a vulnerable position in academia and vulnerability of their professional status with implications on their own career prospects and university research management and development (Ion & Castro, 2017).

In spite of their important roles in higher education institutions, their academic career trajectories are characterized by uncertainty resulting some interrelated issues.

One is related to their role and functions in the HEI, due to the lack of specific regulations regarding their research, teaching and managerial tasks. The relationship between teaching and research is one of the topics in depth analyzed (Horta, 2009; Tomàs, Castro, & Feixas, 2012) but how are they distributed in the workload of PDR and how they perceive their performance.

In second place, the new university model oriented to the market focuses attention on the need to create and work in networks within the same HEI and externally in order to make research more visible and accessible to the potential users (Mohram, Ma, & Baker, 2008, among others). In this context researchers face new challenges and highlight the need to understand how PDR deal with this new function and understand how they establish and maintain relationships and networks with other researchers.

Thirdly, the change in the university model based on research and the increasing role of external and internal quality control system scholars face some loss of professional autonomy as they increasingly must negotiate their work with external funding agencies seeking to influence certain decisions of the research process (data sharing, influence priorities or require prompt results) (Lucas, 2009; Felisberti & Sear, 2014). In addition, it identifies other costs such as limiting collegiality and control of the academics themselves on decision-making processes and professional practices with influences on their career prospects and expectations (Fitzenberger & Schulze, 2013; van der Weijden, Teelken, de Boer, & Drost, 2015).

WHO ARE THE KNOWLEDGE PRODUCERS IN HIGHER EDUCATION?

THE DEVELOPMENT OF RESEARCH ACADEMIC TRAYECTORY IN SPANISH HIGHER EDUCATION

The political orientations of the European Union are progressively based on the idea of knowledge economy where public organizations move towards market-orientation. In this line, universities, as producers of knowledge, are expected to become part of the development and innovation system where the final goal is to contribute to the international competitiveness of the European economy (Hayrinen-Alestalo & Peltola, 2006).

The increasing scientific aspirations of universities in Spain under the external pressures and control, indicate a new situation where the largest Spanish universities have seriously begun to think of their scientific importance and societal relevance (De Miguel, Caïs, & Vaquera, 2001). By putting emphasis on a good scientific basis as a source of new university model and institutional dynamic, the Spanish universities adopted new modes of knowledge production (Ion & Castro, 2017).

Recent studies published in Spain analyze the relationship between the university system's quest for productivity and how the research-intensive Spanish universities function (Tomàs, Mentado, & Ruiz, 2015). These institutions possess strong institutional structures that support research activity and have established systems to promote research and scholarship, such as funding opportunities, transfer networks, systematic support for publication, project presentations and the visibility of successful results. As with any process of transformation, the move to a market-oriented university takes time and requires effort and dedication from the entire academic community. Consistent with market-oriented trends in higher education, Spanish universities are increasingly interested in the intensification of the research function (Castro & Tomàs, 2011).

Consistent with European trends, Spain has recently promoted reforms to strengthen higher education institutions and their organizational logic intended to make them more responsive to current societal challenges and to orient the environment's demands to market (Pérez-Díaz & Rodríguez, 2001).

The mentioned reforms of the higher education system and especially of the research profiles of the academic staff affected differently the different categories of academics. Doctoral researchers, postdoctoral encountered in the first phases of the academic career or senior researchers are facing in different manner the consequences of the changes of the academic culture and logic.

In order to better understand the higher education academic trajectories in the Spanish system, we will summarize the main categories:

In the first category represented by postdoctoral academics, are included especially academics with a PhD degree and situated in the initial phase of their career. In this group there are two subgroups as follows:

- *"Profesor Ayudante Doctor"* (assistant professor PhD) posts are temporary positions (4 years) for which a PhD degree is required. Candidates must obtain the necessary accreditation from the ANECA, the national evaluation agency.

This position may adopt a variety of forms, from a postdoctoral grant to the more formal "Ayudante Doctor". It is a temporary position entailing both research and teaching.

- "*Contratado Doctor*" (Lecturer) is a temporal position regulated by standard labour legislation. In order to be hired as such, one needs the specific accreditation from the ANECA. To obtain this accreditation, one typically has to prove at least 3 years of postdoctoral experience. This is a temporal and non-civil servant position. Lecturers are expected to do both teaching and research and have full autonomy for teaching and developing research programmes.

In the second category of staff usually representing the professorship level, according to the consolidation of the position, we include two subgroups:

- "*Profesor Titular*" (tenured civil servant position or Associate Professor): It is necessary to obtain a national accreditation made by quality agencies and to pass the selection made at institutional level. The criteria on which merit is judged include teaching, research, coordination and supervision of academic activities and administration.
- "*Catedrático*" (Full Professor): Normally one needs to have been associate professor for at least three years to be able to apply, and far from all tenured staff reach this level.

Professors in this category are usually permanent civil servants or contracted. They are expected to do both teaching and research. A high level of initiative towards general development and running of the department is also expected. In general, the teaching load for all academic positions at Spanish universities is relatively high, but may be reduced by successful research activities. Teaching activities are controlled by the universities, whereas research is normally more independent usually done in the framework of a research group.

In this chapter we understand by postdoctoral researchers, all the researchers which are in the period after their PhD thesis, independently if they are in early researchers or experienced researchers.

In our study we set Spanish universities in the context of the knowledge economy and analyze the challenges for the academics in this context addressing issues as: function performed in their work, the relationships formed and maintained with other researchers and their host institution, the role and experience of autonomy in their research, the perceptions of career prospects and future and the interplay of professional/academic and personal lives and demands.

In this context, our chapter aims to fill this gap and provide new insights on the postdocs from a qualitative perspective focusing mainly in study 5 queries related to the role of postdocs as knowledge producers in academia:

- functions performed in their work;
- network system (relationships formed and maintained with other researchers);

WHO ARE THE KNOWLEDGE PRODUCERS IN HIGHER EDUCATION?

- perceptions of career prospects and future;
- role and experience of autonomy in their research.

METHODS

In depth interviews were conducted at five Spanish universities that are renowned for their productivity in research (Buela-Casal et al., 2012): Autonomous University of Barcelona (UAB), University of Barcelona (UB), Complutense University of Madrid (UCM), University of Granada (UGR) and Pompeu Fabra University (UPF) in Spain.

The respondents were postdoctoral researchers in consolidated and high prestigious research groups. Between 1 and 2 research groups from each of the 5 universities were selected from different fields of knowledge and that are highly productive. A total of 17 postdoctoral researchers participated, representing all the disciplinary fields. According to the professional development scale explained in the previous parts of the chapter, the postdoctoral researchers are academics in the initial and middle level of their career equivalent to lecturer and assistant professor. Table 9.1 presents the distribution of the sample by university of origin. In order to ensure the anonymity of the sources we coded the universities participating in the study with codes as illustrated in the table below.

Table 9.1. Sample of respondents

Respondents/Universities	U1	U2	U3	U4	U5	Total
Postdoctoral researchers	4	4	2	3	4	17

RESULTS

Functions Performed as Postdoctoral Researcher

The functions performed by the postdoctoral researchers are directly linked with the university mission. All the respondents strongly agree that the university's principal missions are teaching, research and the transfer of knowledge. The respondents also emphasized that the connection between teaching and research has flaws. Specifically, participants argue that both functions are equally important, at least in the formal discourse, although tension is experienced in the transition from a university culture with a strong teaching component towards a more research-oriented approach, socially in the recent years marked by the university preoccupation for competitiveness in a globalized higher education scenario.

> We come from a university model that is clearly addressed to teaching where the faculty was selected according to teaching needs, and all this points to the fact that we are now moving to a university model focused on the productivity

113

of the research. Yet we are now in a paradigm shift and, hence, much confusion and many contradictions are perceived. (Postdoc_U4)

This argument is put into context by the postdoctoral researchers who suggest that more importance is currently accorded to research than to teaching, given that research grants a greater level of prestige and professional recognition to the university.

> In the current financial crisis, some research projects can mean a significant source of income for the university and the research groups. It also involves greater prestige, greater social recognition, and helps to assure academic promotion. (Postdoc_U1)

Researchers noted that because each university has a mission that emphasizes teaching or research, each institution adopts different decisions.

> Not all the universities, faculties, departments and research groups rate both functions equally. There are traditions, institutional approaches and different career paths, and hence, the values of the mission of each university and department are very different. (Postdoc_U5)

In the process of the institutional mission, those who most urgently demand a change are the postdoctoral researchers because they argue that they suffer the most from the dysfunctions of the change from one model to another.

> I get the feeling that I am right in the middle, given that some senior researchers still demand certain past requirements. However, we also have to face the new demands of productivity with which the system will evaluate us in the near future. (Postdoct_U2)

A new management model more in keeping with the approach of intensifying research coexists with the traditional model since the change in approaches and practices themselves is not automatic and academics need more time to adopt and internalize it. This explains why in some cases; participants perceive that they are in a process of adaptation and internalization of the new "rules of the game" and the new academic culture. In this sense one of the principal investigators points.

> The culture of publishing articles is already very common in college. This culture is not automatically acquired. When there were no sections of research items were evaluated. It is a system that penalizes innovation teaching, because penalizes what is new. (Postdoc_U3)

The new approach of intensifying research is leading to a reconfiguration of the teaching function of academic and professional development. Scholars believe that the new model of university research-oriented influences the ways of doing and understand their function. In this scenario some conflicts arising from the difference between the perceptions that academics have about their professional work at the university and the new approach that the university is taking to manage academic research shows. So while academics still perceive research as a function related to knowledge creation, updating teaching and creativity, from an institutional perspective this serves to control productivity, transfer to the socio-economic sector and positioning institution in the context.

In relation to the different perceptions of academics interviewed on this subject their responses can be placed between two complementary positions. On one side are those scholars who recognize the advantages of the new approach, highlighting the improvement in competitiveness and the prominent role of the university in the process of raising funds.

> I think the university is doing well, for example our university is the first in international projects. The latest news I have is that all Andalusian universities together had obtained 35 million euros, of which thirteen and a half are for that of Granada. We now have 48 active projects. (Postdoc_U4)

On the other hand, we find the most contrary to the approach focused on productivity positions. Critics say the new approach with it greater difficulties occur in the professional development of researchers due to the high pressures and higher competency standards required.

> We are giving too much importance to productivity and that does not seem right. We are obsessed with rankings, with lists of journals, to know where and how many publications do, how many are missing me and how many have placed the field. It is a model that adds nothing, just stress. (Postdoc_U2)

The university mission and vision has changed in the last years in order to adapt to the requirements of the knowledge economy. The university opened to the society and economy needs and the research carried out tried to respond to these needs. One of the participant's summaries the university role.

> The university has a diversity of roles in the society. Firstly, has to produce "brains". Secondly has to produce, use and transfer knowledge. Because the society has changed in the last years. We have to adapt to this and focus on a knowledge society able to grow up through the knowledge produced. The university has to be engaged with this role. (Postdoc_U3)

The university has changed its mission and the new model of academic management has been implemented. The intensification of the research dimension of the university it is recognized by all the agents involved in the academic life. Researchers are the agents most involved in this process and they recognized their role in the research production and transfer, but claim for more institutional support and structures. They consider that their work depends on the coherence between all organizational units and bodies. One of the researchers stated:

G. ION & M. TOMÀS-FOLCH

> Currently, the vice-rectorate responsible for research is mainly an administrative body not a scientific one. In my opinion this unit is working really bad, they need an upgrade to the new requirements. There is no coordination between rectorate and departments and also there is missing a better connection between university level and schools level and also between different research units. (Postdoc_U3)

A defining element of scientific productivity is related to the transfer of knowledge to society. Participants recognized the significant progress made by the university with the current research-oriented model, but warn about the lack of resources or institutional support for these initiatives. The perception of the participants is that a university connection – company is required to ensure good transfer activity.

> Here, we transfer because we work a lot with companies and there is a lot of contact, we make contracts with companies. (Postdoc_U2)

Academics denounced a profound change in their role in recent years have diversified their tasks and responsibilities have increased. The pressure generated by the high demand for academic productivity and the stress generated by the continuous evaluation exercised imply a review of their own professional identity. These multiple facets of professional identity are attributable to the ways of understanding the information received by the institution. Its multiple realities are obvious, but not always the institution knows them communicate and explain properly.

> This is distorting the objects themselves and publishing goals: for many young people who come today to do the thesis it is important to publish and seek only to directors who know that published in major journals. I find it a horror. (Postdoc_U1)

Relationship and Networks

Most of the postdoctoral researchers are working in research groups formed by academics mainly from the same institution. Connections with another groups and professionals form other universities or disciplines are seen as good practices.

> Connections with other groups we have especially in teaching innovations, but not in research yet. In the last years we try to open our group to other universities and other contexts because there are funding opportunities which required it. (Postdoc_U5)

The collaboration within and between institutions is increasing its presence, in "hard" disciplines has a certain tradition. The benefits are essential to the success of the intensification of university research: sharing information, establishing and maintaining exchange programs (teachers and students), improve the chances of international funding, collaborate on research proposals, etc.

WHO ARE THE KNOWLEDGE PRODUCERS IN HIGHER EDUCATION?

The connections with the industry are determinate by the knowledge transfer process and the university seems it is not prepared yet to respond to the society demands. Participants consider that the industry doesn't require for research results in the same rhythm as the university is able to produce.

> The company has not been enhanced research. Here is a different mindset, the company wants to make money fast in this model is very difficult to fit research. This has resulted in a lack of understanding. The company does not demand this research at the same pace. Researchers believe more work to outside companies, publishing articles in magazines and it is likely that companies take strange ideas there. It is possible that the Spanish company miss this opportunity to incorporate quality research we do in Spain. The lack of practice relating to the company enables research to be conducted in other subjects. (Postdoc_U3)

The interest for the research transfer changed the focus of the academic life according to participants and sometimes the participants experiment difficulties to meet their expectations or to identify themselves with the institutional developments.

> Today I recognize myself less within my university few years ago. I recognize myself less because I think he's having a transition towards the business world at the university. College is an unemployed factory, nor do I think he should be attached exclusively to the interests of the market, and we run some danger he be transformed into a higher level of training. I think the university should have other missions as critical of art and scholarship. The research is in danger of lack interest if we are governed by economic criteria, both the output. (Postdoc_U2)

Networks with social context or industry depends, according to researchers to the field of knowledge where the research is conducted.

> We make a kind of work that does not bind us to any company. We as theoretical linguistics in different areas and specializations (phonetics, phonology) but what we do is agreements with companies. What we do is theoretical. I understand that in other faculties, for example veterinary, yes you can do. But we do not, we have no relationship with companies or entities outside. (Postdoc_U1)

Career Prospects

Postdoctoral researchers experiment job pressures and instability and some succeed in finding a potentially or actually tenured position, while others lack clear career prospects and tend to accumulate a number of postdoc positions and eventually leave academia. Mobility is mandatory in order to achieve experience but also to enlarge professional networks. Also, mobility represents a requirement in order to

G. ION & M. TOMÀS-FOLCH

advance in the career, according to the criteria established by the external assessment agencies.

Mobility is not always seen as an opportunity but with some anxiety. Postdocs have to leave their social capital and move to an uncertain future. When asked about their career aspirations and expectations, most respondents prefer to continue working in their university or research institute after their postdoc period finishes. However, this is not always possible especially in the Spanish economic crisis context when the new vacancies are very few in the last years. However, the postdocs with academic career ambitions are dissatisfied with their opportunities to continue working in academia and most of them have to search for new opportunities abroad. This mobility represents also a way to open the university to new contexts as a principal investigator states, but not all of them are willing to do so.

> When a postdoc research leaves our university will not close the door but opened the possibility to come or to work together or collaboration between universities of countries. (Postdoc_U1)

A number of postdocs spent time during their postdoc positions to further develop additional skills in order to expand their eligibility for career options beyond research. Postdocs are aware that networks are critical in preparation for the labour market; more than half who responded are actively networking in and outside the university.

> We communicate with firms and other centres across networks what we do and we hire private companies. (Postdoc_U4)

Work Autonomy

The research- centred university approach also marks a change in the external control systems and is considered as an attempt to their research and teacher autonomy and freedom. From this perspective are put in place new strategies for evaluating and monitoring of research activity: external agents adopt a leading role, is attentive to rooted collegiality in the university and the "locus" of university institutions from the bottom up. Perceived academic decisions related to the evaluation of its research as a process heavily influenced by external administrative structures and other external agents. This also affects the financing of their projects, especially since public funding sources have been cut due to the economic crisis. One of the principal investigators points in this direction.

> So far no research assessment is not made within the university. Everything is based on evaluations of external agencies that make accreditations. (Postdoc_U1)

Respondents also noted the presence of a progressive external control over the resources that the universities allocate to research activities with implication on their

WHO ARE THE KNOWLEDGE PRODUCERS IN HIGHER EDUCATION?

professional life due to the interferences with the recruitment process of academics based on the capacity to attract funds.

> We have become part of a scenario where the external political system has each time received more decision-making capacity in university life. There was a time when the system only controlled economic issues, and a certain amount of freedom was given to everything else. In contrast, lately, we are experiencing greater control over the recruitment processes of academics, the size of the teams, the budget, etc. (Postdoc_U2)

Postdoctoral researchers agreed that the university currently pressures research groups to intensify their research productivity to address external demands. This pressure leads to different strategies to manage research groups, as mentioned by one of the participants.

> I think we are facing a new model of university oriented to the market, which acts as a bank, because the productivity and obtaining funds became the main priorities. The research groups should manage new relationships and networks in order increase the financial sources. (Postdoc_U5)

CONCLUSIONS

In this chapter we analyzed the perception of the postdoctoral researchers in relation to different contextual condition shaping their academic trajectory: perception of their roles in the new academic context influenced by the intensification of the research dimension of the academic work, the relationships established through networks, the prospects and the perception of work autonomy. The results clearly point out that there have been significant changes in the institutional dimension, which are reflected the changes experienced by the intensification of the research dimension of the university and an increased internal and external control of different stakeholders.

The institutional and organizational changes lead to changes also in the individual dimension from perceived transformation in their academic profile to the alteration of their perceived professional autonomy.

The results showed that postdocs are feeling pressured to face the new challenges of high performance demands and especially external mechanisms of accreditation and control, pressure which is translated in some occasions to the high requirements to publish in high-impact journals, to create a solid professional networks within and outside of their university, and to constantly have to seek funding sources that will sustain their research.

The results also demonstrated that the challenges experimented in the vision of the university research approach has generated changes that affect academics' professional definition and development marked by the need to generate resources for research and to demonstrate high levels of productivity and the impact evidences

119

of their work. This vision also considers collaboration, research management, the identity and the role of the researcher and to be able to face these challenges, researchers require more transfer training and institutional support. In the same line of the challenges postdocs stated publications seem to be the main challenge faced by researchers at because of the intensification of scientific productivity. All of these phenomena have determined a reorganization of their academic priorities and have involved an increase in scientific productivity in recent years. These researchers have already entered into a university that is clearly research oriented; therefore, they have not had to modify their cultural references, and they feel that the university policy clearly promotes the development of research.

The study brings to the light some implications of the new conception of the professional development in the academic world. In the first place, the implications are related to the organizational aspects of the academic life and pointed out changes in the organizational university values and culture towards the adoption of elements derived from the market-oriented university model. So while academics still perceive research as a function related to knowledge creation, updating teaching and creativity, from an institutional perspective this serves to control productivity, transfer to the socio-economic sector and positioning institution in the context.

The results of the study advise reviewing mechanisms of professional development to the extent that the new approach modifies substantial aspects of the academic function: autonomy, tasks, dedication, networks, etc. Faculty selection, training, promotion, and evaluation systems should be reviewed through the new lens of the university priorities that intensifies research.

In spite of their important roles in higher education institutions, their academic career trajectories are characterized by uncertainty resulting some interrelated issues: One is related to their role and functions in the HEI, due to the lack of specific regulations regarding their research, teaching and managerial tasks. The relationship between teaching and research is one of the topics in depth analyzed but how are they distributed in the workload of PDR and how they perceive their performance. In second place, the new university model oriented to the market focuses attention on the need to create and work in networks within the same HEI and externally in order to make research more visible and accessible to the potential users bringing the attention the role of the knowledge transfer to society and the development of research useful for the practices and policies. In this context researchers face new challenges and highlight the need to understand how PDR deal with this new function and understand how they establish and maintain relationships and networks with other researchers.

Thirdly, the study moved forward the debate on the analysis of the university model based on research and the increasing role of external and internal quality control system affecting scholars and which has to adapt their professional path to the exigencies of external funding and evaluation agencies seeking to influence certain decisions of the research process (data sharing, influence priorities or require prompt results). In addition, it identifies other costs such as limiting collegiality and

WHO ARE THE KNOWLEDGE PRODUCERS IN HIGHER EDUCATION?

control of the academics themselves on decision-making processes and professional practices with influences on their career prospects and expectations.

Despite the inquiry in the postdoctoral researcher's life, this study is far to be exhaustive and for sure represents just the beginning of field of study with implications not only at personal level but deeply connected to the organizational and structural landscapes.

REFERENCES

Buela-Casal, G., Paz, P., Sierra, J., Quevedo-Blasco, R., Castro, A., & Guillén-Riquelme, A. (2012). Ranking de 2011 en producción y productividad en investigación de las universidades públicas españolas. *Psicothema, 24*(4), 505–515.

Castro, D., & Tomàs, M. (2011). Development of manager-academics at institutions of higher education in Catalonia. *Higher Education Quarterly, 65*(3), 290–307.

Dale, R. (2005). Globalisation, knowledge economy and comparative education. *Comparative Education, 41*(2), 117–149.

Davis, G. (2009). Improving the postdoctoral experience: An empirical approach. In R. B. Freeman & D. L. Goroff (Eds.), *Science and engineering careers in the United States: An analysis of markets and employment.* Chicago, IL: University of Chicago Press.

De Miguel, J., Caïs, J., & Vaquera, E. (2001). *Excelencia. Calidad de las Universidades españolas.* Madrid: CIS.

Etzkowitz, H., Ranga, M., Benner, M., Guaranys, L., Maculan, A. M., & Kneller, R. (2008). Pathways to the entrepreneurial university: Towards a global convergence. *Science and Public Policy, 35*(9), 681–695.

Felisberti, F. M., & Sear, R. (2014). Postdoctoral researchers in the UK: A snapshot at factors affecting theirresearch output. *PLoS One, 9*(4), 938–990.

Felt, U. (2007). Change management. The new meaning of leadership in autonomous universities. In B. Conraths & A. Trusso (Eds.), *Managing the university community: Exploring good practices* (pp. 11–12). Brussels: European University Association.

Fitzenberger, B., & Schulze, U. (2013). Up or out: Research incentives and career prospects of postdocs in Germany. *German Economic Review, 15*(2), 287–328.

Hayrinen-Alestalo, M., & Peltola, U. (2006). The problem of a market-oriented university. *Higher Education, 52*, 251–281.

Hazelkorn, E. (2005). *University research management. Developing research in new institutions.* Paris: OECD.

Horta, H. (2009). Holding a post-doctoral position before becoming a faculty member: Does it bring benefits for the scholarly enterprise? *Higher Education, 58*, 689–721.

Ion, G., & Castro, D. (2017). Transitions in the manifestations of the research culture of Spanish universities. *Higher Education Research and Development, 36*(2), 311–324.

Lucas, L. (2009). Research management and research cultures: Power and productivity. In A. Brew & L. Lucas (Eds.), *Academic research and researchers* (pp. 66–79). Maidenhead: McGraw-Hill International.

Mitchell, J. S., Walker, V. E., Annan, R. B., Corkery, T. C., Goel, N., Harvey, L., et al. (2013). *The 2013 Canadian Postdoc Survey: Painting a picture of Canadian postdoctoral scholars.* Toronto: Canadian Association of Postdoctoral Scholars and Mitacs.

Mohrman, K., Ma, W., & Baker, D. (2008). The research university in transition: The emerging global model. *Higher Education Policy, 21*, 5–27.

O'Grady, T., & Beam, P. S. (2011). Postdoctoral scholars: A forgotten library constituency? *Science & Technology Libraries, 30*(1), 76–79.

Pérez-Díaz, V., & Rodríguez, J. C. (2001). *Educación superior y futuro de España.* Madrid: Fundación Santillana.

G. ION & M. TOMÀS-FOLCH

Slaughter, S., & Leslie, L. (1997) *Academic capitalism. Politics, policies, and the entrepreneurial university.* Baltimore, MD: Johns Hopkins University Press.

Tomàs M., Castro, D., & Feixas, M. (2012). Tensiones entre las funciones docente e investigadora del profesorado en la Universidad. *REDU, 10*(1), 343–367.

Tomàs-Folch, M., Feixas, M., Bernabeu-Tamayo, M. D., & Ruiz, J. M. (2015). La literatura científica sobre rankings universitarios: una revisión sistemática. *REDU-Red universitaria de docencia universitaria, 13*(3), 33–54.

Van Balen, B., Van Arensbergen, P., Van der Weijden, I., & Van den Besselaar, P. (2012). Determinants of success in academic careers. *Higher Education Policy, 25*(3), 313–334.

Van der Weijden, I., Belder, R., Van Arensbergen, P., & Van den Besselaar, P. (2015). How do young tenured professors benefit from a mentor? Effects on management, motivation and performance. *Higher Education, 69*(2), 275–287.

Van der Weijden, I., Teelken, C., de Boer, M., & Drost, M. (2015) Career satisfaction of postdoctoral researchers in relation to their expectations for the future. *Higher Education, 72*(1), 25–40.

LILIANA DONATH, MONICA BOLDEA AND ANA-MARIA POPA

10. NUDGING GENERATION Y TOWARDS EDUCATION FOR SUSTAINABILITY

INTRODUCTION

Education is fundamental for the economic and social progress and a core determinant of human capital development as well as social justice enhancer. But, when education is sustainability driven, it acts as a remarkable resource for *collective capacity building*. Since, by definition, sustainable development concerns durable economic growth, social justice and environment safeguarding, education for sustainable development (ESD) equips graduates with skills and competences to meet future challenges.

For the present adult generation (dubbed generation Y or millennial), reaching these goals means implementing a complex approach of education, knowing that its outcome touches the quality of the labour demanded by businesses. The question that remains is the manner the education system is able to adjust in order to create a chain reaction with positive externalities for the community. The issue becomes even more stringent given that generation Y has certain characteristics that trigger the need of new educational policies.

Studies indicate that, by 2025, more than 75% of the labour force will be supplied by Generation Y, meaning that it has to be equipped for the challenges posed by sustainability issues (Donston-Miller, 2016). Other extended researches (Delloitte, 2018) stress that millennials do not perceive that business success should be reflected only by financial and economic performance, but also by the positive impact they make on society, by supporting creativity, life improvements, capacity building, etc. The generation that dominate the workforce nowadays have gone through economic and political crises becoming aware that it takes more to succeed than financial wellbeing, are career changers and most of them reluctant to embrace rigid corporate structures (PWC, 2011). As the transformation of the millennial workforce is an ongoing process, most of the studies are based on surveys that, at some point, should trace the main features of the generation and approach it in a normative rather than a positive one.

When introducing globalization into the equation, it can easily be argued that it changes the everyday approach of labour mobility and, consequently, the deconstruction and reconstruction of the social capital. As compared to previous generations, the current labour force has experienced life differently, being mostly subject to uncertainties.

© KONINKLIJKE BRILL NV, LEIDEN, 2020 | DOI: 10.1163/9789004422209_011

In today's consumerism, there is a direct connection between social media and globalization, i.e. the media indicate a wide range of (consumer) lifestyle choices from all over the world; thus, youngest individuals, nowadays, tend to develop networks based on mutual interests rather than on neighbourhood. Unless closely watched and/or regulated, on the long run, these tendencies may become harmful for the economy and society. These social developments introduce new dimensions for collective capacity building, thus driving a new sustainability oriented education.

Historically, younger generations had always encouraged new ideas that impacted on businesses and the society at large and often proved to be disturbing for older generations. Yet, globalization and technology have radically changed the game, requiring a change of perception in filling the intergeneration gap.

The generation gap also conflicts work attitudes, millennials preferring to work flexible hours, expect higher recognition of their work and easily embrace international mobility. A trend towards individualism can also be observed, the younger generation seeking personal happiness and well-being and looking for a personal lifestyle that fits the ambiguities of the current society (Fenn, 2010; Kilber et al., 2014; Jerome et al., 2014; Hom, 2009).

In the current business environment, economic and technological changes have brought about a shift in the basic structure of many companies, change that can be considered job-specific. A young generation of professionals is about to take on new roles, to accept wider responsibilities and assume leadership. Generation Y, as part of these changes, is grasping innovation opportunities, thus contributing to the implementation of sustainable development requirements.

Under these circumstances, the above mentioned changes are important to be considered by the education system, in the pursuit of the best methods to meet the needs of future graduates (Shaw & Fairhurst, 2008; Jerome et al., 2014; Erickson, 2008).

The chapter approaches ESD through the lenses of economic and financial education given that there are few studies that regard this field. From economists' perspective it means identifying the trends of businesses that are able to contribute to the implementation of sustainable development at large. The question the chapter poses concerns the identification of the best ways ESD can be embraced and applied in a quantification prone and rational field as economic and business education. Considering the characteristics of the millennial generation, nudging seems to be the best possible way, since it avoids any imposition of a single solution, but offers alternatives that lead to the desired outcome. Though there are many differences as well as similarities between consecutive generations, the chapter does not make a cross-generation comparison, per se, rather emphasizing the main characteristics of generation Y, their education needs and investigates the possibilities to adapt economic education to sustainable development requirements.

There is a large emerging literature that stresses the need of a different paradigm in approaching education governance, the skills and competences students should acquire as well as the most appropriate teaching methods. The main challenge of education is to equip new generations with the ability to adapt to *the circular economy* requirements, including collective capacity building for promoting sustainability, the latter ensuring an in-depth, progressive insight and a perceptive understanding of complex matters.

A BRIEF VIEW ON GENERATION Y

Over the past 60 years, three generations of labour force have succeeded: the baby boomers, Generation X, and the emergence of Generation Y. The differences between individuals, according to the generation they belong to, result from the different economic and social circumstances they grew up in, which influenced their views on progress.

It is essential to understand the typology of individuals belonging to different age groups, since their economic and social performance impacts on personal development and social capacity building. Each generation reflects attitudes, ideals and behaviours as pillars of their labour effectiveness and life satisfaction. From a wellbeing perspective, the *prosperity paradox* is noticeable, adding to the generation gap.

According to researches (Bresman & Rao, 2017) there are significant differences between generations concerning leadership and entrepreneurial ambitions, technology reliance, training and fitting in and no clear conclusions are drawn, since other characteristics, such as the country of origin, cultural and economic background sometimes becoming prevalent. From a business perspective, while boomers are work centric, goal oriented, ambitious, have the ability to handle crisis, are most educated, have strong work ethics, generation X do not favour advancement as a main career objective but rather a better work-life balance, are flexible and brand loyal, willing to take responsibility. Further on, millennials are more inclined towards innovation, are at ease working in teams, heavily rely on technology, are open to new ideas, wish to improve society and environment etc.

Specifically, generation Y exhibits many significant behaviours compared to other generations. While there are still debates about the exact time-frame that defines Generation Y, they may be dubbed the "digital generation" globally oriented, and equipped with multitasking skills.

As Figure 10.1 shows, Generation Y is the largest, meaning that there is a critical mass that has the capacity to enforce changes in the evolution of the economy and society. Although it varies widely according to education and region of origin, Generation Y brings some unique skills and capabilities that certainly differentiate them from other age groups.

Being the largest dominating group, they will not only be the future investors, but employees to. According to Ernst & Young, 75% of the global labour force will be millennials by 2025, a considerable percentage (62%) being already involved in management (BNP, 2017). Therefore, generation Y is readily in a position to implement and promote sustainable businesses. If previous generations, i.e. baby

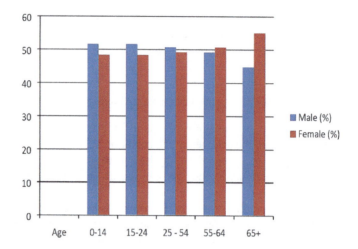

*Figure 10.1. The structure of generations by age groups
(based on https://www.worldometers.info/demographics/world-demographics/#age-structure)*

boomers and generation X, have triggered technical innovation, the generation Y has entirely propelled it, promoting digitalization in all areas.

Understanding attitudes is vital, since they are beliefs that shape the perception of facts and matters in a positive or negative manner. On the other hand, values are abstract and general, transcending specific situations in a durable manner.

Most researchers have attempted to analyze individual values on different scales and measures, given that they influence cognition, attitude and human behaviour. It should be noted, however, that values, being subjective in nature, differ among various cultures claiming interpretations across and within geographic areas, as well as age, gender and race groups.

Among the most relevant features shared by young individuals of Generation Y (Altinbasak-Farina & Guleryuz-Turkel 2015; Leelakulthanit, 2014; Yeaton, 2008; Martin, 2005) the following could be considered:

- confident, optimistic, tolerant;
- energetic and goal oriented;
- inventive and constantly looking for information;
- globally oriented;
- show less respect for hierarchy;
- satisfaction at work is enhanced by a positive environment;
- favour transparency and are not afraid to question authority;
- competitiveness, personal and professional development;
- casual attitude;
- do not consider lifelong careers;
- strive for success, are ambitious and determined to succeed.

The literature describes Generation Y as one of a different kind of trust, optimism, self-esteem and, to a certain extent, are more educated, making them open towards a more tolerant society (Tulgan & Martin, 2001; Yeaton, 2008); the same studies, however, stress the fact that the majority have been brought up in environments – either home or school-settings – designed to build high self-esteem, having quite high expectations about their future and, in many cases, rather unaware of their own limitations, thus not being able to take responsibility for their shortcomings.

Researchers argue that Generation Y are creative, enjoy freedom and flexibility and are less adjustable to micro-management. Some studies stress that their system of values includes – above all – loyalty and respect, dynamism and adaptability.

They also claim to be independent and autonomous and manifest a great desire for recognition. The general conclusion of most studies is that millennials manifests a strong social consciousness, but are inclined towards consumerism, though not remaining loyal to the same brands which makes them more difficult to control.

THE INFINITE GAME OF EDUCATION FOR SUSTAINABLE DEVELOPMENT

The Core of the Issue

The life span of generation Y overlaps a time frame when sustainability emerged as the new paradigm for all the area of the modern world. This is why an entire generation is called forward to face the challenges and change behaviours.

In order to be effective, ESD should consider the typology of the generation it addresses. Education is often analyzed within the context of complex systems dealing with a constant flow of changes, unpredictability, a need for creating space for emerging ideas, knowledge transfers to the community. Its complexity stems from the fact that it is a multi-level and time scale system consisting of individuals and institutions that interact, creating added value. Value is created as a result of individual interactions, and often the emergent result is more than, or qualitatively different from, the sum of individual actions (Haffeld, 2012).

In order to equip the Generation Y with the skills and competences they need to face the challenges posed by sustainability, the education must shift from the *finite to the infinite game approach.*

Approaching ESD as an infinite rather than a finite game (Carse, 1986), meets the need to treat all aspects of life in a "borderless" manner and acknowledge cross-section issues related to: Economic wealth, Environment, Ethics, Equity, Health, Finance, and Politics. It allows an integrative, holistic, interdisciplinary, out of the box and critical thinking. Students are guided to understand their field of expertise as part of a larger system that invites for flexibility, creativity, emphasizes anticipation and fulfilment of expectations without replicating well established past strategies. It supports the approach of the prospect theory (Kahneman, 2013) understating that actions are subject to bounded rationality, bounded willpower, bounded selflessness. Onwards, an open end, or circular approach impacts on the long term learning process.

L. DONATH ET AL.

Table 10.1. Finite and infinite games (based on Carse, 1986)

Finite game	Infinite game
Purpose: to win the game	Purpose: continue the game
Participants: includes only selected people	Participants: invite others in
Process: all alert participants are needed	Process: any single participant cannot finish the game
Perspective: assumes that past strategies reoccur/replicates past winning strategies	Perspective: looks to the future
Rules: do not change during the game	Rules: must be flexible and consistent with the circumstances
Discourages creativity	Encourages and supports creativity

Considering the demands of generation Y this approach could be more appropriately applied since it fosters creativity and teamwork. UNESCO cites various examples of countries that implement ESD, each of them focusing on specific issues, rather than adopting a holistic approach.[1]

The New Skill Requirements

The employability of generation Y highly depends on the extent they can operate in sustainability driven businesses, considering that, presently, companies are on trend to extend the Environment, Social and Governance (ESG) strategies. It encompasses methods, i.e. *exclusionary screening, best-in-class screening norm-based screening, ESG integration* (inclusion by asset managers of ESG factors into financial analysis and investment decisions), *sustainability-themed investing* that revolve around sustainability (BNP, 2017).

Between 2012 and 2014 exclusionary screening was the largest strategy (USD 14.4 trillion), followed closely by ESG integration (USD 12.9 trillion) and corporate engagement/shareholder action (USD 7 trillion).

As statistics show, such an approach produces positive externalities, i.e. enhances the reputation of the company, impacts on the improvements of the regulatory framework (i.e. green bonds guidelines, security and exchange commissions, financial stability task force, etc.), sustainable banking become a mainstream paradigm, consolidates risk – return – performance indicators, climate related projects are embraced. According to The Forum for Sustainable and Responsible Investment (2016) the is an unprecedented increase of value of sustainable investments (Figure 10.2).

Promoting ESG adds value to long term investments, sets the foundation for funding sustainable projects, enhances the reputational stance of the company encourages

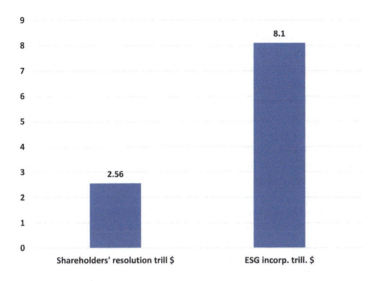

Figure 10.2. Sustainable investments (2016). (Source: http://www.ussif.org)

long term business strategies and supports business regulation improvement as well as wide range screening.

The path towards ESD is not straightforward, countries preferring different approaches of the issue. Some allot specific curricula and syllabuses; others attach sustainability problems to the existing curricula. Either way, a number of barriers may occur, some educational systems rather relying on teaching about sustainability, which often means explaining theory at length rather than stressing on factual case studies and problem solving. In this case, experimentation proves to be the most effective tool, given the complexity and multi-facets of sustainability (McKewon, 2002). Reorienting education obviously cannot be full-fledged unless is it strongly demanded by the community. If it is determined to address core issues of sustainability than a bottom up implementation of the curricula becomes easier

NUDGING TOWARDS SUSTAINABILITY ORIENTED EDUCATION

The Tool Kit

The new sustainability business approach recommends ESD as the major trend in education all over the world. This shift is induced by the current generation of students' expectations, new communication technology, the unprecedented dynamic of the labour market that requires new skills and competences, etc. The growing trend of sustainable investments around the world triggers ESD that is called upon to provide the necessary skills and competences to effectively support and extend sustainable business and portfolio projects. A straightforward way to reach this objective is to build collective capacities in the education system that requires institutional commitment and accountability.

Institutional commitment means leading by example, i.e. building sustainable campuses: revisiting all the operations according to sustainable development, i.e. management, curriculum and community (Fadeeva et al., 2010). The concept of *whole institution is promoted*, considering the quality assurance indicators that presently are quantitative ones, but should be extended with qualitative ones that often are marginalized or left out.

Since it is conceivable that the employability of future graduates will depend on their ability to comply with the sustainability approach of major companies, they should be accommodated with *critical thinking, creative problem solving, teamwork, equity, responsibility*. The level at which ESD should be employed depends on the foundations acquired in previous learning levels. Raising awareness on sustainability issues among students means already to plant the roots of positive spill-over, since later on they will be able to transfer the acquired knowledge in businesses.

The extent to which students perceive and apply this information depends, among others, on the teaching methods. According to UNESCO, the key aspects to promote quality education consist of:

- seeking out the learner
- acknowledging the learners' knowledge and experience
- making the teaching content relevant
- enhancing the learning environment

This approach becomes even more important since sustainability is directly linked to the concept of equity and, therefore, teaching techniques should enhance social equity among the students.

Globally oriented generation Y have a holistic vision and assume competition and risks in everyday situations. Considering the characteristics of the generation, nudging is preferred to other enforced, mandatory teaching and learning methods. Therefore, when shifting from traditional education to ESD, one should rely on the tools that are most familiar: *simple procedures, choice architecture, visualization, default learning, active choosing, personalized, default*, etc. (Sunstein, 2012).

Default frameworks are preferred in unclear, confusing circumstances, or standardization is induced by the shared customs, habits, and needs of the community.

On the contrary, when the context is familiar but customs and habits differ and identification of preferences is difficult, *active choosing* is preferred and *learning* is promoted as a long term beneficial lever then active choosing is preferred.

Personalized default rules, on the other hand, allow freedom of choice and take centre stage in a heterogeneous context with well informed choice architects.

ESD invariably requires adaptive teaching methods that foster new skills. The first step is to screen and map the needs of the students and stakeholders by identifying the core issues: what knowledge is already available, is there a general commitment,

130

are decisions taken on rational or emotional grounds, are they influenced by herd behaviour or noises, are there immediate or long term benefits?

Literature, often describes *choice architecture* as the main technique to change behaviours. It allows a libertarian-paternalistic approach, leaving as much freedom as possible, but hinting towards the desired outcome. In addition, but not opposed, *visualization*, by attaching mental models for the desired outcome, is able to emphasize the incentive.

Visualization may take the shape of various educations for sustainable development (ESD) pedagogies, i.e. drama, play, music, design, simulations, scenario, drawing to stimulate creativity and imagine alternative futures. Visualization (drawings, diagrams, etc.) envisages various mapping with different purpose, abstraction, notation, spatial meaning, verbal and visual spectrum. (Varga-Atkins & O'Brien, 2009). Under the present educational circumstances, reflection becomes indispensable, either within or out of the class: it allows for *self-evaluation* (as objective as possible) and also *introspection.*

Nevertheless, successfully implementing any pedagogical techniques in sustainable education should consider the following influences on generation Y's ability to respond to the nudge:

- the personality of the messenger influences choices;
- responses to incentives are influenced by framing, anchoring and rule of the thumb;
- other people's habits are important;
- defaults define pre-set options;
- salience draws attention on the new and relevant;
- anchoring strongly influences emotional associations;
- commitments are important as well as self-contentment.

Nudging involves an iterative approach, i.e. Test-Learn-Adapt. ESD is increasingly connected to education and learning sciences (integrative learning facilitating the understanding of this complex issue) and triggering emotional moral, creative connections. Small, bite size learning units support the repeated ability to *respond-reflect-rethink-recalibrate.* On the other hand, progressive pedagogy encourages discovery-based, collaborative, interdisciplinary, system based, social learning.

The Infrastructure

ESD needs, *per se*, a specific teaching and learning infrastructure that can accommodate the entire set of requirements for such a procedure.

Since research is the main driver in creating knowledge, integrating a multidisciplinary and transdisciplinary approach, it means that *sustainability centres, nudge units and behavioural insight teams* are to be promoted as a possibility to reunite integrated learning throughout the entire educational establishments (e.g. universities). Any of these structures, as global learning spaces, are able to involve all stakeholders in the governance process that can be broken down, further on, to the governance of *knowledge production, mediation and utilization.*

Knowledge being produced in the educational system throughout teaching/ learning and research for the benefit businesses, communities and policy makers, it is obvious that these entities will seek the highest effectiveness from the educational system in order to minimize further actions in preparing their experts. On the other hand, universities are not able to provide the entire set of competences required by practitioners and, consequently, a tighter collaboration within clusters is beneficial.

If the line of thinking and objectives provided by businesses, as stakeholders, is followed, then the positive spill-over of education that is sought after would summarize in improving the quality of higher education – a better communication among stakeholders – increased attractiveness of local education.

Literature cites the possibility of clustering between various stakeholders, considering that it is an effective way to apply and verify common educational policies that would meet the requirements of the entire set of stakeholders. If such an experiment proves to be beneficial than it can be further extended with minimum costs, since the learning curve has already reached its maximum.

In promoting ESD, at regional or national level, the various centres of expertise are meant to support and drive education in the pursuit of the desired outcome. They also endeavour to transfer the knowledge acquired through research towards the community and the region.

The main aim of the above mentioned infrastructure is to add value to the formal education by covering issues that are not sufficiently elaborated. They may also act as link factors within regions that share common cultural values and can address sustainability issues within the local economic and social environment, or creating a local/regional knowledge base in which universities play the key role and provide guidance.

The ESD infrastructure, as global learning space, may be organized in various manners, from encouraging face-to face communication to multi-sector platforms and networks, but promoting a *partnership approach* in its entirety.

The architecture of the centres varies widely, but one common approach is to blur the frontiers among universities (and research centres), secondary and primary schools (as representatives of formal education) and the non-formal education provided by local/regional stakeholders (businesses, NGOs, communities, media, etc.).

The most important result is that the centres allow the networking of a significant number of participants, intensifying the dialog horizontally and vertically. According to UNU-IAS (2015) the ESD infrastructure encourages a bottom-up, pyramidal approach starting from the wider base of different social groups. Nevertheless, the core institutions should be identified that have the ability to ensure the widespread dissemination of information and have an interlink profile (Figure 10.3).

The main outcomes that result following an effective cooperation among stakeholders are:

Figure 10.3. A multi-stakeholder approach of ESD

- enhanced leadership that promotes sustainability, social responsibility, working in complex multicultural systems, bridging the gap between education-research-stakeholders-community, green procurement, etc.;
- greening the curricula (case study and simulation projects, lifelong learning, creative thinking, research driven learning;
- greening initiatives (promoting entrepreneurial skills, effective use of resources, bridging intergenerational gap, etc.;
- promoting regional culture/values thus raising awareness on local specificities and their global connection;
- promoting sustainable campuses that serve as model for future business behaviours (Donath, 2017).

To implement the requirements of ESD, the Faculty of Economics and Business Administration (FEAA) Timisoara has set up an innovative lab (The Minds Hub that stands for a global learning space) – where major stakeholders, i.e. students, companies, academics, NGOs collaborate in pursuit of the above mentioned outcomes. According to a Survey conducted among students, the quality of information in the field of sustainable development is given in Figure 10.4.

CONCLUSIONS AND POLICY LESSONS

Considering the shifts of businesses towards social responsibility and the attributes of generation Y in a broader context of sustainable education, a libertarian paternalism approach can be considered as a key instrument in nudging millennials towards ESD. An inclusive vision states that public authorities, in their way of influencing

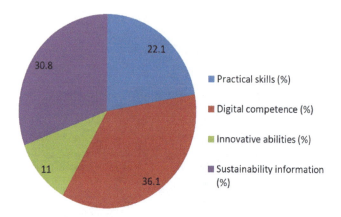

Figure 10.4. Quality of information acquired by students

the decision making process of individuals, have to intervene in a non-abusive way, letting people sort information and help grow the knowledge-based society. This will ultimately give power to people since an educated nation can better develop and become sustainable in educational terms. Designing policy in a "phishing" way (i.e. nudging behaviour that serves self-interests, rather than collective ones) is easy, because policymakers in the public sector might have the tendency to follow their own objectives, being effortlessly biased, sometimes selfish and easily corrupted, if their moral values aren't strong enough.

Nevertheless, the true challenge comes when the public sector is concerned with doing the best for its citizens and wants to design policies that serve the societal needs.

Since implementing a nudging technique, eventually, means elevating beneficiaries to a higher social status or reputation, education should support:

- better skills;
- increased employability;
- higher innovation capacity;
- development of citizenship;
- equality and social cohesion.

Therefore, the EU considers that education should be a life learning process, being the responsibility of the Member States. Literature shows that, in order to reach sustainable development, ESD should be encouraged to equip millennials with the required knowledge and skills.

From this perspective, the main priorities at EU level are:

- encourage networking between education institutions, businesses and the community;
- policy implementation in global learning spaces;
- innovation projects;

- strategic partnership;
- mobility.

To provide relevant social responsibility knowledge for employability, decision makers should encourage increased transparency and recognition of skills and competences, strong support for educators and innovative learning. These may serve as support for sustainable and efficient investments in education and training systems, inclusive education, equality, non-discrimination, civic competences.

In the nudging process, setting the objective of education policy in a straightforward manner is obvious. According to Thaler (2015) and Thaler and Sunstein (2015) in order to design nudges, three principals have to be followed:

- nudges should be transparent and never misleading;
- opt out of the nudge should be easy, preferably a mouse clicks away;
- nudges are meant to improve welfare and wellbeing.

The benefits of nudging as resulted from experiences around the world are vast: it preserves the liberty of individual choice among the offered alternatives, improves the economic and social status of the beneficiaries, avoids mandates and bans, promotes transparency and effectiveness. Since it relies on simplification, default rules and acknowledged social norms, it increases ease, convenience and disclosure that are widely valued by generation Y.

From an educational perspective nudging may better answer the modern requirements of capacity building since it involves a shift from pure knowledge transfer to creativity, dynamism and heavily relies on governance principles, all actors being actively involved (academics, students, management, community). It has the potential of coagulation skills and mutual support in reaching goals. In this respect, methods like recognizing and acknowledging an existing problem, visualization, experimentation, problem solving case studies, debates are useful in developing critical thinking. Researchers have developed toolkits that are useful in ESD implementation. But, there are no *one fits all* solution. It highly depends on the degree the community is willing to pursue sustainability principle, thus triggering the reformation of curricula.

ESD is at various stages of implementation, some countries paving the way others lagging behind. The chapter raises awareness on the necessity for speeding up the reformation of educational systems to meet the demands and expectations of millenials who will be the major work force in the decades to come.

NOTE

[1] See https://en.unesco.org/greencitizens/our_stories

REFERENCES

Altinbasak-Farina, I., & Guleryuz-Turkel, G. (2015). Identifying the needs of gen Y by exploring their value systems: A qualitative study. *International Journal of Trade, Economics and Finance, 6*(6).

L. DONATH ET AL.

Bresman, H., & Rao, V. D. (2017). A survey of 19 countries shows how generations X Y and Z are and aren't different. *Harvard Business Review. Generational Issues.* Retrieved from https://hbr.org/2017/08/a-survey-of-19-countries-shows-how-generations-x-y-and-z-are-and-arent-different

Carse, J. (1986). *Finite and infinite games.* New York, NY: Macmillan.

Deloitte Millennial Survey. (2018). *Millenials disappointed in business, unprepared for industry 4.0.* Retrieved from https://www2.deloitte.com/global/en/pages/about-deloitte/articles/millennialsurvey.html

Donath, L. (2017). A sustainability approach of higher education. In J. Beracs, G. Kovats, L. Matei, P. Nastase, & M. Szabo (Eds.), *Central European Higher Education Conference Proceedings* (2nd ed.). Corvinus University of Budapest Digital Press.

Donston-Miller, D. (2016). *Workfoce 2020: What you need to know.* Retrieved from https://www.forbes.com/sites/workday/2016/05/05/workforce-2020-what-you-need-to-know-now/#10f862d42d63

Erickson, T. J. (2008). *Plugged in: The generation Y guide to thriving at work.* Boston, MA: Harvard Business School Press.

European Commission. (n.d.). *Strategic framework – Education & Training 2020.* Retrieved from https://ec.europa.eu/education/policy/strategic-framework_en

Fadeeva Z, Gakute, L., Mader, C., Scott, G., & Mohun, S., (Eds.) (2010). *Sustainable development and quality assurance in higher education.* London: Palgrave, MacMillan.

Fenn, D. (2010). *Upstarts: How gen Y entrepreneurs are rocking the world of business and 8 ways you can profit from their success.* San Francisco, CA: McGraw-Hill.

Haffeld, J. (2012). Facilitative governance: Transforming global health through complexity theory, Global Public Health. *International Journal for Research, Policy and Practice, 7*(5), 452–464.

Hom, S. (2009). *Ystory: The real truth about gen Y and what it means for marketers.* BookSurge Publishing.

Jerome, A., Scales M., Withem, C., & Quain, B. (2014). Millennials in the workforce: Gen Y workplace strategies for the next century. *E-Journal of Social & Behavioural Research in Business, 5*(1), 1–12.

Kahneman, D. (2013). *Thinking fast and slow.* New York, NY: Farar, Straus and Giroux.

Kilber, J., Barclay, A., & Ohmer, D. (2014). Seven tips for managing generation Y. *Journal of Management Policy and Practice, 15*(4), 80.

Leelakulthanit, O. (2014). Life satisfaction of gen Y shoppers. *Journal of Business & Economics Research, 12*(3).

Martin, A. C. (2005). From high maintenance to high productivity. What managers need to know about generation Y. *Industrial and Commercial Training, 37*(1), 39–44.

McKewon, R. (2002). *ESD toolkit.* Retrieved from http://www.esdtoolkit.org/authnote.htm

Millennials at work. (n.d.). Reshaping the workplace. Retrieved from https://www.pwc.com/co/es/publicaciones/assets/millennials-at-work.pdf

Shaw, S., & Fairhurst, D. (2008). Engaging a new generation of graduates. *Education & Training, 50*(5), 366–378.

Sunstein, C. R. (2012). *Impersonal default rules vs active choices vs personalised default rules: A tryptisch.* Unpublished. Retrieved from http://nrs.harvard.edu/urn-3:HUL.InstRepos:9876090

Thaler, R. H. (2015). *The power of nudges, for good and bad.* Retrieved from https://www.nytimes.com/2015/11/01/upshot/the-power-of-nudges-for-good-and-bad.html

Thaler, R. H., & Sunstein, C. R. (2015). *Nudge: Improving decisions about health, wealth and happiness.* New Halen, CT & London: Yale University Press.

Tulgan, B., & Martin, C. A. (2001). *Managing generation Y: Global citizens born in the late seventies and early eighties.* Amherst, MA: HRD Press.

Varga -Atkins, T., & O'Brien, M. (2009). From drawings to diagrams: Maintaining researcher control during graphic elicitation in qualitative interviews. *International Journal of Research & Methods in Education, 32,* 53–67.

Yeaton, C. (2008). Recruiting and managing the 'why?' Generation: Gen y. *The CPA Journal, 78*(4), 68.

IRINA MASLO AND MIKAEL CRONHJORT

11. CAPACITY BUILDING IN INITIAL TEACHER EDUCATION (ITE)

Collaboration for Collective Capacity Building

INTRODUCTION

The shift from content teaching to learning outcome paradigm, from teaching of individuals to creation of workforce collaborative leaning spaces, from knowledge control to formative assessment of competences has to be seen as a complex of challenges. Due to these challenges, it is difficult to implement educational reforms in higher education (HE), and in ITE practice in particular. The complexity of these problems requires new solutions. However, it is a challenge for one separate country alone to transform this problem into an opportunity to reform ITE. Thereby, the demand on strengthening the collective international capacity in personalization and internationalization perspectives of ITE (FICIL, 2017) becomes increasingly significant nowadays.

The aim of this chapter is to analyze the concept and the model of the Latvian HE best practice – Master degree programme on Educational Treatment of Diversity (ETD) of the University of Latvia (LU). The competence-based ETD was elaborated in 2007 by UNED (Spain), LU (Latvia), Charles University (Prague) and PH Ludwigsburg (Germany). It is unique in its 10 years of practical experiences, accredited twice in Spain and Latvia as sustainable and innovative. In 2012 the ETD was selected as best practice on opening HE to adults (European Commission, 2013). In 2017 it was selected as one of the 15 best practice cases for preparing teachers for equity treatment of diversity in educational settings (European Commission, 2017;). We wish to benefit from the experience in ETD for development of ITE, by a deep analysis.

The use of *pedagogy of collaboration* as the theoretical basis of this best practice and as a model for implementation has not been analyzed so far. How is collaboration as idea and purpose for building collective capacity used in the current HE case? How is collaboration as means for collective capacity building implemented in practice? What implicants for ITE policy making and educational practice are evident? To respond to these questions, an in-depth interpretative analysis of the concept of pedagogy of collaboration will be carried out in this chapter. The evidence-based model of collaborative learning will be examined for explanatory and interpretive purposes and demonstrated by students' narratives.

© KONINKLIJKE BRILL NV, LEIDEN, 2020 | DOI: 10.1163/9789004422209_012

I. MASLO & M. CRONHJORT

COLLABORATION AS IDEA AND PURPOSE OF ITE

The selected case of HE is based on the idea of pedagogy of collaboration. Pedagogy of collaboration was developed by a group of Russian novel teachers, who created original empirical educational systems in the time-space of 'perestroika' in the 20th century. Most of the authors of this idea had more than 25 years working experiences at school, among them Amonashvili, Lysenkova, Nikitiny, Shatalov and others. The initiators of their cooperation became the editors of the *Teacher's Newspaper* Matveyev and publicist Soloveichik (Amonashvili et al., 1989; Kerr, 1991).

Collaboration as Idea of ITE

The core of the pedagogy of collaboration is that collaboration is the idea, purpose and means of education, where the teacher-student relationship empowers the learners to involve themselves in leaning supported by teachers. The success in learning inspires their confidence in overcoming learning difficulties and achieving success. Thereby, relationships play the dominant role in learning as collaborative process. On the one hand, collaboration is the idea behind the concept of pedagogy of collaboration. On the other hand, collaboration is a means to ensure the success in learning through support by teachers.

Inspired from this idea, doctoral studies for the first five Latvian novel teachers were offered at the end of 1980s at the LU, initiated by the director of the Institute of Psychology and Pedagogy Professor A. Spona. The author of this chapter, being one of them, habilitated by developing the concept of individualization of the school pedagogical process as personalized multidimensional collaboration process in 1995 (Spona & Maslo, 1991; Maslo, 1995). The concept has been developed further in collaboration with professors and doctoral students (Maslo, 2003; Rubene, 2004; Tilla, 2004) in an extended international cooperation with colleagues in Germany and Spain.

Collaboration as Purpose of ITE

Compared to the original Russian concept of pedagogy of collaboration, two main differences in conceptualization of collaboration have to be pointed out. First, collaboration is in fact a relationship, but not only between teacher and student. The relationship between a teacher and a student is always determined by the relationship between students and teachers themselves in their micro-, meso-, macro- and meta-environments, "increasing the collaboration with experts, community and peer groups, and by fostering connections that are often global in reach" (McLoughlin & Lee, 2008, p. 17). Second, collaboration does not always impact on personal learning success. Only personalized relationships of trust and confidence lead to successful collaboration. Therefore, collaboration is a multidimensional process of creating personal, interpersonal, institutional, regional, national, and international relationships in a multifaceted environment resulting in personal capability and

138

CAPACITY BUILDING IN INITIAL TEACHER EDUCATION (ITE)

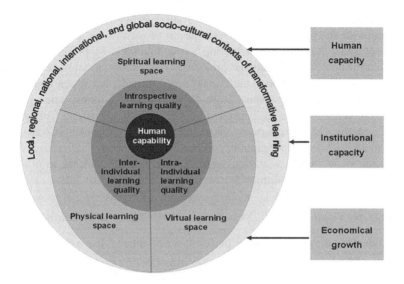

Figure 11.1. A multidimensional model of personal capability and collective capacity building (modified from Maslo et al., 2014)

collective capacity building for diverse learning, communication and collaboration purposes (Figure 11.1).

As we develop the concept of pedagogy of collaboration, the main principles of collaboration in ITE are described in the next section of this chapter: personalized learning; building opportunities of collaboration (creating diverse collaborative learning spaces); free choice of collaboration tools, place and pace (flexibility); pedagogical leadership of collaboration versus teaching; formative assessment of collaborative activities.

COLLABORATION AS MEANS FOR COLLECTIVE CAPACITY BUILDING IN ITE

The created pedagogical knowledge on collaboration for collective capacity building was implemented in 2007–2017 in Master studies on Educational treatment of diversity, enhancing modernization of HE through personalization and internationalization (FICIL, 2017) (see Figure 11.1).

The main principles of pedagogy of collaboration were implemented with an emphasis on organization, planning, and other factors determining quality of HE.

Personalized Learning

Personalized learning constitutes the central element of the model of pedagogical leadership of collaborative learning. Personalization of collaboration has been

139

I. MASLO & M. CRONHJORT

viewed as intra-personal, inter-personal, and introspective processes. Inter-personal communication in collaborative processes has to be seen as the substantial element of intra-personal learning. Collaboration as an introspective process means that socio-cultural contexts (institutions, projects, social networks, and teams at local, regional, national, international, and global level) provide and widen opportunities for transformative learning (Wells, 1999; Wygotski, 1978). Introspection promotes reflective looking inwards, an inspection of one's own thoughts and feelings about himself. Thereby, it has an important impact on the creating of personality. Consequently, the international Master's Programme "Educational Treatment of Diversity" focuses on personal basic, generic, and transversal competences of students, as a basis for development of professionalism of teachers. For more details, see Tables 11.1–11.3.

Building Opportunities of Collaboration (Creating Collaborative Learning Spaces)

Most students of the programme are performance orientated. It is a challenge to shift the mind, from the ambition to be the best in the group, to active participation in collaborative activities through constructivist mutual learning. Individualization of the mastering pathways of collaborative learning is the key. Collaborative activities are organized and planned in the form of challenging situations through all modules of the programme. Each module offers five practical situations, oriented towards subject content, to be solved in collaborative learning for personal benefits by applying existing and creating new knowledge, skills and attitudes.

Pedagogical Leadership of Collaboration Versus Teaching

Pedagogical leadership should provoke students to "a shift from the need for an individual to learn something which everyone agrees he would wish to know, to the will of some individual to teach something which it is not agreed that anyone has any desire to know. Such a shift in emphasis could only come with the breakdown of self-contained and self-regulated cultural homogeneity" (Mead, 1970, p.92). Rangachari (2011) continued this work and stressed the value in making students autonomous and self-directed learners. Therefore, the collaborative learning activities need pedagogical leadership, rather than teaching, to empower the transformational effects in students' intrapersonal, interpersonal and introspective learning at diverse spiritual, physical and virtual learning spaces by providing the formative feedback timely and continuously (Figure 11.2).

An effective pedagogical leadership of collaborative learning requires the providing of objective and subjective conditions for successful implementation: (Maslo et al., 2014):

- the integration of students' informal knowledge of ITC;
- implementing pedagogical leadership in tandems for developing students' intrapreneurship (Fernández González & Vostrikovs, 2012);

CAPACITY BUILDING IN INITIAL TEACHER EDUCATION (ITE)

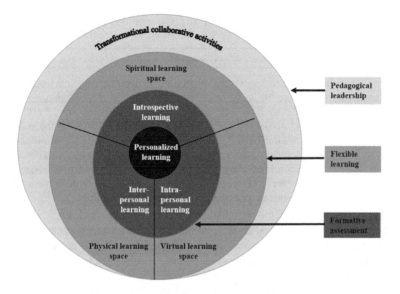

Figure 11.2. A model of pedagogical leadership of collaborative learning

- formative internal, external and self-assessment of competences;
- self-enhancement;
- personal involvement of teachers and students;
- supportive social climate;
- eagerness and grit for transforming challenges into new learning opportunities.

Formative Assessment of Collaborative Activities

Students systematically make self-evaluations of their competences, providing the evidence on effects of personalized learning in collaborative activities. They also plan their self-enhancement, based on formative assessment by tutors and professors. Examples of self-evaluations, provided in Tables 11.1–11.3, demonstrate the typical evidence of efficiency of pedagogy of collaboration in practice.

COLLABORATION FOR COLLECTIVE CAPACITY BUILDING IN ITE

Due to the transdisciplinary character of the ETD programme, it attracts a wide variety of professional practitioners from diverse fields: they are economists, lawyers, school teachers, sociologists, journalists, seaman staff managers, college teachers, leaders of non-governmental enterprises, special education teachers, foreign language teachers, translators, designers, project managers, preschool teachers, parents of children with special needs, social workers, sport coaches, etc.

I. MASLO & M. CRONHJORT

Table 11.1. Evidence of efficiency of pedagogy of collaboration in practice in self-evaluation rubric of generic competences in the module on cultural diversity

Generic competences	Evidence of efficiency of pedagogy of collaboration in practice
Using knowledge in social and cultural context	I really used my knowledge in a multicultural environment as the university of Latvia as I have contacts with people, mates, colleges and professors for other countries. I also used my knowledge in Latvia primary school but after the new knowledge I believe that I can response in a full multifaceted environment some time in my life as a teacher. This module offered to me some basic characteristics which are needed in the structure of school's class. Here we refer to implement of this knowledge it will be proven in practise. I did that in a collaborative survey.
Extending and disseminating knowledge in scientific, cultural and practical contexts	Retention of the person's values. Cultivation of his abilities via his personal strategies. Via understanding of cultural diversity, high quality of cooperation and then. Implementation of social culture teaching is succeeded. Enrichment of my teaching methods and understanding of multicultural environments via values as mutual respect of equal rights and empathy. Promotion of supportive environment resulting in everyone's activate participation in learning through the modification of the ways of learning. Implemented multifaceted knowledge. Using effectively multicultural results, interpreting new knowledge and more open-minded.
Integrating new theories and approaches for educational treatment of diversity	Everyone had some existing knowledge but I think after this module we enrich our knowledge, differentiate them and put them in a right queue. In every unit we expressed our previous knowledge, the new knowledge and our opinions how we implement them in the future.

Table 11.2. Evidence of efficiency of pedagogy of collaboration in practice in self-evaluation rubric of pedagogical competence in the module on cultural diversity

Critical and innovative thinking	Evidence of efficiency of pedagogy of collaboration in practice
Knowing how to apply the acquired knowledge and problem-solving capacity in new or relatively unknown environments and in wider or multidisciplinary contexts related to area of study	The universal principles of inclusion of diverse social learning cultures are absolutely understandable and I can apply the new knowledge in multifaceted environments for creating the supportive environments and activating the role of everyone in the most effective way of learning involving my own.

CAPACITY BUILDING IN INITIAL TEACHER EDUCATION (ITE)

Table 11.3. Evidence of efficiency of pedagogy of collaboration in practice in self-evaluation rubric of transversal competences in the module on cultural diversity

Transversal competences	Evidence of efficiency of pedagogy of collaboration in practice
Assuming risk of implementing new challenges	We have discussed a lot about the implementation of new methods, ways in different environments either in Skype web conference or in the face-to-face meetings.
Taking initiative to face and solve problems	It is necessary, we have a qualitative dialogue all the time of our cooperation as colleagues.
Assessing impact of knowledge development and learning	We succeed that with conversations about our conclusions, with the homework and with this particular evaluation.
Giving advice and counselling	We exchanged opinions, I often expressed my opinion and generally there was a constructive dialogue.
Empowering feeling of membership in groups, communities and society	… we worked as group, we cooperated all together, in groups of 4–6 people, we made presentations and activated participation. I believe that is the most important, and I really thank our professor.
Using information ICT in order to give opinions and make decisions	We used Skype, records, videos. We made documents in Google drive, survey and we used practical new technologies.
Assuming the role, functions and tasks of professionals dedicated to educational treatment of diversity for improving continually own occupational activities	We referred to the ways and the methods extensively. We also presented the basic characteristics one's supportive and prosper environment. We understood the best ways of active participation for everyone. At the end we discussed how can we do that in action.
Using the most appropriate approaches for inclusive education of people with diverse needs	Incorporation and inclusion are the basic points in this course and we analyzed that and we agreed that we have to keep their values. The most appropriate methods for creating supportive environments for inclusion of everyone.
Empowering people with diverse needs to promote their own personal abilities	Of course, we are taught how important are the people's personal abilities (values) and we based on them in order to receive the best by themselves.
Promoting integration attitudes and inclusive behaviour in different educational, familiar and social contexts	Protection of everyone's personal values, understanding of culture diversity. Flexibility, understanding of principle "it's normal to be different", empathy. Learning for everyone, feedback, inclusion. Participate creative.

By using temporal learning analytics and their potential for future computer assisted qualitative analyses, collaborative learning experiences have been observed over time. We have selected discourse data demonstrating collaborative learning constructs, and analyzed them temporally (Chen et al., 2018, p. 7). In the next two online-forum discourse data extracts from ETD, we explore the evidence on collective capacity building by mastering the collaborative activity in personalization and internationalization discourses, respectively.

Collective Capacity Building in Personalization Perspective

The current module personalization discourse data shows how the intended LO are reached. The extract covers three weeks. The number of students is four and all four are involved in active participatory personalized learning through the collaborative activity. Nine anonymous responses provide evidence of the efficiency of the pedagogical leadership of collaborative learning:

08.09.2017, 14:00: (Student 1) I just went through the materials of last years' students – very useful for an insight. After all – that is a job that has been done already and we can elaborate and form our understanding on these conspectuses. Also, a series of case-studies have been implemented, applying these methods, so I'm trying to get an access to these studies – maybe something useful/new comes out of them – I'll keep you posted :).

08.09.2017, 14:15: (Professor) – is there an advised form of providing the group results after all the research? Should that be a description or, if we come up with something unusual, we can provide the results as an info-graphics or something else?

08.09.2017, 19:19: (Student 1): Team – what do you think – could we gather our findings (main differences between both models) on a GoogleDoc and present them visually, as an info-graphic? It would be a more visual material, with less text but emphasizing the main things. I would be happy to prepare the info-graphics; we just have to come to a conclusion regarding the contents. A link for a document that we can prepare all edit simultaneously at …

08.09.2017, 19:57: (Student 1): That's the thing – I can make it! We have to come up with the key points of the differences between these methods and I'll make a few drafts of how they could look. And then we can decide together – TeamWork at its best :).

011.09.2017, 14:38: (Student 1): Team – it would be perfect if we could finish the task this week, so it does not last into the next module :). Is anyone willing to combine all information that has been prepared by team members individually? I think it would be perfect to use GoogleDocs for creation of common team files – all information will be stored here, in one place, and

CAPACITY BUILDING IN INITIAL TEACHER EDUCATION (ITE)

all changes will be done in the original document so no duplication and less confusion with downloading files etc. A link to the editable doc.

011.09.2017, 18:56: (Student 2) Hi! I'm having trouble opening the file – could you, please, send it again …? :).

13.09.2017 13:08: (Student 1) A Team-Skype date then! :) 18:00 on Skype – let's agree on the final info that we want to include in the Infographics.

13.09.2017, 13:08: (Student 3) I focused on TQM – my main findings are attached here. Love it that it comes from "real life" – manufacturing & business – and is then applied to pedagogy and is not some abstract theory that is experimented directly on children in education :). When we meet today 18:00 on Skype, it would be perfect to combine what all of us have and decide the key aspects that we wish to emphasize.

14.09.2017, 12:15: (Student 4) Attached you will find the DRAFT solutions for the result demonstration. Comments, suggestions and necessary amendments are more than welcome – perfect if we can finish by tomorrow. There are two files: 1) The historical file focuses on the origin of each method. I thought it would be important to know where each method comes from to understand them better. We miss info about the origin of the effectiveness theory, but with your help I'm sure we can finish it today :) 2) The comparison file focuses on the comparison table, but is more visual, thus easier to understand. We can also skip the historical comparison and leave only the model comparison, of course. How do you think?

20.09.2017, 14:46: (Student 3–4) Sorry for the delay – here are two files that each of us submits as course result – comparison and main conclusions that we made last Friday.

Compared to individual studies, the collaborative activity provides the group with a starting idea and purpose of collaboration (What? How? Why?). A professor is an active participant in the group with hints or own ideas and supports students' confidence in collaboration. However, all students achieved the intended aim timely and demonstrated own autonomy and responsibility for team learning, transforming their attitude on own learning into responsibility for the team.

Collective Capacity Building in Internationalization Perspective

The international discourse data of the same forum shows the outcome quality achieved during four days, strengthening the collective capacity of international students from different countries and Latvian host students with and without international mobility backgrounds (2 international students from America and Asia, and 3 students from Latvia. The extract consists of 14 anonymous responses:

145

05.09. 2017 11:34: (Student 1 from Latvia) Never mind my e-mail. I found it! Who would like to join me?

05.09. 2017 12:34: (Professor) My congratulation, A., for initiating studies. B. and C. please join! E. does not have access at the moment, ERASMUS students do not have it either.

05.09. 2017 01:00: (Student 2 from America) Hello everyone! It was really complicated to reach here but I managed to do it! I wanted to share a good document which was posted last year for a student for the same course (Student of previews year X.) It is about effectiveness and total quality model. At the beginning it was hard to understand what those words mean, but now, many questions pop up in my mind. Due to the fact that in my country (America) the educational system is trying to change the perspective about the real aim of education. Most of the time the educational system is looking for good results, but in order to reach the quality model it needs to have certain factors, as are mentioned in both documents. Quality, as UNICEF paper presented in X. says, has many aspects to consider as, "healthy learners ready to participate, a safe environment, relevant curricula and materials, well managed classrooms, and outcomes related to skills and attitudes". However, nowadays it is very difficult to concrete those aspects. As an example, in my home university we have a "Tutoring Program" where students from different pedagogies help students (from the age of 7 to 16) to study, but all these students are in social risk. As much as the school tries to motivate them to have a different perspective of what school is, they are influenced for several factors that disrupt the vision that they have about the school. Most of the kids come from a family that don't support them (no participation of the families) … On the other hand, we have the "quality" model that the educational system really wants (which is more like an efficient one, low cost, short time, good results), but most of the teachers are so under pressure because the government expectations related to get more good results and a bunch of contents, that they forget to create new thinkers' citizens. If I misunderstood the words effectiveness and quality, I would like to read your opinions. =).

06. 09.2017, 10:44: (Student 1 from Latvia) HEY! V., are you in this group? Group X: D., B., C.). Later today I can start doing things.

07. 09.2017, 00:38: (Student 3 from Latvia with mobility background) Hi, V., and student 5, nice that you started discussion. I could not agree more with what you said about 'problematic' kids – they do not fit anywhere (society might think that they are kind of 'lowering' the quality, as well as harms efficiency). About the topic of practical activity – it made me to get familiar with Total Quality Management and whole idea of that movement. I also got to read some very nice and inspiring articles on TQM in schools (but unfortunately my computer broke down totally and all the stored information there must be

CAPACITY BUILDING IN INITIAL TEACHER EDUCATION (ITE)

recovered by some specialist, so sadly I can't add those nice articles here :(My other technical problem is that now I can only type with I-pad or smart-phone what is not really comfortable and impossible to create new documents :(Really hope to solve that by the next week. The one I really liked was article by Winn, Green (1998) – Applying TQM in educational process. I can only give a link https://www.i... Total quality as an idea in general is related to the fundamental change in attitude of each and every person involved in the process. The main focus of the model is the client/product (student in case of education) and his satisfaction with the service. Each and every person have agreed on common goal and keeps in mind it in every step of their work. Efficiency (I choose this word instead of effectiveness) model from my point of view is absolutely different (however there might be areas where both models overlap). I liked the article of Lockheed, Hanushek (1994) – Concepts of Educational Efficiency and Effectiveness. I see that those two models have plenty of differences. Both are seen as good. Still – I have a feeling that wish for efficiency in reality prevails over wish for total quality. Efficiency is quite easy to measure and test (one must only have to compare costs to outcomes/results). Quality evaluation is very difficult topic and results might not show the real results of education. ... OK, that's a lyric from my side :) I believe that we have to write a word doc about differences/common of both models and to publish it here, where others could add their ideas and view. I can start with such paper work after my computer will be recovered (but anyone else also can be the first who starts writing).

07. 09.2017, 01:04: (Professor) In order to find differences, please have a look at course material. In Spanish – V. can do this perfectly, and in course material Summary in Latvian you can find the easy way.

07. 09.2017, 12:51: (Student 1 from Latvia) Hey! Great intro to our work! Sorry for the delay with my views. I'll get there as soon as I get free of work.

07. 09.2017, 23:13: (Student 2 from America) Thanks for your materials and also for your opinion about the topic. Unfortunately, I don't have access to the great material uploaded to read (I don't know the reasons) but it asks me to pay in order to read the document that the teacher had uploaded. It's a pity because I cannot contribute that much: (hope tomorrow I can find something else in the library and I can keep sharing ideas.

08. 09.2017, 00:31: (Course Professor) I checked, V., where is the problem. Maybe you click not the right link? Please check: Pedagogical leadership ... and then: X Course material in Spanish and Summary of the main content in Latvian. This will be the right link. If any problems again, please ask me in SKYPE.

08. 09.2017, 10:18: (Student 4 from Latvia with mobility background) V., I initially had the same feeling that I have no access to materials. But just click

I. MASLO & M. CRONHJORT

this link – ... and then scroll down – in the very end of the material are 2 pdf files, one of them in Spanish.

08. 09.2017, 14:00: (Student 3 from Latvia with mobility background) I just went through the materials of last years' students – very useful for an insight. After all – that is a job that has been done already and we can elaborate and form our understanding on these conspectuses. Also, a series of case-studies have been implemented, applying these methods, so I'm trying to get an access to these studies – maybe something useful/new comes out of them – I'll keep you posted :). ... Professor (asked by first name) – is there an advised form of providing the group results after all the research? Should that be a description or, if we come up with something unusual, we can provide the results as an info-graphics or something else?

08. 09.2017, 18:16: (Professor) Thank L. for this question, I had waited of it. Great!!! What do you mean? Is the description (text) the best way to visualize the differences? One of the ways is the creation of a table. Maybe you can find out another way what you find as most appropriate? Here you can find the other visualization forms of comparing (but please don't use the concept-map than we use it in the activities of the Unit 3): http://www... Here you have the full freedom to your creativity!!!

08. 09.2017, 17:27: (Student 1 from Latvia) When looking at any kind of terminology I like consulting dictionaries. This is how 'effectiveness' and 'total quality' are defined by Oxford English dictionary: *Effectiveness*- The degree to which something is successful in producing a desired result; success. *Total quality* – A theory of management based on the principle that the highest standards of work must be maintained throughout every level of an organization's operations, especially in order to guarantee efficient working practices and high-quality products and services. Although, these definitions are general and aren't connected directly to educational terminology, one can see that effectiveness is more goal orientated, whereas total quality is looks more at the process. When we understand the basics, we can look at those terms from the perspective of education. According to the UNESCO, *effectiveness* is 'an output of specific review/analyses (e.g., the *WASC Educational Effectiveness Review* or its *Reports on Institutional Effectiveness*) *that measure* (the quality of) *the achievement of a specific educational goal* or the degree to which a higher education institution can be expected to achieve specific requirements. And here I can add, that the UNESCO confirms efficiency model being different from effectiveness (this is what Santa said), since *efficiency is measured by the volume of output or input used.* On the other hand, there is total quality model, which is defined in Kristina Toll-Road's paper in a profound way. In addition, since quality model pays attention rather to the process, it is important to understand that the environment is changing and

148

all the 'components' (students, teachers, administrators, board of education) of educational system should adapt to the new. There's a file with English translation of course materials for those who can't access something or don't understand Latvian.

08. 09.2017, 18:56: (Student 4 with mobility background) D., Hi! I'm having trouble opening the file – could you, please, export and upload it once more? For me, hi? :).

08. 09.2017, 19:15: (Student 1 from Latvia) Here it goes [link].

Compared to individual studies, the new knowledge developed in collaborative activity is over expectations of the teachers. The international discourse data shows how the strengthening of collective capacity supports the personalized learning of an international student who, however, has challenges in access of the e-environment in the institution. The support from host students is essential for the active participation of one international student. The other international student did not participate in the conversation during the four days covered in this extract but participated later. The discourse data also demonstrates the changing role of professor, from teaching into pedagogical leadership, and building relationships of trust and confidence between professor and students.

CONCLUSIONS

The main purpose of ITE is to equip student teachers to be pedagogical leaders. The temporal discourse analysis displays the advantages of using collaborative learning. Respecting student diversity helped to consolidate existing knowledge, and to gather new evidence on how student teachers can be prepared for diversity in the classroom. Among others success factors of this programme, the effective cooperation between the universities as co-creators of this programme on one hand, as quality of the collaboration of programme students and professors – on the other hand, were evident.

The temporal record of the online-forum discourse data enables us to identify the potential implicants for ITE policy making and educational practice. These results will be tested for conformation by computer supported qualitative analyses in further secondary analyses on subsequent forums, considering sequence-oriented features in the construction of personal competences (personalized learning outcomes) in collaborative activities.

Implicants for policy making. In the selected case of analyzed HE practice, the cooperation implies a consolidation of individuals and institutions (at academic and administrative university levels) in acting groups aimed to enrich one-unit output, in our case the described best practice. The consortium of four universities (Spain, Germany, Czech Republic and Latvia), led by National Distances University (UNED), strengthens the collective capacity for development of this best practice.

I. MASLO & M. CRONHJORT

In turn, to collaborate means to actively participate in a personalized communicative process focusing on learning outcomes. The process is aimed at the collective capacity building and creative mastering of self-organized team activities. Pedagogical leadership and formative assessment play important roles in this process. So then, cooperation and collaboration are different but effective means for building the collective capacity in ITE.

Implicants for educational practice. Collaboration, being an interactive process with emphasis on its communicative nature and arisen from human relationships, is closely connected with opportunities for participation. Collaboration creates new opportunities to master activities together, combining the assets every human has. Acting together, we get the time to do more and more important things, better than it can be done by everyone alone.

REFERENCES

Amonashvili, S, Volkov, I., Ivanov, I., Ilin, E., Kurkin, E., Lysenkova, S., Nikitina, L., Nikitin, B., Shatalov, V., & Shchetinin, M. (1989). The methodology of reform. Reports on the third meeting of experimental educators in Moscow. *Soviet Education, 31*(7), 44–76.

Care, E., Griffin, P., & Wilson, M. (2017). *Assessment and teaching of 21st century skills: Research and applications.* New York, NY: Springer Publishing.

Chen, B., Knight, S., & Wise, A. F. (2018). Critical issues in designing and implementing temporal analytics. *Journal of Learning Analytics, 5*(1), 1–9.

European Commission. (2013). *Developing the adult learning sector. Lot 3: Opening higher education to adults* (pp. 93–126). Luxembourg: Publications Office of the European Union.

European Commission. (2017). *Preparing teachers for diversity: The role of initial teacher education. Final report.* Luxembourg: Publications Office of the European Union.

Fernandez González, M. J., & Vostrikovs, S. (2012). Students' intrapreneurship in higher education settings and its relevance in the formation of entrepreneurship attitudes: A case study from Latvia. In C. Martin & E. Druica (Eds.), *The proceedings of the International Conference "Entrepreneurship Education – A Priority for the Higher Education Institutions – CREBUS"* (pp. 90–94).

FICIL. (2017). Position paper on higher education policy. *Position Paper. The Foreign Investors' Council in Latvia, 4.*

Hopping, D. (2001). Building collective capacity: New challenges for management-focused evaluation. *Children and Youth Services Review, 23*(9–10), 781–804.

Kerr, S. T. (1991). Beyond Dogma: Teacher education in the USSR. *Journal of Teacher Education, 42*(5), 332–349.

Lytras, M. D., Daniela, L., & Visvizi, A. (2018). *Enhancing knowledge discovery and innovation in the digital era.* Hershey, PA: IGI Global.

Malloch, M., Cairns, L., Evans, K., & O'Connor, B. (Eds.). (2011). *The Sage handbook of workplace learning.* London: Sage.

Maslo, E. (2003). *Mācīšanās spēju pilnveide.* Riga: RaKa.

Maslo, I. (1995). *Skolas pedagoģiskā procesa diferenciācija un individualizācija.* Rīga: Raka.

Maslo, I., Surikova, S., & González, M. J. (2014). E-Learning for widening participation in higher education. In V. Zuzevičiūtė, E. Butrimė, D. Vitkutė-Adžgauskienė, V. Vladimirovich Fomin, & K. Kikis-Papadakis (Eds.), *E-learning as a socio-cultural system: A multidimensional analysis* (pp. 21–42). Hershey, PA: IGI Global.

McLoughlin, C., & Lee, M. J. W. (2008). Three P's of pedagogy for the networked society: Personalization, participation, and productivity. *Journal of Teaching and Learning in Higher Education, 20*(1), 10–27.

Mead, M. (1970). *Culture and commitment: A study of the generation gap.* Garden City, NY: Natural History/Doubleday.

150

CAPACITY BUILDING IN INITIAL TEACHER EDUCATION (ITE)

Rangachari, P. K. (2011). Steps to pluripotent learning: Provocative teaching. *Advances in Physiology Education, 35*, 323–329.

Riel, J., Lawless, K. L., & Brown, S. W. (2018). Timing matters: Approaches for measuring and visualizing behaviours of timing and spacing of work in self-paced online teacher professional development courses. *Journal of Learning Analytics, 5*(1), 25–40.

Rubene, Z. (2004). *Kritiskā domāšana studiju procesā.* Rīga: LU Akadēmiskais apgāds.

Scott, C. L. (2015). *The futures of learning 3: What kind of pedagogies for the 21st century?* UNESCO Digital Library. Retrieved from https://unesdoc.unesco.org/ark:/48223/pf0000243126

Spona, A., & Maslo, I. (1991). *Skolas pedagoģiskais process.* Rīga: Latvijas pedagogu biedrība.

Tiļļa, I. (2004). *Sociālkultūras mācīšanās organizācijas sistēma.* Rīga: RaKa.

Uskov, V. L., Howlett, J. R., & Jain, L. C. (2017). *Smart education and e-learning. Proceedings of SEEL International Conference on Smart Education and Smart E-Learning.* New York, NY: Springer.

Wells, G. (1999). *Dialogic inquiry: Towards a sociocultural practice and theory of education.* New York, NY: Cambridge University Press.

Wise, A. F., & Chiu, M. M. (2011). Analysing temporal patterns of knowledge construction in a role-based online discussion. *International Journal of Computer-Supported Collaborative Learning, 6*(3), 445–470.

Wygotski, L. S. (1978). *Mind in society: The development of higher psychological processes.* Cambridge, MA: Harvard University Press.

MARIA N. GRAVANI

12. BUILDING COLLECTIVE CAPACITY FOR ADULT LEARNING IN DISTANCE EDUCATION

INTRODUCTION

The chapter, which is part of the book on collective capacity building – shaping education and communication in knowledge society, critically discusses the challenges of building collective capacity for adult learning in distance education. In particular, it aspires to analyze and explore the ways with which collective capacity for adult learning is built in distance learning universities through online learning communities and, consequently, adult learners, by engaging in collaborative activities, enhance their learning and improve their practice. In doing so, the chapter critically presents, as 'good' practice the approach taken to collective capacity building in the online module: 'Teaching adult education online' delivered by the Open University of Cyprus (OUC) for the International Masters in Adult Education for Social Change (IMAESC).

As my recent research (Gravani, 2015, 2018) identifies, a number of dimensions influence adult learning in distance education, such as: *personality,* i.e. participants' educational background, past experience in distance education, individual needs, interests, learning styles and experiences; *mutuality,* the extent to which participants are involved in the preparation and delivery of the courses; *emotionality*, emotions triggered throughout the courses; *formality,* the educational context, approaches and models adopted in the organization and delivery of the courses (Gravani, 2015, pp. 188–189). Likewise, Cercone (2008), Makoe et al. (2008) draw on comparable conclusions and underline that adult learning in distance education is culturally and contextually dependent. Amongst the personal, social and contextual factors that interrelate and can either promote or hinder adult learning identified in the research literature, prominent is the need for sharing power, values, trust, knowledge and collaborating on many levels (Knowles & Associates, 1984; Brookfield, 1986; Knowles, 1990; Merriam & Caffarella, 1999; Cercone, 2008; Makoe et al., 2008; Lee, 2018; Lee et al., 2019). This consists of the basis for building collective capacity (Pallot & Pratt, 2010; Fullan, 2010; Harris, 2011; Amini & Oluyide, 2016; James & Figaro-Henry, 2017).

However, building collective capacity for adult learning in distance education is a factual challenge and not a laid-back process, as this is interrelated to the context, structured curriculum, relationships developed, dispositions, institutions. Pallot and Pratt (2010, p. 7) recognize distance education and on-line environment as a lonely

© KONINKLIJKE BRILL NV, LEIDEN, 2020 | DOI: 10.1163/9789004422209_013

M. N. GRAVANI

place, as learners and educators experience often feelings of isolation, when working online. Similarly, recent research (Gravani & Karagiorgi, 2014; Gravani, 2015, 2018) on adult teaching and learning in distance learning universities highlights that adult learners often complain about being remote and isolated and not being able to cooperate with colleagues since in most cases they do not see each other and rarely have the opportunity to connect and share feelings and learning experiences. Besides the distance factor, as barriers to close interaction and collaboration among adult learners in distance education are recorded adult learners' different ways of learning, individual differences and needs, family and professional compulsions (Gravani, 2018). Also the prearranged curriculum for most of the courses in the distance learning universities (Keegan, 1996; Peters, 1998; Yiayli et al., 2010; Christidou et al., 2012) does not allow to adult learners and their educators spaces for discussion, exchange, negotiation.

There are, of course, benefits in teaching and taking online class, such as flexibility, adjustability and other. For example, Pallot and Pratt (2010, p. 7) accurately argue that participants are able to connect any time and place, from their bedroom in pajamas and bunny slippers or their library or computer lab via technology and twenty-first century digital tools. Nonetheless, technologies and innovations, even if they are good, advanced and attract all the attention at the outset, they are doomed to fail and are unlikely to be beneficial, without attention to proper implementation and collective capacity building (James & Figaro-Henry, 2017). As Kollias (2018) claims technologies alone can never change education as it is known.

Following the above, the chapter critically addresses the challenges and the ways with which collective capacity for adult learning is built in distance learning universities through online learning communities by using as an example the 'Teaching adult education online' course delivered by the OUC. Such an investigation is valuable and contributes to the ongoing discussion of an under researched area. It also makes a clear point about the importance and possibility to build collective capacity in distance education.

In what follows, the main concepts of the chapter are visited. Then the OUC context and the 'Teaching adult education online' course are critically presented and the approach taken as well as the ways with which collective capacity is built in the above module are critically discussed and evaluated. Finally, conclusions are drawn about the significance and prospects of building collective capacity for adult learning in distance learning universities by changing the culture through using online learning communities and collaborative behaviours.

COLLECTIVE CAPACITY BUILDING, RELATED CONCEPTS AND RESEARCH FRAMEOWRK

The chapter draws on a number of concepts including collective capacity building, adult learning, distance education, online learning communities. Capacity building, as a notion, according to Harris (2011), is far from new, as it has been consistently

154

pointed out in relation to school improvement and change (Harris, 2011; Stringer, 2013). It has also been recently used and examined with respect to leadership (James & Figaro-Henry, 2017), e-learning expertise (Aczel et al., 2008; Kosioma Eli, 2015), open learning (Amini & Oluyide, 2016), population health improvement (Welter et al., 2017). However, 'capacity building' has not been easy to pin down conceptually, as different organizations define the term within the context of their activities (Amini & Oluyide, 2016). For example, UNESCO (2013) identifies capacity in education as the process through which stakeholders in the delivery of education develop, maintain and apply various capacities to achieve their targets. In the EU (2011) toolkit for capacity development, it is seen as "an attribute of people, individual organizations, and group or organizations; shaped by, adapting to and reacting to external factors and actors". The United Nations Development Programme (UNDP) (1994, as cited in Aczel et al., 2008, p. 339), defines capacity as "the ability of individuals, organizations and societies to perform functions, solve problems, and set and achieve goals". For Fullan (2010 p. 57) capacity building concerns competencies, resources and motivation. Individuals and groups are high in capacity if they possess and continue to develop the knowledge and skills and do important things collectively and continuously. The latter is widely postulated in the education literature (Sharrat & Fullan, 2009; McKinsey, 2010; Levin, 2010; Fullan, 2010, 2011; Hargreaves et al., 2011, as cited in Harris, 2011).

From the above, it is evident: first, that capacity is located at three levels: individual, organizational and institutional that interrelate and are interdepended, and; second, that in order to build capacity, collective, systematic work and responsibility are required. It is beyond the purpose of the present chapter to discuss separately the three levels, as it is considered that there is an interaction and synergy among them (Harris, 2011), when applying to the learning of adults in distance education. Also while investing in individuals and human capital is important, there is greater return from building social capital, and the latter resides in the relationships and interactions rather than in the individuals themselves (Harris & Jones, 2011). As Wenger (2000) argues, some people know things that others do not know and collective knowledge exceeds that of any individual. Also according to Fullan (2010a, p. 72), "working together generates commitment ... and collective capacity gets more and deeper things done in shorter periods".

In the chapter, following Harris's (2011) paradigm, rather than expanding the description and deconstructing the concept of capacity building, the focus is on the mechanism for building it. For Harris (2011) and Harris and Jones (2011) who focused their research on teachers as professionals, this comes down primarily to professional learning communities and "collective responsibility where professionals are working together to improve practice through mutual support, mutual accountability and mutual challenge (Harris, 2011, p. 627). They argue that this does not happen by default but has to be created by design. This draws heavily on Wenger's (2000) notion of communities of practice, in which, through collaboration, "groups of people who share a concern, a set of problems, or a passion about a topic, deepen their knowledge, expertise and improve their practice by interacting on an ongoing basis" (Wenger, 2000, p. 4).

Therefore, by analogy with the aforementioned, how can we build collective capacity to enhance adult learning in distance learning universities? This is feasible through online learning communities (Lee, 2018; Lee et al., 2019; Pallof & Pratt, 2010; Thorpe, 2002) that are discussed below after defining the concepts 'adult learning' and 'distance education', also central in the analysis presented. The former is seen as being "both the process which individual adults go through as they attempt to change or enrich their knowledge, values, skills or strategies, and the resulting knowledge, values, skills, strategies and behaviours possessed by each individual" (Brundage & McKeracher, 1980, p. 5, as cited in Gravani, 2015). The latter refers to the educational delivery method which is characterized by "a semi-permanent separation of teacher and learner; it is influenced by the educational organization in both the preparation of the teaching materials and students' support; it uses technical media and is a two-way process" (Keegan, 1990, p. 44, as cited in Gravani, 2015). In the chapter 'distance education' is used interchangeably with 'distance learning' and 'online learning', and are considered synonymous terms, although they have slightly different meaning.

Online learning communities are based on a social constructivist learning paradigm, according to which learning is a social practice and involves learners participating in collaborative knowledge construction processes (Scardamalia & Bereiter, 2014). Collaboration is the "heart and soul" of online learning communities, according to Pallof and Pratt (2010). It is a complex intervention and it is both a process innovation and a product innovation (Lawson, 2004, cited in James & Figaro-Henry, 2017). It accomplishes a number of outcomes: assists with deeper level of knowledge generation, promotes initiative, creativity, critical thinking and dialogue (Brookfield, 1995); allows students to create a shared goal for learning and forms the foundation of a learning community, addresses all learning styles and issues of culture (Pallof & Pratt, 2010, pp. 6–7). Pallot and Pratt's (2010) model of online collaboration builds around the notions of *social presence*, i.e. the social context, online communication, and interaction (Tu & Corry, 2002, cited in Pallot & Pratt, 2010), *constructivism*, and the use of an *online learning community* to accomplish constructive outcomes in an online course. The online learning community consists of a number of components, such as: *people*, the students, tutors, staff involved in the online course; *shared purpose,* the sharing of interests and resources amongst the participants in the course; *guidelines*, the structure of the online course, which provides the ground for interaction and participation; *technology*, which is the vehicle for course delivery and a place where participants can meet; *collaborative learning*, participants' interaction which supports socially constructed meaning and creation of knowledge; and *reflective practice*, which promotes transformative learning (Pallof & Pratt, 2010, pp. 7–8). Elements of their proposed model, which is based on connectivism and social constructivist perspective, are used in the present chapter as a guiding heuristic, as they provide a framework for the critical analysis of the module: 'Teaching adult education online' delivered by the OUC. In what follows a critical description of the context within which the module is offered is attempted.

SETTING THE SCENE

The 'Teaching adult education online' module has been designed and delivered by the Open University of Cyprus (OUC), since 2017, as part of the Erasmus Mundus 'International Masters in Adult Education for Social Change' (IMAESC) programme. The OUC is a State distance learning university that has operated since 2006 and has as its strategic mission to furnish adults with equal opportunities to learn, regardless their age, place and physical condition, and to indorse science, knowledge, research, lifelong learning and adult education (Gravani, 2015). As a coordinator of distance education in Cyprus, the OUC offers alone or jointly with other universities more than 30 programmes of study, graduate (Masters and Doctoral) and undergraduate, and other short vocational training courses, which operate on a modular degree system (Gravani, 2018). These are delivered within a highly structured and centralized system, in which every aspect of the programmes is centrally controlled from the government, via the Agency for Quality Assurance in Higher Education, the Ministry of Finance, the General Auditor, and the university (Gravani, 2018). Therefore, in most of the cases there is not much space for learners and educators to be involved in a meaningful dialogue and co-create the learning contract.

The IMAESC programme has been offered jointly with the Universities of Glasgow (programme leader), the University of Malta and Tallinn University. It builds from students' interests in adult education to deepen and broaden their knowledge and understanding of adult education in a globalizing world from an international perspective and with a focus on social change. Social change cannot be attained without cultivating critical and reflective thinking, mutual trust, support, mutual accountability and mutual challenge, and without working collectively to improve things. In IMAESC adult students receive a theoretical grounding in adult education, as well as intercultural and practical skills development through teaching placements, focused seminars and online courses (University of Glasgow, 2019). Students are mobile, as each semester they are located in one of the aforementioned universities, starting from Glasgow (semester one), moving to Malta (semester two), then Tallinn (semester three), while they choose to locate themselves in one of the above places for the final semester for writing up their master's dissertation. There is also an optional summer school in the Universiti Sains Malaysia (USM) and a limited number of internship options in UNESCO (UIL), PRIA (Participatory Research in Asia) and DIE (German Institute for Adult Education). In the IMAESC programme the OUC contributes with two online modules of 15 ECTS each, the: 'Research Methods' and 'Teaching adult education online'. For the delivery of both certain educational tools and methodology are used.

M. N. GRAVANI

The educational methodology adopted at the OUC as presented by Epiphaniou et al. (2015, cited in Gravani, 2018, p. 179), consists of the following basic components. The *thematic unit* or *module*, which is the core organizational unit of each programme; *student group*; the *group advisory meetings* that are organized through the Web conferencing service; the *student assessment*, which takes the form of written assignments and final exams with physical presence; and the *educational tool*, which is the eClass eLearning Platform based on Moodle. The latter is hierarchically structured and provides to adult learners, tutors and OUC administrators possibilities for posting, downloading and distributing multimodal educational material, assigning activities and exercises, receiving comments and queries, submitting assignments, interacting, through synchronous and asynchronous communication (Gravani, 2018, p. 184). The eClass eLearning Platform has the capacity to bring people together by employing a number of services that endorse communication and collaborative learning. The most important of them are discussed below: a*synchronous learning* service which permits participants in the platform to have twenty-four hours' access to the educational resources, activities and tools such as forums, instant messaging, chat, links, webpages, folders, questionnaires. Availability and accessibility of course materials via the asynchronous learning service has numerous benefits and enhances adult students' participation in the course. The *synchronous learning* service in which educators and learners interact closer to each other, organize lectures, thesis presentations, short seminars. This builds on Elluminate Live! and as commented in Gravani (2018, p. 181), it creates a class-like environment for participants to chat, talk, see each other, exchange emotions and provides opportunities for dialogue and cooperation. T*he video lecture and streaming service* based on Panopto for capturing, recording and delivering lectures to different audiences. The *assignment submission and plagiarism detection* service; the *learning activity management system* for the creation of visually learning activities for the modules; the *mobile learning* service which furnishes students with the possibility to attend modules through their tablets or smartphones (Rodosthenous et al., 2016, as cited in Gravani, 2018, p. 180).

From the above it becomes palpable that the available services at the OUC and especially the eClass Platform supports the conditions for building collective capacity by providing the setting for a collaborative environment for learning and the co-construction of knowledge. This echoes Vygotsky's social constructivism or socio-cultural approach to learning, which highlights that the origins of knowledge creation should not be sought in the mind, but in the social interaction among individuals (Kollias, 2018). It also conforms to the adult learning principles that favour learner centred approaches and the creation of cultures of learning where adult learners learn together and are jointly dedicated to the enhancement of learning. Nevertheless, recent research focused on some modules delivered by the OUC has revealed some challenges and complications in the development of opportunities for social interaction and collaboration via the eClass Platform, as learning through the Platform can be highly mechanical and might not grasp the authenticity of learning in social settings (Gravani, 2018). Moreover, complications were caused

CCB FOR ADULT LEARNING IN DISTANCE EDUCATION

due to the broader centralized and inflexible system, the fixed curriculum of the modules and the incompetence, inexperience, lack of available time and training on behalf of the educators to work towards adjusting the courses to the online and adult learning principles and to use the resources available to make them more interactive (Gravani, 2018, pp. 184–185). Certainly, there are good examples of modules at the OUC of using the educational methodology and tools available to build online communities of learners where the focus of concern is the construction of knowledge as a collective accomplishment situated in the exchanges amongst them. One of this is the 'Teaching adult education online' module which is critically presented in the subsequent section as a 'good' practice in terms of the approaches it adopts to build collective capacity through online learning communities. This is depicted in the design of the curriculum and assessment, the selection of the educational activities and online tools and overall approach to learning adopted in the module.

BUILDING COLLECTIVE CAPACITY IN THE 'TEACHING ADULT EDUCATION ONLINE' MODULE

As stated in its study guide, the course is about teaching adults online (Kollias, 2018) and its curriculum evolves around three central themes. These are: the 'Critical issues in online teaching and learning', focusing on online pedagogies, distributed learning in social media, ubiquitous learning, adult educators' and students' role in online learning environments, online teaching in multicultural contexts and many more. The 'Trends in open learning online', examining the logic and recent developments in the open educational resources (OER) movement and related concepts, as well as focusing on massive open online courses (MOOCs), from a pedagogic and social perspective. Finally, the 'Online course design considerations in practice' focusing on the design of a mini pilot course. Students by working in small groups obtain an extensive hands-on experience in structuring, planning and delivering an online course using Moodle. Among others, they decide on their preferred pedagogic approach, remix, repurpose and upload learning materials, specify learning activities and choose assessment techniques (Kollias, 2018). It is evident from the above that the curriculum of the module combines both theoretical and practical aspects, for which students are invited to work in small groups and practice collaborative work. As specified in the study guide, it is oriented towards blending the study of sound academic research and theorizing on adult online education with the development of practical skills needed by competent adult educators working in online programmes and by e-course and e-learning content developers (Kollias, 2018, p. 4).

The pedagogic approach adopted for the module, as again reported in the study guide, is influenced by the connectivist approach to online adult teaching and learning and, also the socio-cultural approach to learning (Kollias, 2018), which both consists of the basis for the development of online communities, as they complement each other. In the connectivist approach, one the one hand, it is the connections that enable us to learn more that are more important than our current state of knowing

(Siemens, 2005), and much learning can happen across peer networks that take place online. The socio-cultural approach to learning, on the other hand, proposes that learning is essentially a distributed and mediated phenomenon located in the interactions between people and the activities they engage in, as we learn from the action and behaviour of other people in the society. In this learning is negotiated (Kollias, 2018).

Succeeding the connectivist approach to learning, in the explored module the educator guides students to information and answers key questions as needed, in order to support students' learning and sharing on their own. Students, in their turn, are encouraged to seek out information on their own, online, and express what they find creating personal learning environments. Thus, each week students are expected to study a set of learning materials and extra resources for further exploration and engage in small individual and group projects on the weekly topic and its wider theme. This is also important because it helps students to follow the pace of the course, provide a good ground for collaboration and sharing, and help them identify areas of interest for further exploration and skills development. The result of such activities is a connected community around this collective achievement (Kollias, 2018). For example, in week 4 of the academic year 2018–2019, the tutor uploaded in the discussion forum of the eClass Platform the following note for the students titled 'what kind of …'?:

Based on your study of the papers above and other learning materials you may find as relevant, please, post a contribution (and or comments on others' contributions) on the following questions:

- What kind of online teacher you would like to be?
- What kind of online students would you like to have?
- How you think you could change their lives through your teaching?
- Do you like the students you would like to have?

The above is indicative of the tutor's attempt to guide students in trying to search for information, answer questions, comment and critically discuss other students' comments and contributions, in order to make them interact with each other and work collaboratively. Following the above post on behalf of the tutor, 35 posts were uploaded in the platform from the 27 students of the module, and a joint accomplishment has emerged. For this to happen, students throughout the course are asked to explore and use different kinds of online tools and environments for practicing their skills in e-learning content and course development, communication and sharing. Thus, it is expected that they are already familiar with the most common internet technologies and uses such as: Google searching, e-mailing, social media, etc. (Kollias, 2018, p. 4).

Moreover, students, in the light of the socio-cultural approach to learning, are encouraged to explore the affordances, meditational roles, cultural and epistemic orientations of new massive online teaching and learning practices (e.g. MOOCs); informal learning and knowledge sharing practices (e.g. crowdsourcing, peer learning) and different types of online technologies and tools (e.g. social technologies), and; reflect upon their limitations and the possibilities in adult teaching and learning for social change (Kollias, 2018). For this to happen, students are encouraged to participate in a number of collaborative educational activities that encourage the development of practices and promote critical reflection requiring:

- *aggregation*, i.e. searching and accessing a wide variety of online resources to read, watch, or play;
- *remixing*, i.e. keeping track and organizing bookmark collections (e.g. tags) of internet findings, through social bookmarking (e.g. Pinterest), blogging (e.g. in Wordpress); posting to a related discussion in the course's Moodle platform, etc.;
- *repurposing*, i.e. enabling the reusability of existing openly available learning content into new teaching/learning contexts; and
- *sharing* their work and ideas with other students and groups in the course and make them freely available over the internet (Kollias, 2018, p. 4).

The weekly activities, described above, in which students are invited to participate on an optional basis, are directly linked to the two compulsory assignments that students need to submit in order to be formally assessed for the course. These have a formative form, and aim, on the one hand, to develop a deeper understanding of critical issues related to the teaching of adults online and make students familiar with tools and processes that can make their understandings and ideas visible to others. On the other hand, the second assignment aims to develop a practice-based understanding of the challenges involved in the collaborative design and co-construction of an online mini-course (Kollias, 2018). Assessment is also completed by written exams at the end of the course, as this is a requirement for distance learning modules centrally imposed by the university and the Agency for Quality Assurance in Higher Education. Of course, the traditional exam in a written form, in a distance learning module that employs formative assignments throughout its duration, is inconsistent and disconnected from its philosophy, and negatively criticized by the students.

Summing up it can be argued that the 'Teaching adult education online' module is a thoughtfully designed course, which builds around the notions of social presence, constructivism and the use of an online learning community (Pallot & Pratt, 2010), based on people, a shared purpose, specific guidelines, technology, collaborative learning and reflective practice (Pallof & Pratt, 2010). For the above it consists of a 'good' example of building collective capacity.

CONCLUSION

The chapter has discussed the challenges involved in building collective capacity for adult learning in distance education by presenting a 'good' practice of collective capacity building implementation in an online module provided by the Open University of Cyprus. Such an investigation is valuable as it highlights the ways with which collective capacity is built, and provides prospects and ideas for building it in distance learning universities, by changing the culture through using online learning communities and collaborative behaviours. The investigation contributes to the discussion of an under researched area and makes clear points about the possibility to enhance adult learning in distance learning environments via encouraging collaborative exchange and practice among learners where they work together to improve learner outcomes and the practice of others and their own. Thus, as Lave and Wenger (1991) argue, the focus is not on the individual as learner, but on learning as participation in the social world. Participation in a community of learners becomes the 'potential curriculum' with the circulation of information among the participants as a 'condition for the effectiveness of learning' (Lave & Wenger, 1991).

In pursuing the above, the chapter has critically reviewed the concept of collective capacity building and has extensively discussed the mechanism of building it in distance education. Then, it has critically presented the context of the distance learning university within which the 'Teaching adult education online' module is offered with emphasis on the educational methodology and available tools used to build online communities of learners. Finally, the chapter has analytically discussed how in the context of the selected module online communities of learners for collective capacity building are created with the use of the proper design of the curriculum and assessment, the selection of the educational activities and online tools and the overall connectivist and socio-cultural approach to learning adopted in the module.

Undoubtedly, the 'good' example presented has shown, although imperfectly, that building collective capacity through online communities of learners is a powerful component in enhancing adult learning in distance education and links to sustainability. However, as this is only a small case study presented, in order for 'best' cases of collective capacity building in distance education to be designed, more empirical investigation is needed in the field and systematic work and changes towards educational systems and programmes underpinned by open, flexible and embracing approaches to learning, such as the connectivist and socio-cultural approach. Of course, as Schweisfurth (2013) argues, a critical mass of actors is also needed, who will actively and determinedly involve in this through empowering students to take responsibility of their own and collective learning via designing a flexible curriculum that allows exploration and collaboration.

REFERENCES

Aczel, J. C., Peake, S. R., & Hardy, P. (2008). Designing capacity-building in e-learning expertise: Challenges and strategies. *Computers and Education, 50*(2), 499–510.

Amini, C., & Oluyide, O. (2016). Building capacity for Open and Distance Learning (ODL) in West Africa sub-region: The pivotal role of RETRIDAL. *Open Praxis, 8*(4), 337–350.

Brookfield, S. (1986). *Understanding and facilitating adult learning: A comprehensive analysis of principles and effective practices.* Milton Keynes: Oxford University Press.

Brookfield, S. (1995). *Becoming a critically reflective teacher.* San Francisco, CA: Jossey-Bass.

Cercone, K. (2008). Characteristics of adult learners with implications for online learning design. *AACE Journal, 16*(2), 137–159.

Christidou, V., Gravani, M. N., & Hatzinikita, V. (2012). Distance learning material for adult education: The case of the OUC. *Ubiquitous Learning: An International Journal, 4*, 33–46.

European Commission (EU). (2011). *Reference document No 6: Toolkit for capacity development.* Luxemburg: Office for Official Publications of the European Communities. Retrieved January 29, 2019, from https://europa.eu/capacity4dev/file/13622/download?token=QvdLHLwH

Fullan, M. (2010). *All systems go: The change imperative for whole system reform.* Thousand Oaks, CA: Corwin Press.

Gravani, M. N. (2015). Adult learning in a distance education context: Theoretical and methodological challenges. *International Journal of Lifelong Education, 34*(2), 172–193.

Gravani, M. N. (2018). Use of technology at the Open University of Cyprus (OUC) to support adult distance learners: To what extent is being informed by the Learner-Centred Education (LCE) paradigm? In A. Anjana (Ed.), *Technology for efficient learner support services in distance education* (pp. 173–188). Singapore: Springer.

Gravani, M. N., & Karagiorgi, Y. (2014). Underpinning principles of adult learning in Face to Face (f2f) meetings employed by distance-teaching universities. *Journal of Adult and Continuing Education, 20*, 53–67.

Harris, A. (2011). System improvement through collective capacity building. *Journal of Educational Administration, 49*(6), 624–636.

Harris, A., & Jones, M. (2011). *Professional learning communities in action.* London: Leannta Press.

James, F., & Figaro-Henry, S. (2017). Building collective leadership capacity using collaborative twenty-first century digital tools. *School Leadership & Management, 37*(5), 520–536.

Keegan, D. (Ed.). (1996). *Foundations of distance education* (3rd ed.). London: Routledge.

Knowles, M. S. (1990). *The adult learner: A neglected species.* Houston, TX: Gulf Publishing Company.

Knowles, M. S., & Associates. (1984). *Andragogy in action: Applying modern principles of adult learning.* San Francisco, CA: Jossey-Bass.

Kollias, A. (2018). *Teaching adult education online* (IMAESC611, Study guide). Nicosia: Open University of Cyprus.

Kosioma Eli, O. (2015). E-learning as a veritable tool for capacity building in adult education and open distance education in Nigeria. *Journal of Educational and Social Research, 5*(1), 137–144.

Lave, J., & Wenger, E. (1991). *Situated learning: Legitimate peripheral participation.* Cambridge: Cambridge University Press.

Lee, K. (2018). Everyone already has their community beyond the screen: Reconceptualising online learning and expanding boundaries. *Educational Technology Research and Development, 66*(5), 1255–1268. Retrieved January 25, 2019, from https://link.springer.com/article/10.1007/s11423-018-9613-y#citeas

Lee, K., Choi, H., & Cho, Y. H. (2019). Becoming a competent self: A developmental process of adult distance learning. *The Internet and Higher Education, 41*, 25–33.

Makoe, M., Richardson, J. T., & Price, L. (2008). Conceptions of learning in adult students embarking on distance education. *Higher Education, 55*(3), 303–320.

Merriam, S. B., & Caffarella, R. S. (1999). *Learning in adulthood: A comprehensive guide* (2nd ed.). San Francisco, CA: Jossey-Bass.

Pallof, R. M., & Pratt, K. (2010). *Collaborating online: Learning together in community* (Vol. 32). New York, NY: John Wiley & Sons.

Peters, O. (1998). *Learning and teaching in distance education. Pedagogical analyses and interpretations in an international perspective.* London: Kogan Page.

Scardamalia, M., & Bereiter, C. (2014). Knowledge building and knowledge creation: Theory, pedagogy, and technology. In K. Sawyer (Ed.), *Cambridge handbook of the learning science* (2nd ed., pp. 397–417). New York, NY: Cambridge University Press.

Schweisfurth, M. (2013). *Learner-centred education in international perspective: Whose pedagogy for whose development?* London: Routledge.

M. N. GRAVANI

Siemens, G. (2005). Connectivism: A learning theory for digital age. *International Journal of Instructional Technology and Distance Learning, 2*(1), 3–10.

Stringer, P. (2013). *Capacity building for school improvement: Revised.* Rotterdam, The Netherlands: Sense Publishers.

Thorpe, M. (2002). Socio-cultural perspectives. In. J. C. Aczel (Ed.), *H802 study guide.* Milton Keynes: The Open University Press.

UNESCO. (2013). *Towards effective capacity development: Capacity Needs Assessment Methodology (CAPNAM) for planning and managing education.* Paris: UNESCO. Retrieved from https://unesdoc.unesco.org/ark:/48223/pf0000226090

University of Glasgow. (2019). *Erasmus Mundus International Master Adult Education for social change.* Retrieved from https://www.gla.ac.uk/postgraduate/erasmusmundus/imaesc/ theprogrammeandhowtoapply/programmestructure/#/year1,year2,aimsandintendedlearningoutcomes

Welter, C., Jacobs, B. A., Jarpe-Ratner, E., Naji, S., & Gruss, K. (2017). Building capacity for collective Action to address population health improvement through communities of practice: A distance-based education pilot. *Pedagogy in Health Promotion: The Scholarship of Teaching and Learning, 3*(1), 21–27.

Wenger, E. (2008). *Communities of practice: Learning, meaning, and identity.* Cambridge: Cambridge University Press.

Yiayli, S., Yiaylis, G., & Koutsoumba, M. (2010). Autonomy in learning in a distance educational environment. *Open Education: The Journal of Open and Distance Education and Educational Technology, 2*(1&2), 92–105.

IOANA DARJAN, LOREDANA AL GHAZI, ANCA LUSTREA,
MIHAI PREDESCU AND MARIANA CRASOVAN

13. NURTURING THE WELL-BEING OF UNIVERSITY STUDENTS FOR IMPROVED CAPACITY BUILDING

INTRODUCTION[1]

Universities are complex organizations, with clear aims, well-defined functions, and professional responsibilities for the society and the communities in which they exist. Seen in this light, universities should be permanently sensitive and responsive to all societal changes, to the new demands and challenges. Therefore, their preoccupation with the constant development and improvement of their capacity building is of the utmost importance. Capacity building aims at three main dimensions: individual, organizational, and institutional.

This chapter focuses on the individual dimension of capacity building, mainly on how to create and improve a set of efficient strategies for responding to the demands of our society and community. It also explains how we can create a number of teaching staff skills necessary for such an enterprise.

The main aim of universities is to facilitate and improve the student's learning and their self-development. To fulfil their aims, universities develop practical measures to be further implemented. This process begins with the identification of the crucial interconnected factors that facilitate or impede learning. They have individual, environmental, and relational characteristics. One vital factor is the psychological well-being of students and their mental health.

Psychological well-being and the state of mental health have a high impact on all our human actions, influencing our motivations for self-development and self-actualization. For the last few decades, researches have been investigating the positive effects of well-being on academic progress and successful learning outcomes, on the development of positive social and emotional environments and on building and maintaining qualitative relationships in different contexts. In the end, capacity building is concerned with the creation of the right premises for better self-development and successful academic pathways for university students. In this chapter, the relationships between psychological well-being and mental health will be closely examined in the context of real situations that are potentially stressful, such as the beginning of academic studies. For this purpose, we will use the Ryff's Psychological Well-Being Scale, the Warwick-Edinburgh Mental Well-being Scale

© KONINKLIJKE BRILL NV, LEIDEN, 2020 | DOI: 10.1163/9789004422209_014

I. DARJAN ET AL.

(WEMWBS), and Counselling Centre Assessment of Psychological Symptoms CCAPS 34. Our subjects are 90 first-year university students in the Educational Department of WUT.

DIMENSSIONS OF CAPACITY BUILDING IN UNIVERSITIES

Capacity building has been defined either as "the emergent combination of individual competencies and collective capabilities that enables a human system to create value" (Baser & Morgan, 2008, in van Duren, 2013, p. 15) or as "the evolving combination of attributes, capabilities, and relationships that enables a system to exist, adapt and perform" (Brinkerhoff & Morgan, 2010, in van Duren, 2013, p. 16). Capacity building targets variables at three main levels: the individual one, the organizational one, including systems and subsystems, and the players involved, and the institutional one, including systems and rules. All these variables could be strengthened to develop a more supporting and enabling learning environment.

Capacity building is measured by the level of performance achieved in the society, and, subsequently, the results obtained enhance the society's values. The measure of capacity building lies in its own performance and its further results which can enhance the society's value (van Duren, 2013). Simister and Smith (2010) use the analogy of a stone thrown into the water to express and explain the effects obtained by an increase in the capacity: it creates ripples which can affect the surrounding areas that are closely interconnected.

Different models can be used for assessing the capacity of an organization: the first model is designed by Kapland (1999) that contains six different elements: the context in which the organization functions and its conceptual framework, its vision and strategy, its organizational culture, its structure, the skills mastered by its employees, and its material resources; the second one is the ECDPM '5c'model, which refers to the capability to commit and engage, the capability to carry out technical, service delivery and logistical tasks, the capability to relate and attract support, the capability to adapt and self-renew, and the capability to balance diversity and coherence (van Duren, 2013).

Although many national and international agencies and public administration institutions have been concerned with the concept of capacity building and have kept it on their agendas as a priority subject, they have not been able yet to arrive at a working definition that would be acceptable to them all.

Sustainable communities, which offer exceptional models of living and working together, are thought to be good examples of learning communities that invest a lot in the development of their capacity. In these communities, universities are regarded as reliable partners or leading figures in the process of empowering communities through capacity building.

It is a fact that the university has the potential to be a partner for the community but, more importantly, it has the responsibility to contribute to the development of the community.

166

The Association of University Leaders for a Sustainable Future considers that "universities have a major role in the education, research, policy formation, and information exchange necessary to make these goals possible. Thus, university leaders must initiate and support mobilization of internal and external resources so that their institutions respond to this urgent challenge" (ULSF, 1999). ULFS indicates the 10 main actions that universities have agreed to develop:

1. Increase Awareness of Environmentally Sustainable Development;
2. Create an Institutional Culture of Sustainability;
3. Educate for Environmentally Responsible Citizenship;
4. Foster Environmental Literacy for All;
5. Practice Institutional Ecology;
6. Involve all Stakeholders;
7. Collaborate for Interdisciplinary Approaches;
8. Enhance Capacity of Primary and Secondary Schools;
9. Broaden Service and Outreach Nationally and Internationally;
10. Maintain the Movement (ULSF, 1999).

Capacity building in universities focuses on two main directions:

- Developing internal capacities, building a more sustainable university and campus; and
- Promoting capacity building of the local community, by offering know-how strategies for sustainable development (Shiel et al., 2016).

The principles and responsibilities of universities that aim at supporting their communities are presented in several important documents, such as. "University Charter for Sustainable Development", produced by COPERNICUS (1994), and the Magna Charta of European Universities (Magna Charta Universitarium, 1988).

Van Duren (2013) investigates the capacity development of higher education institutions in developing countries and concludes that universities need to increase their performance due to a number of external and internal pressures and requests, which are the following: the massification of higher education since the late twentieth century, the increasing relevance and impact of higher education for larger groups of population for helping them attain their aspirations, changing demographics, requests for a diversification of educational services for larger and more diverse groups of students, for new labour-market needs, the crucial importance of research studies showing support for the society's progress and adaptability.

CAPACITY BUILDING – STEPS TAKEN AT WEST UNIVERSITY OF TIMISOARA

The WUT is the largest higher education institution in the Western region of Romania and it is also an important agent for regional growth. The following principles guide the development of the WUT and its institutional actions: public responsibility, social and educational equity, student-centred education, transparency, and social inclusion.

I. DARJAN ET AL.

The WUT, acting in its capacity of an agent of development and growth at regional and national levels, is determined and dedicated to enhancing its capacity building, which shows that the WUT is an advanced research and educational organization.

Our University's interest in developing capacity building is illustrated in the structure it has implemented, in the actions conducted, and in the institutional relationships that it has developed recently. The principles that create capacity building in the WUT are the result of a long process of reflection and a series of concrete measures:

- The first principle shows a focus on a pragmatic ideology, which is shared both at an institutional level and at the level of the faculties. The WUT preserves the national and regional values, originating in European values and missions. Our University places a great emphasis on the needs of our community and on the particular nature of the local and regional labor market, constantly adapting our educational offer and curriculum to their real needs. In short, the construction of our university capacity building is based on a constant adaptation and adjustment of the existing resources to the latest social demands and challenges. In addition, the WUT invests constantly in training programs that encourage and inspire the staff to reach beyond their level. A large body of specialized professionals in various fields of activity contribute to the new goals set by the WUT and to its latest mission. These specialists use their knowledge and expertise to initiate educational programs for the students who take full advantage of such programs, but also the local community derives substantial benefits from them. In contrast with the reactive model that the WUT used to promote, for the past last years, it has embraced a proactive model, setting the public agenda and offering a new understanding of the latest issues in our society.
- The second principle focuses on the means and processes that aim to identify the University's main objectives, which also measure the expected impact and sustainability of the measures adopted the WUT Charter (WUT Charter, p. 6) states the university mission, as a catalyst for the development of the Romanian society through fostering an innovative and highly participative environment of scientific research, an environment of learning and artistic creation, dedicated to excellent sport performance, and finally ensuring the transfer of the competence and knowledge output towards the community, through a set of educational, research-oriented, and consulting services offered to its partners in the economic and socio-cultural environment. The WUT's objectives are relevant for the community's development, since its practice-based research constantly contributes to the social, economic and cultural well-being of the regional community. The WUT has an educational, but also a social mission, aiming to innovate and generate social changes, with a great impact on the community. In 2018, the WUT researchers in the economic and social fields conducted a Public Opinion Barometer which aimed to ascertain the needs of the citizens of Timisoara and to propose measures accordingly. Also, several other projects

NURTURING THE WELL-BEING OF UNIVERSITY STUDENTS

("Cultural Leadership", "Living heritage", art shows) have been developed by the WUT, contributing to our mutual community project that promotes Timisoara as the European Capital of Culture in 2021.

- The third principle of direct participation shows that all the members of our educational organization are involved in the process of capacity building. From this perspective, each university member has a direct impact on the decisions and the general institutional policy affecting each management level. For all important decisions, the academic community, including teaching and research staff, but also our students, are informed and consulted. The WUT provides a high level of organizational transparency, as shown by its general regulation requiring that all the official documents, decisions, projects be posted online and disseminated. The participation of students and staff is highly encouraged, both in the scientific life and in social action. For instance, students are rewarded for their voluntary work for the local community.
- The fourth principle of multi-dimensionality shows that capacity building can and should be applied to three different levels: the individual level, the organizational level, and the institutional/relational level. The WUT is interested in developing knowledge and skills in all its university members, teaching, research and administrative staff. A lot is invested in training sessions, academic projects, national and international mobilities, which have excellent results on the quality of our staff. At the same time, our students are encouraged to participate in learning and practical experiences, in national and international mobilities, in artistic and scientific events, while their curricula are designed to meet the demands required by such activities.
- The fifth principle of the environment shows that our University's actions are conditioned by the quality of the offers made by the stakeholders and the domain they wish to transform through capacity building. The WUT is always in close contact with several local stakeholders, labor market representatives, local, national and international public figures, who are invited to round tables, conferences, and formal meetings. The aim is to stay in touch with the real needs of the community and then to adapt our actions accordingly. The environment is regarded as a transformable element, which helps the WUT to improve the quality of our life in the community, by translating the amount of scientific and empirical knowledge into a set of real physical actions and realistic measures.
- The sixth principle of flexibility and adaptation in different contexts designs a number of complex strategies, methods and resources used for changing mentalities, developing knowledge, creating technical skills, and for facilitating an exchange between knowledge and skills.

The West University of Timisoara is a good example of a medium-sized university located in a dynamic community, with a steady economic growth. The social environment, energized by the students studying here and the thriving local industry, indicates that our university facilitates the students' integration into the labour market

I. DARJAN ET AL.

and the development of innovation and creativity. In actual fact, our university has struggled to refocus its mission from a more traditional role as the primary deliverer of culture and instruction to an active agent of social change. It focuses on 'smart' solutions and constantly enhances the quality of its intellectual output. In this way, it is not only the community that grows and thrives, but also its members. For the past last ten years, the WUT has moved away from the image of a traditional, fairly isolated, science-oriented institution to a more dynamic educational institution, which has been improving its educational offer for its students and for the local industry. The WUT is now more inclusive and has become an active member in regional, national and European networks.

IN SEARCH OF WELL-BEING

Positive psychology, a new domain of psychology, which was developed in 1998 by the work of Seligman, Csikszentmihaly and Peterson, can be defined in many ways. It can be seen as the "scientific study of what makes life most worth living" (Peterson, 2009) or as "the scientific study of positive human functioning and flourishing on multiple levels that include the biological, personal, relational, institutional, cultural, and global dimensions of life" (Seligman & Csikszentmihalyi, 2000), or as the study of happiness. Positive psychology incorporates Seligman's theory of PERMA, Csikszentmihalyi's theory of flow, and Seligman and Peterson's methodology of studying character strengths and virtues.

Initially known as 'the three paths to happiness theory' (Seligman, 2002), this theory states that there are three different types of what can be called a happy life, according to their main purpose: first, the pleasant life, which is a life of sheer enjoyment, focused on experimenting positive emotion and experiences; secondly, the good life, which is a life of engagement, consisting in the immersion and absorption in the flow of current activities; thirdly, the meaningful life, which is a life of affiliation, for which happiness and well-being can only be attained if you are a small cog that contributes significantly to a permanent and collective sense of happiness. Seligman (2011) refines this theory and creates the PERMA model of well-being. This model claims that well-being is a combination of five major elements: positive emotions and experiences, active engagement, important and relevant relationships, meaning and purpose in life, and personal accomplishments.

The theory of character strengths and virtues (Park, Peterson & Seligman, 2004; Peterson & Seligman, 2004) offers a framework for identifying positive psychological traits. It proposes a model containing six virtues (wisdom, courage, humanity, justice, temperance, and transcendence) and their correspondent personal strengths, such as creativity, love of learning, bravery, integrity, kindness, social intelligence, citizenship, fairness, forgiveness, humility, appreciation of beauty, etc.

Carol Ryff (1989, 2014) develops a theory of well-being rooted in the Aristotelian philosophy and ethics, which considers that the main purpose in life is not the pursuit of happiness but acting virtuously. According to Ryff (1998, 1995), psychological well-being is determined by six distinct factors: self-acceptance, personal growth, purpose in life, environmental mastery, autonomy, and positive relations with others.

Diener (1984) proposes a tripartite model of subjective well-being. The term 'subjective well-being' highlights the relevance of personal experience and personal appraisal of one's well-being. Our personal appraisals involve both emotional reactions and cognitive judgments. Subjective well-being, which tends to be stable over time and is influenced by our personality traits, is defined by three distinct, yet often interrelated, components of the general well-being: frequent positive affect, infrequent negative affect, and cognitive evaluations.

The existential type gives a more comprehensive approach to well-being (van Deurzen, 1997, 2009; Leijssen, 2009). It takes into account the whole complexity of our human existence, ranging from the physical, social, and personal reality to the non-physical or spiritual reality. These four dimensions of our existence (physical, social, personal, and spiritual) are interconnected, therefore they are all equally important to our well-being and to our healthy functioning.

Researchers from the Universities of Warwick and Edinburgh have developed a measurement tool for assessing our mental well-being. In their views, mental well-being expresses the quality of individual psychological functioning, a high rate of life satisfaction, and an ability to develop and maintain mutually benefiting relationships. So, psychological well-being is generated by a sense of autonomy, self-acceptance, personal growth, purpose in life, and self-esteem (Parkinson, 2008).

The concept of mental well-being can be defined from two distinct perspectives: the hedonistic perspective and the eudaimonic perspective (Bauer & McAdams, 2010; McMahan, 2011; Ryff et al., 2008). From a hedonistic perspective, mental well-being expresses a subjective experience of happiness and life satisfaction, while the eudaimonic perspective views mental well-being as positive psychological functioning, good relationships with others, and self-realization.

Another ongoing debate tries to decide if subjective well-being and psychological well-being are two distinct dimensions or just two different perspectives on the same general construct (Chen et al., 2013). Subjective well-being seems to have a more hedonistic orientation, pursuing a pleasant and happy life. On the other hand, psychological well-being takes a more eudaimonically orientated approach, its focus being on the fulfilment of human potential and on guiding our lives according to real and meaningful purposes. Yet, both are fundamentally concerned with the subjective nature of our well-being (Keyes et al., 2002).

In the end, mental well-being can be conceived in two distinct ways: it can be seen as a single continuum model, with the mental well-being at the one end of the spectrum and the mental illness, at the other. Conversely, it can be seen as a two continua or dual continua model, which regards mental well-being and mental illness as two separate dimensions. The two continua model can explain why people with mental illnesses often experience good mental well-being.

MENTAL HEALTH AND HIGHER EDUCATION

The positive paradigm in psychology shifts the focus away from mental illness and its negative characteristics (negative thinking style and maladaptive behavioral patterns) to the promotion and fostering of happiness, well-being, and positivity in our life.

Seligman and Csikszentmihalyi (2000) conclude in their study that psychology should move beyond 'a disease model' of correcting what is wrong, repairing what is broken, and eliminating the worst effects.

Acknowledging the increase in the incidence of depression and anxiety disorders in children and youth, and also the decreasing age of their onset, Seligman (2009) supports the view that young children's well-being must be nurtured appropriately in schools in order for children to have better learning results (successful adaptability, high rates of literacy, more discipline), and to achieve better personal development as social beings and citizens. Schools can be the best place to teach well-being. Three important goals can be attained by nurturing well-being in schools: it can be an antidote to depression, can enhance life satisfaction, and it can facilitate better learning outcomes and more creative thinking (Seligman et al., 2005). Seligman considers that well-being promotes better learning.

'Positive' schools are those concerned with the psychological distress of students for which they propose a proactive approach, with the focus on building protective factors, functioning as a buffer system against adversity and pain (Terjesen et al., 2004, as cited by Ong, 2013; Predescu et al., 2017; Darjan et al., 2017). Positive education builds excellent abilities for emotional self-regulation and improves resilience; it can reduce anxiety and stress and can also develop personal strengths and virtues, such as hope, kindness, social intelligence, self-control, and the ability to broaden one's perspective. It is true that positive education produces positive outcomes which, in turn, generate further positive developmental outcomes in the young person (Park, 2004, as cited in Ong, 2013; Darjan et al., 2016).

As regards university students, it is a fact that the rate of mental disorder incidence is the highest between the ages of 16 and 24 years old. From this point of view, university students can be considered as a 'high risk' population for mental health difficulties.

Many studies (Roberts et al., 2000; Stewart-Brown, 2000; Adlaf et al., 2001; APS, 2014; Stallman, 2010) report that the university student population experiences higher levels of psychological distress than the non-student population.

The highest level of distress is reported to begin at the start of the first year of the university studies. Students often report less distress in the subsequent years, which indicates that well-being declines mostly during the first year of the university studies. However, this decline might persist if it is not professionally addressed for the whole period of the degree studies (Stallman, 2010).

More importantly, it seems that students who are less motivated to study or have negative learning motivations are at a higher risk for experiencing mental health disorders and difficulties (Larcombe & Fethers, 2013; Sheldon &Krieger, 2007).

University students might suffer from a wide spectrum of mental disorders, ranging from mild to severe intensity. Even short or long-term disorders might impact negatively on the student's functioning and well-being. It is important to mention that mental disorders might fluctuate over time, and some students who experience short periods or episodes of mental disorder still manage to control these difficulties and further lead active and fulfilling lives. The Disability Discrimination Act (DDA, 1995, 2015) considers students with mental health difficulties affecting them negatively for a year or more as disabled. Temporary distress, generated by stressful events, such as bereavement and failures, might also impact negatively on the studies of the students and their good functioning.

It is important to identify the internal and external factors that affect our students' mental health and their well-being in order to develop effective interventions for assisting them throughout their university studies. In this way, school drop-out can be prevented and also the escalation of personal difficulties, but at the same time personal development and academic progress and success can be promoted and valued. It is important to have access to the information regarding the students' well-being and their mental health in order to assist and counsel them during the transition periods from high school to university or from the undergraduate degree to the postgraduate life.

FOSTERING THE WELL-BEING OF UNIVERSITY STUDENTS– PHASES AND ACTIONS

In the process of developing an organizational strategy for fostering the well-being of university students, it is vital to follow a pre-established logic and the steps that are necessary in this series of cyclic phases (Figure 13.1):

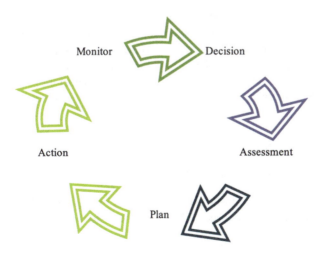

Figure 13.1. Phases of developing an organizational strategy

I. DARJAN ET AL.

- Decision;
- Assessment;
- Planning;
- Acting/implementing procedures;
- Monitoring and refining procedures.

The decision phase has the following stages:

- Acknowledging the relevance of the students' well-being and their mental health for their personal development and academic progress;
- Setting one important objective of the university which involves fostering and supporting the students' well-being and mental health;
- Decision making at the level of the university's management to take action towards attaining this goal.

This last decision phase focuses on documenting the scientific and empirical arguments that show the positive effects of building a sound institutional environment, the right procedures, and positive relationships in order to foster the well-being of the students and strengthen their mental health. At an organizational level, all these rationalities help to legitimize and support the decision-making process.

The assessment phase focuses on identifying a set of instruments and methods suitable for the identification of the actual state of well-being and mental health among university students, their intercorrelations, and their impact on the students' academic adjustment and progress. The result and conclusions obtained in this phase will generate the main objectives, the necessary solutions and further directions, and will guide the subsequent action phase.

The action phase implements the organizational strategy, through a research-in-action approach.

The monitoring phase uses systematic assessment, thus being able to offer the necessary data and a number of suggestions for a polished refinement or improvement of the actions, which are constantly adapted to the features of the given environment and the particular characteristics of each individual and the challenges they might face.

In this chapter, we will present the results and the conclusions of the assessment phase and the preliminary conclusions and suggestions for planning the strategy of action.

A PILOT-STUDY AT THE WEST UNIVERSITY OF TIMISOARA

Aims and Objectives of the Pilot Study

The aims of this study are to investigate the level of the well-being in university students and to assess the impact of the academic distress on the students' general well-being.

In addition, this study aims to identify the relationships between the well-being of the university students and their potential psychological disorders and distress. There are further benefits of this study concerning, for example, an improvement in the early identification of any evidence of psychological disorder and the particular nature of the university students' well-being. The early identification of any risk factors will have positive effects on the counseling practices, meant to reduce the prevalence of psychological disorders and their negative effects on the students' academic progress and their personal development (Darjan, 2017; Darjan et al., 2016).

The research objectives are:

- To identify the levels of subjective and mental well-being of university students.
- To identify the types of psychological disorders and their severity in the first-year university students.
- To identify the possible correlations between the well-being and any potential psychological disorders manifested in the first-year university students.

The assumption is that academic distress has a significant impact on our general well-being. Our claim is that even low levels of mental and subjective well-being will correlate positively with symptoms of psychological disorders and distress.

Another important implication of this study is the adaptation and validation of technical assessment instruments for the Romanian university student population, the early identification of students at risk of academic failure and school drop-out, and the development of sound preventive and interventional strategies at the university level.

Participants

This study was conducted on 90 university students, enrolled in Educational Sciences specializations at the West University of Timisoara, at the bachelor (95.6%) and master (4.4%) degree levels. The age of the participants varies between 18 and 43 years old, with a mean of 21.43 and a standard deviation of 4.31. Only one male student participated in the research study (1.1%) and 89 females (98.9%). Out of the total number of participants, 62 (68.9%) were enrolled in the first study year, 16 (17.8%) in the second year, and 12 (13.3%) in the third year of university studies.

Instruments and Procedures

The instruments used are the Ryff's Psychological Wellbeing Scale (PWBS), long-form (84 items), the Warwick- Edinburgh Mental Wellbeing (WEMWBS) Scale (14 items), and the Counselling Centre Assessment of Psychological Symptoms CCAPS 34 (34 items).

I. DARJAN ET AL.

The subjects completed the instruments on-line, via the Google-Sheets application. Before completing the questionnaires, the participants had been informed about the research aims and objectives, the research team, and the confidentiality policies.

The Ryff's PWBS, long-form (84 items) is a theoretically grounded instrument which focuses on measuring various aspects of psychological well-being. It has 6 subscales (14 items on each scale): autonomy, environmental mastery, personal growth, positive relations with others, purpose in life, and self-acceptance.

The second instrument, The Warwick-Edinburgh Mental Wellbeing Scale (WEMWBS), is a 14 item scale, designed to assess the state of mental well-being during the course of the past two weeks. Scores can range from a minimum of 14 to a maximum of 70 points. Higher scores are associated with higher levels of mental well-being. The WEMWBS is available free of charge and can be downloaded from the developers' website.

The third instrument, the Counselling Centre Assessment of Psychological Symptoms (CCAPS-34), is an instrument with seven subscales, assessing possible psychological symptoms or distress among university students. It also includes a Distress Index. The seven subscales are: Depression, Generalized Anxiety, Social Anxiety, Academic Distress, Eating Concerns, Hostility, and Alcohol Use.

The participants took part in this study on a voluntary non-compulsory basis, and they were not paid. Also, the participants' confidentiality and ethical conditions were warranted, and they were asked to give their full consent to participate in the study. From a total of 556 students, 90 chose to complete the questionnaires.

RESULTS OF THE PILOT-STUDY

Well-Being in University Students

The state of the mental well-being of the sample used in our research study was determined using the scores at the Warwick MWB scale. The mean score was 55.78, at 8.77 standard deviations. Comparing this result with the test value reported by the developers as a mean score for the group aged between 16–75 years old, 50.7, a statistically significant difference was identified between our sample and the general population data. The study's conclusion is that our sample shows a significantly higher level of mental well-being, much above the average scores. The results of Ryff's PWB scale are presented in Table 13.1.

According to the results presented, our sample proves a high level of well-being. Furthermore, our students show a good ability to be autonomous, they feel competent, involved in the process of personal growth and personal potential development. Also, they consider themselves able to build warm and harmonious relationships with others, based on mutual trust and capable of self-acceptance. They consider their life as being meaningful.

176

NURTURING THE WELL-BEING OF UNIVERSITY STUDENTS

Table 13.1. Descriptive statistics for Ryff scale and subscales

	N	Minimum	Maximum	Mean	Std. Deviation
Ryff's_score	90	2.93	5.55	4.5914	.62115
Autonomy_scale	90	3.00	5.50	4.2468	.86541
Envinromental_mastery_scale	90	1.86	5.71	4.4143	.82824
Personal_growth_scale	90	3.43	5.93	4.9817	.60444
Positive_relations_scale	90	2.64	6.00	4.6937	.71511
Purpose_in_life_scale	90	2.38	5.85	4.5624	.65927
Self_acceptance_scale	90	2.79	5.71	4.6111	.74824
Valid N (listwise)	90				

Academic Distress, Well-Being, and Psychological Disorders

Using CCAPS – 34, we have assessed the psychological symptoms and academic distress of the sampled university students, as well as their own personal evaluation of the emotional state of well-being.

Reported depressive symptoms are significantly lower than those manifested in the general population (t = –2.58, at sig = .011). While the test value reported by the developers as a mean score for the elevated cut-point for depression was 1.75, our sample had a mean of 1.55.

For the generalized anxiety symptoms, the developers reported a mean score for the elevated cut-point of 2.10. With a mean score of 2.07, the amount of generalized anxiety symptoms found in our sample is similar to the one reported for the general population (t = –.30, sig. = .76), which indicates that our sample presents elevated generalized anxiety symptoms.

Regarding the social anxiety, the mean score of our sample was 2.5644, while the test value reported by the developers as a mean score for the elevated cut-point for social anxiety was 1.75. As there are no statistically significant differences (t = .95, sig. = .346) between our sample results and the general population data, we can conclude that our sample presents elevated symptoms of social anxiety.

There are significant differences (t = –7.60, sig. = .000) between the amount of academic distress reported by our sample (m = 1.82), compared with the score for the elevated cut point reported by the developers (m = 2.50). Our students seemed to be less distressed by academic issues.

The eating concerns of our sample (m = 2.11) are significantly greater, compared with the general population data (m = 1.50). The differences are statistically significant (t = 5.87, sig. = .000).

I. DARJAN ET AL.

Table 13.2. Comparative results on CCAPS 34 between study sample and the etalon

	CCAPS 34	Research Participants
Mean	1.85	1.82
Std. dev	1.11	0.84
Low cutpoint (percentile)	1.45 (44)	1.5 (44.4)
High cutpoint (percentile)	2.5 (72)	2 (71.1)
No. subjects low cutpoint		40
No. subjects high cutpoints		30

The analyzed signs of hostility are significantly higher in our sample, with a mean score of m = 1.63.

The difference is statistically significant (t = 3.63, sig. = 000), as the value test reported by the developers as a mean score for the elevated cut-point for hostility in the general population is 1.33.

In conclusion, the psychological symptoms and concerns reported by our sample are, with a very few exceptions, quite similar to those reported for the general population (Table 13.2).

The Impact of Academic Distress on Well-Being and Mental Health

Academic distress can be a very important risk factor for the emergence of psychological symptoms, for reducing the individual efficacy and level of functioning, and for altering the quality of interrelation.

In our sample, a statistically significant negative correlation (r = −.64, p = .000) was found between academic distress and mental well-being.

High levels of academic distress have a significantly negative effect on the ability of environmental mastery (r = −.77, p = .000) and on self-acceptance (r = −.70, p = .000).

The academic distress reported by our participants has an important impact on their mental well-being and on all the dimensions of their psychological well-being (Figure 13.2).

The quantity of reported academic distress (low and high levels) has statistically significant effects on well-being, social functioning, and positive self-assessment (Table 13.3).

Figure 13.3 presents the effects of low and high levels of academic distress on reported psychological symptoms and concerns. High levels of academic distress generate more psychological symptoms, while low levels of academic distress correlate with fewer psychological symptoms.

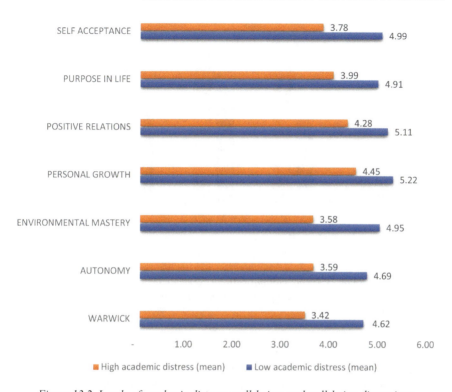

Figure 13.2. Levels of academic distress, well-being, and well-being dimensions

Table 13.3. Impact of different levels of academic distress on well-being and mental health

	Warwick	Autonomy	Environmental mastery	Personal growth	Positive relations	Purpose in life	Self-acceptance
Low academic distress (mean)	4.62	4.69	4.95	5.22	5.11	4.91	4.99
High academic distress (mean)	3.42	3.69	3.58	4.45	4.28	3.99	3.78
Difference (t)	6.77	6.23	9.80	7.04	5.11	5.11	6.68
Significance level (p)	0.000	0.000	0.000	0.000	0.000	0.000	0.000

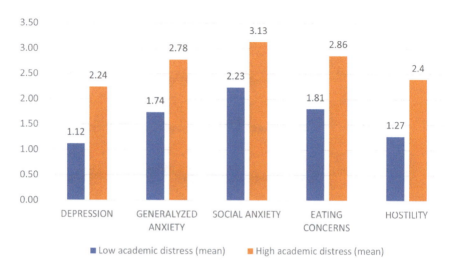

Figure 13.3. The relations between levels of academic distress and psychological symptoms

CONCLUSIONS

Capacity building at the individual level means an enhanced life experience that nurtures the development of the individual's potential and stimulates creative action. The postmodern shift in learning, industry, and social life has developed tremendous opportunities but also a lot of stress. We need to choose constantly between the many options we are given and then put them into practice immediately. The preservation of good mental health, the prevention of burnout, the personal involvement in meaningful and relaxing activities and finally the preservation of our well-being are essential to our daily coping with an intense lifestyle. In the case of the university students, a vulnerable group by definition, in transition to adulthood and trying to adjust to their new social status and roles, the promotion of well-being involves not only the preservation of mental health but also the strengthening of new social relationships that will have an impact on their future life.

Universities, regarded as learning and social communities, should be concerned with the well-being of their students. It is a fact that our well-being impacts positively on our learning processes and outcomes and on our personal growth and happiness; they act like a buffer and a protective factor against mental disorders.

While mental illness can beset anyone and at any time, individuals with underlying disorders are more vulnerable, especially when they are faced with new, unfamiliar and potentially stressful situations and contexts. Life periods of transitions, like the beginning of university studies, are extremely vulnerable and could mark the onset of mental disorders.

Even in the absence of clear psychological symptoms and concerns, a reduced sense of well-being could impact negatively on the level of personal self-acceptance, functioning, self-efficacy, and life satisfaction.

The results of this pilot-study demonstrate the debilitating effects of academic stress on our students' well-being and mental health. Consequently, damaged well-being and mental illnesses may lead to school drop-out, academic failure, and personal dissatisfaction.

Universities should develop and run programs and mental health services to promote students' learning and academic success. The focus should be on developing clear and appropriate support strategies for helping students to have better access to counselling and on constant adjustments of their learning and living environments. The final objective should be to enable students to achieve personal, social, and professional success.

While the enrolling procedures in university studies can be rather stressful, they can also have positive effects which further influence the individual well-being (Universities UK [UUK] & GuildHE, 2000). They relate to the opportunity of living in a new environment with a clear purpose and structure and to other opportunities created for better academic and personal achievements, new learning opportunities, reduced social isolation, while students are able to enjoy the company of new friends and peers.

In conclusion, the university environment creates new opportunities but also challenges, which may impact individuals differently. However, the main task of a university is to enhance the positive effects of the academic experience while constantly offering appropriate support and guidance for those who are more vulnerable. In the end, assisting students to fulfil their own potential is not only beneficial for them, but for the whole society at large.

NOTE

[1] The authors take public responsibility for the content and contributed equally in the concept development, design, analysis, writing, and revision of this chapter.

REFERENCES

Adlaf, E. M., Gliksman, L., Demers, A., & Newton-Taylor, B. (2001). The prevalence of elevated psychological distress among Canadian undergraduates: Findings from the 1998 Canadian Campus Survey. *Journal of American College Health, 50*(2), 67–72.

Association of University Leaders for a Sustainable Future. (1990). *The Talloires declaration 10 point action plan.* Retrieved from http://ulsf.org/wp-content/uploads/2015/06/TD.pdf

Authentic Happiness. (2011). Retrieved June 19, 2018, from https://www.authentichappiness.sas.upenn.edu/learn/wellbeing

Bauer, J. J., & McAdams, D. P. (2010). Eudaimonic growth: Narrative growth goals predict increases in ego development and subjective well-being 3 years later. *Developmental Psychology, 46*(4), 761–772. https://doi.org/10.1037/a0019654

Bewick, B. et al. (2010). Changes in undergraduate students' psychological well-being as they progress through university. *Studies in Higher Education, 35*(6), 633–645.

I. DARJAN ET AL.

Chen, F. F., Jing, Y., Hayes, A., & Lee, J. M. (2013). Two concepts or two approaches? A bifactor analysis of psychological and subjective well-being. *Journal of Happiness Studies, 14*, 1033–1068. doi:10.1007/s10902-012-9367

CRE-Copernicus. (1994). *COPERNICUS – The University charter for sustainable development.* Retrieved from http://www.iau-hesd.net/sites/default/files/ documents/copernicus.pdf

Csikszentmihalyi, M. (1990). *Flow: The psychology of optimal experience.* New York, NY: Harper & Row.

Darjan, I. (2017). *Therapeutic community networks for children and youth at risk.* Saarbrücken, Germany: Edition Universitaires Europeennes.

Darjan, I., & Lustrea, A. (2010). Promoting social competence development to reduce children's social aggression. *Procedia – Social and Behavioral Sciences, 2*(2), 3297–3302.

Darjan, I., Lustrea, A., & Predescu, M. (2016). Rolul şcolii în promovarea rezilienţei copiilor cu dificultăţi de invatare. In M. Craşovan (Ed.), *Educatie-evaluare-integrare.* Timisoara, Romania: Editura Universitatii de Vest.

Darjan, I., Predescu, M., & Tomita, M. (2017). Functions of aggressive behaviours – Implications for intervention. *Journal of Psychological and Educational Research, 25*(1a), 74–91.

Diener, E. (1984). Subjective well-being. *Psychological Bulletin, 95*(3), 542–575. doi:10.1037/0033-2909.95.3.542

Diener, E. (1994). Assessing subjective well-being: Progress and opportunities. *Social Indicators Research, 31*(2), 103–157. doi:10.1007/BF01207052

Disability Discrimination Act. (1995, 2015). London: HMSO.

Kaplan, A. (1999). *Organizational capacity: A different perspective* (Development dossier, No. 10). Geneva, Switzerland: Non-Governmental Liaison Service, United Nations.

Keyes, C. L. M., Shmotkin, D., & Ryff, C. D. (2002). Optimizing well-being: The empirical encounter of two traditions. *Journal of Personality and Social Psychology, 82*, 1007–1022.

Larcombe, W., & Fethers, K. (2013). Schooling the blues: An investigation of factors associated with psychological distress among law students. *UNSW Law Journal, 36*, 390–436.

Leijssen, M. (2009). Psychotherapy as search and care for the soul. *Person-Centered & Experiential Psychotherapies, 8*(1), 18–32.

Locke, B. D. et al. (2012). Development and initial validation of the Counseling Center Assessment of Psychological Symptoms-34 (CCAPS-34). *Measurement and Evaluation in Counseling and Development, 45*, 151–169.

Magna Charta Universitarium. (1988). Retrieved from http://www.magna-charta.org/resources/files/the-magna-charta/english

McMahan, E. A., & Estes, D. (2011). Hedonic versus Eudaimonic conceptions of well-being: Evidence of differential associations with self-reported well-being. *Social Indicators Research, 103*(1), 1–34. https://doi.org/10.1007/s11205-010-9698-0

Ong, C. (2017). *Towards positive education: A mindful school model.* Retrieved from http://repository.upenn.edu/ma

Park, N., Peterson, C., & Seligman, M. (2004). Strengths of character and well-being. *Journal of Social and Clinical Psychology, 23*(5), 603–619.

Parkinson, J. (Ed.). (2008). *Warwick-Edinburgh Mental Well-being Scale (WEMWBS) user guide version 1.* Retrieved from http://www.mentalhealthpromotion.net/resources/user-guide.pdf

Peterson, C. (2009). Positive psychology. *Reclaiming Children and Youth, 18*(2), 3–7.

Peterson, C., & Seligman, M. E. P. (2004). *Character strengths and virtues: A classification and handbook.* New York, NY/Washington, DC: Oxford University Press/American Psychological Association.

Predescu, M., & Darjan, I. (2017). A follow-up study of implementation of a positive approach to discipline at school and classroom levels. *Journal of Educational Sciences, 35*(1), 95–105.

Roberts, R. J. et al. (2000). Mental and physical health in students: The role of economic circumstances. *British Journal of Health Psychology, 5*, 289–297.

Ryff, C. D. (1989). Happiness is everything, or is it? Explorations on the meaning of psychological well-being. *Journal of Personality and Social Psychology, 57*, 1069–1081. doi:10.1037/0022-3514.57.6.1069

Ryff, C. D. (2014). Psychological well-being revisited: Advances in the science and practice of Eudaimonia. *Psychotherapy and Psychosomatics, 83,* 10–28. https://doi.org/10.1159/000353263

Ryff, C. D., & Singer, B. (1998). The countours of positive human health. *Psychological Inquiry, 9*(1), 1–28.

Ryff, C. D., & Singer, B. H. (2008). Know thyself and become what you are: A eudaimonic approach to psychological well-being. *Journal of Happiness Studies, 9,* 13–39. https://doi.org/10.1007/s10902-006-9019-0

Ryff, C. D., Lee, C., & Keyes, M. (1995). The structure of psychological well-being revisited. *Journal of Personality and Social Psychology, 69*(4), 719–727. Retrieved June 18, 2018, from http://midus.wisc.edu/findings/pdfs/830.pdf

Seligman, M. E. P. (2002). *Authentic happiness: Using the new positive psychology to realize your potential for lasting fulfillment.* New York, NY: Free Press.

Seligman, M. E. P. (2009). *Authentic happiness.* New York, NY: Free Press.

Seligman, M. E. P. (2011). *Flourish: A visionary new understanding of happiness and well-being.* New York, NY: Simon & Schuster.

Seligman, M. E. P., & Csikszentmihalyi, M. (2000). Positive psychology: An introduction. *American Psychologist, 55,* 5–14.

Seligman, M. E. P., Steen, T. A., Park, N., & Peterson, C. (2005). Positive psychology progress: Empirical validation of interventions. *American Psychologist, 60,* 410–421. Retrieved June 18, 2018, from https://www.researchgate.net/publication/259956843_Do_Positive_Psychology_Exercises_Work_A_Replication_of_Seligman_et_al

Senatul UVT. (2010). *Carta Universitatii de Vest din Timisoara.* http://www.obis.ro/wp-content/uploads/2011/10/carta5.pdf

Sheldon, K. M., & Krieger, L. S. (2007). Understanding the negative effects of legal education on law students: A longitudinal test of self-determination theory. *Personality and Social Psychology Bulletin, 33,* 883–897.

Shiel, C., Leal Filho, W., Paço, A., & Brandli, L. (2016). Evaluating the engagement of universities in capacity building for sustainable development in local communities. *Evaluation and Program Planning, 54,* 123–134. http://dx.doi.org/10.1016/j.evalprogplan.2015.07.006

Simister, N., & Smith, R. (2010). *Monitoring and evaluating capacity building: Is it really that difficult?* (INTRAC Praxis Paper 23). Retrieved from http://www.intrac.org/data/files/resources/677/Praxis-Paper-23-Monitoring-and-Evaluating-Capacity-Building-is-it-really-that-difficult.pdf

Stallman, H. M. (2010). Psychological distress in university students: A comparison with general population data. *Australian Psychologist, 45*(4), 249–257.

Stewart-Brown, S., Evans, J., Patterson, J., Doll, H., Balding, J., & Regis, D. (2000). The health of students in institutes of higher education: An important and neglected public health problem? *Journal of Public Health Medicine, 22,* 492–499.

UNDP. (2008). *Capacity assessment. Practice note.* New York, NY: United Nations Development Programme.

UNEP. (2002). *Capacity building for sustainable development: An overview of UNEP environmental capacity development initiatives.* Retrieved from http://www.unep.org/Pdf/Capacity_building.pdf

Universities UK (UUK) & GuildHE. (2000). *Student mental wellbeing in higher education.* Good practice guide.

van Duren, R. (2013). Capacity development in higher education institutions in developing countries (Working Paper No. 2013/30). Maastricht School of Management.

van Deurzen, E. (2009). *Psychotherapy and the quest for happiness.* Newbury Park, CA: Sage Publications.

van Deurzen, E. (1997). *Everyday mysteries: Existential dimensions of psychotherapy.* London: Routledge.

The Warwick-Edinburgh Mental Wellbeing Scales – WEMWBS. Retrieved June 19, 2018, https://warwick.ac.uk/fac/med/research/platform/wemwbs

AURORA CARMEN BĂRBAT

14. THE NORMATIVE VALUE OF HEALTH

Epigenetical, Bioethical and Theological Approaches to Health Education

INTRODUCTION

The chapter examines the interdependent relationship between natural sciences and humanities with reference to the concept of good health as a universally valued asset and the greatest blessing in our life.

The hermeneutical analysis of a number of health aspects, health values and health education in general is grounded in a soul-body theory, which also advocates for an interdisciplinary approach. The analytical-holistic approach presents difficulty for a definition of health. Therefore, building a successful collective capacity in health education involves a genuine interdisciplinary dialogue between distinct disciplines and between how scholars conduct research and then implement their research outcomes in practice.

VIEWS ON HEALTH: TOWARD A COLLECTIVE BUILDING OF CAPABILITIES

According to the first three main principles advocated by WHO (World Health Organization):

(1) Health is a state of complete physical, mental and social well-being and not merely the absence of disease or infirmity. (2) The enjoyment of the highest attainable standard of health is one of the fundamental rights of every human being without distinction of race, religion, political belief, economic or social condition. (3) The health of all peoples is fundamental to the attainment of peace and security and is dependent on the fullest co-operation of individuals and States" (WHO, 2018, Constitution of WHO: principles). Apparently, health has to do only with our physiological and mental well-being. In this sense, the normal functioning of our bodies and our physical independence are crucial values. This would mean that biological dysfunctions should be regarded as conclusive medical evidence for identifying a disease (Rogers & Walker, 2017). However, a more comprehensive view on health includes other factors such as unity, harmony, communion, even happiness, which is evidently more than just the good functioning of our human component parts. Sometimes even for the medical scientist, physiological and physio pathological functions can be only vaguely determined, since they are dependent on the scientific

© KONINKLIJKE BRILL NV, LEIDEN, 2020 | DOI: 10.1163/9789004422209_015

knowledge, societal acceptance and patient-specific normativity rules. Consequently, health approached in an analytical-holistic perspective remains a difficult concept to define. According to current scientific definitions, health can be achieved through a tremendous amount of individual struggle in order to restore the balance in our bodies. In other words, health is a habitus and not a status. In this 'habitus', we do our best so that we may be able to reach and maintain a longer time period of independence and autonomy in our lives.

THE NORMATIVE VALUE OF HEALTH

Due to the increasing costs of health treatments, many international actions regarding our health resources have become a global political and normative issue. They argue that human life is inviolable and each human being has an intrinsic value and personal dignity. This is why the debate about what are our main health care priorities raises delicate ethical issues, involving human convictions, spiritual and religious beliefs, life philosophies, intergovernmental regulations, and genuine intelligence.

Currently, academic debates and medical ethics define health by following two major patterns: firstly, the *analytical-naturalist perspective* and secondly, the *subjective-holistic* approach. In an attempt to release the tension between these two opposing conceptual trends, Yvonne Denier (2005) identifies a third pattern: the *pluralist-holistic approach.* Her main arguments are the following:

- good biological functioning is determined by medical evaluations resulting from standardized medical conventions;
- good and deviated functioning is relative and dependent on our human evolution and medical know-how;
- healthy and unhealthy human conditions remain difficult to determine because of societal and cultural contexts;
- people are interested in their own health condition because it influences their own well-being;
- our well-being is both a moral and normative concept, with objective and subjective features;
- the level of good health determines our overall well-being; take the case of a disabled person who is unable to go on a holiday or to plan his/her own activities without assistance, etc. (Denier, 2005, p. 50).

EPIGENETICS. PSYCHO-NEUROIMMUNOLOGY – A MODEL OF TRANSDISCIPLINARITY

Genes, fundamental physical units of heredity, are a linear sequence of nucleotides in a segment of DNA that provides coded instructions for protein synthesis. Through complex mechanisms, these biochemical processes lead to the expression of our hereditary character. Genes are responsible for producing specific proteins within our

THE NORMATIVE VALUE OF HEALTH

cells, resulting in a unique constellation of blueprint that shapes every human feature: our weight, hair colour, bodily structures, personality traits, etc. Unfortunately, our genetic blueprint is rather vulnerable: the mutations that occur in our genes can produce hereditary diseases or hereditary predispositions to diseases. However, while it has been long accepted that diseases can be produced by genetic mutations, a recent research line seeks to determine how our values, thoughts and lifestyle can influence our basic genetic data (Török-Oance, 2013). This approach suggests that major scientific achievements do not only need key specialized knowledge from one particular scientific field, but they may benefit from close contact with other disciplines:

> The word 'epigenetic' literally means 'in addition to changes in genetic sequence'. The term has evolved to include any process that alters gene activity without changing the DNA sequence, and leads to modifications that can be transmitted to daughter cells (although experiments show that some epigenetic changes can be reversed) [...] Today, a wide variety of illnesses, behaviours, and other health indicators already have some level of evidence linking them with epigenetic mechanisms, including cancers of almost all types, cognitive dysfunction, and respiratory, cardiovascular, reproductive, autoimmune, and neurobehavioral illnesses. Known or suspected drivers behind epigenetic processes include many agents, including heavy metals, pesticides, diesel exhaust, tobacco smoke, polycyclic aromatic hydrocarbons, hormones, radioactivity, viruses, bacteria, and basic nutrients. (Weinhold, 2006, p. 160)

Many unique personal experiences like love, spirituality, environmental status, distress, electromagnetic shifts, etc. can influence our genes (genotype) by shaping our personal responses to how we experience them (phenotype). As life events are changing all the time, the epigenetic processes become the patterns through which we change. Since natural sciences have already proven this fact, neuro-immunology, a relatively new discipline, tries to explain the mystery of this pluri- and transdisciplinary term. Information regarding our health is crucial, creating a complex network of relationships: within ourselves and between ourselves and the environment, too:

> Cell biologist Bruce Lipton, PhD likens cells to miniature people. They have the same systems and receptors as skin so they can perceive their environment and the community of cells at large. Cells are constantly communicating with each other via photons of light in the layer of the human energy field right outside the body. They receive information from the brain and energy field and respond accordingly. When we experience an emotion, our cells experience the same emotion through energy vibrations and changes in body chemistry. (Heart Math Institute, n.d.)

In his own telemedicine project (YouTube documentaries), Bruce Lipton shared with us his insights on stem cell research: "Just like a single cell, the character of our

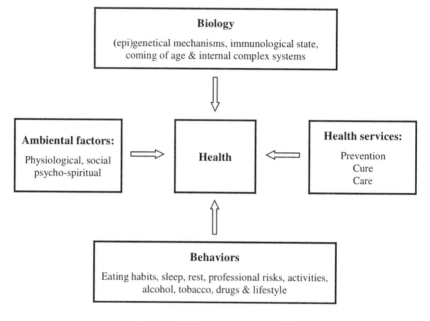

Figure 14.1. Parameters of health

lives is determined not by our genes but by our responses to the environmental signals [...]" (Lipton, 2017). As a consequence, the well-known theological Thomistic expression *Anima forma corporis (The soul forms the body)* is now 'blessed' by the discoveries of the epigenetic mechanisms: *Anima (in)forma corporis*. Saint Thomas Aquinas (1225–1274), a Catholic priest, Dominican brother and Doctor of the Church, was a greatly influential philosopher, theologian and jurist in the tradition of scholasticism. His authority on Western reflection is remarkable, particularly in the fields of ethics, natural law, metaphysics, and politics (Beck, 2008, 2017). Trying to realize a schematic perspective of the above-mentioned facts, we can conclude by developing the model of health shown in Figure 14.1.

ETHICAL INTERFERENCE IN MEDICINE AND HEALTH EDUCATION

All basic principles of bioethics (beneficence, non-maleficence, autonomy and justice) must be applied in association with the practitioner's virtues. Without trying to summarize all core bioethical topics, we have to agree that the patient-therapist relationship, the distinction between clinical practice and clinical research, placebo/ nocebo effects, the preimplantation genetic diagnosis, beginning-of-life issues, end-of-life issues, sex reassignment, and telemedicine remain nowadays at the top of the list (McCullough, 2017). At the same time, despite the difficulties in advocating the role of religion in secular clinical institutions, the relevance of spiritual beliefs for

THE NORMATIVE VALUE OF HEALTH

bioethics cannot be ignored: patients as well as health caregivers are humans with beliefs and spiritual values.

The patient-physician relationship is of great importance and relevance for therapy, teaching us some broad perspectives about ethics in general. If therapy includes also nursing as a dimension of care, the patients' opinions and preference of care often conceal fear, depression or misinformation. Consequently, the question about what the patient thinks and feels has to be further investigated in the still narrow dimension of shared vulnerability within the patient-physician-nurse triangle (Burns, 2017).

In clinical trials, people (whether patients or not) volunteer to help find answers to some health questions. They represent, in some conditions, one of the fastest ways to improve or find new treatments. Concerning the aspect of safety, clinical trials are conducted according to a scientifically and ethically rigorous plan, where researchers and health professionals must follow strict (inter)national rules. These rules make sure that those who agree to participate are treated as safely as possible.

The critique of these trials refers not only to some unreported side effects, but to the controversial medical progress concerning the healthcare itself. Anyway, just as effective clinical progress cannot arise without clinical research, valid clinical research requires clinical practice. As we can understand, defining the patient's safety remains a matter of finding a delicate balance between scientific knowledge and applied research ethics (pharmaceutical drug companies' intentions, drug safety policy, and moral duty of healthcare practitioners). Discovering the strengths and weaknesses of medical knowledge as well as understanding the action of some unknown factors will surely improve the practice of clinical research:

> There has lately been a growing level of interest in assessing the quality of clinical trials, not only with regard to internal validity, but also in terms of a host of parameters that might guide the application of trial results to informing decisions about the development of medical products, medical practice, or health policy. While the critical importance of clinical trials is widely acknowledged, as a scientific tool, they remain a work in progress. (Califf, 2017, p. 25)

As regards the new dimensions and trends in medical practice and education, a special focus lies in what we call e-Health, i.e. the use of information and communication technologies for health. E-Health tools include telephony (mobile and land lines), electronic mail and digital technologies (radio, TV, video, portable disc players and the Internet, while e-learning programs involve different delivery systems from live, interactive telemedicine to computer programs). Programming will be based on students' needs determined by the dialog between educators and students (undergraduate students, residents, fellows, or specialists working in the community or academic setting) (Negruţ, Pavel, & Negruţ, 2012).

In the field of medical ethics in the last decades there have been lots of reactions against paternalism in favour of patient autonomy (self-determination, personal

A. C. BĂRBAT

liberty, and independence). Proceeding from the idea that health includes more than a good physiology and a balanced mental state, we could notice that more and more patients are becoming health consumers. Consequently, in trying to develop some coping strategies, many physicians have been trying to adjust by transforming themselves into health service providers. Both perspectives (paternalism and autonomy) are, in fact, restrictive, since the former tries to protect only the objective and non-evaluating discourse (evidence-based) and the latter is embracing only the patient value concept. But the question that arises focuses on the issue of whether patients should be aware that they can be "the only legitimate source of valuing" (Denier, 2004, p. 50).

As we know, according to the autonomy principle, competent adult patients have the right to control what happens to their bodies: these patients have the right to refuse or accept treatments, drugs, and surgical procedures, even if those decisions are not in their best interest. It certainly remains controversial if health care systems should allow patients unable to understand the risks of their own decisions to determine the steps of their own therapy (without doubt, there were cases when unsatisfied patients or family members started malpraxis debates or scandals, even if at the beginning of the therapy they were not open to being part of the decision process).

Health educators should make it clear that one of the most dangerous attitudes in healthcare is elevating patient autonomy and the subjective-holistic perspective to such heights that we risk accepting the idea that "health services are simply private goods offered to the individuals to be accepted or refused as they see fit" (ibid.).

One of the fundamental challenges of the researcher is that they can be independent from neither the uncontrollability of their own intuition, nor the human ability to assimilate scientific knowledge (ibid.). The same author pointed out some other dangers that shape the confidence crisis within the educative functions of science:

- the scientific incompetence that can ruin popular scientific institutions and universities, based on the incompetence of the scientific agents (researchers);
- the uncritical pressure and unintelligent importation of the market model into the world of science (Denier, 2004, p. 188).

HEALTHCARE ALSO NEEDS COMPETENT PSYCHOTERAPISTS,
INTELLIGENT SPIRITUAL ADVISERS AND VOCATIONAL SOCIAL WORKERS

Since Descartes popularized the notion of mind/body dualism, both mind and body have been considered separate entities. This conviction has influenced theology, as well as medical theory and practice. Many priests focused their counselling only on the spiritual dimension, disconnecting the (un)believer from their own socio-psychological realities. At the same time, our conventional allopathic medicine treats parts instead of the whole person. Fortunately, the holistic perspective on medicine 'converts' many practitioners (physicians, spiritual counsellors, clinical

THE NORMATIVE VALUE OF HEALTH

psychologists, and social workers) in this world of new and beautiful discoveries, such as the following:

> Overall, our data suggest that the heart and brain, together, are involved in receiving, processing, and decoding intuitive information. On the basis of these results and those of other research, it would thus appear that intuitive perception is a system-wide process in which both the heart and brain (and possibly other bodily systems) play a critical role. (McCraty, Atkinson, & Trevor Bradley, 2004, p. 325)

Both clinical psychologists and clinical social workers try to help people deal with suffering. Clinical social workers are active in direct services, helping people cope with problems related to poverty, family issues, abuse, legal issues, and human rights, while clinical psychologists diagnose and treat mental, behavioural or emotional health issues. Sometimes, the work of clinical social workers is more similar to that of a psychologist (Jurca, 2016). As logical consequence, many well-respected psychotherapists in the Catholic world have degrees in both psychology and theology; the best medical doctors are trained in psychology and are excellent social workers who have a complementary degree in psychology or applied theology. A good future collaboration between various therapists requires a supervised pluri- and interdisciplinary academic practice. In very good universities, students should become familiar with real situations encountered in their future work place (Vlaicu & Bălăuță, 2017, p. 53).

The Blamed Christianity and Its Forgotten Contributions to Science

Both the Inquisition – an institution that was established by the papacy and by secular governments to combat heresy – as well as the immoral behaviour of the clergy are on top arguments embraced by many people against Christianity. Unfortunately, many of these Church opponents cannot be forced to study the history of Christianity from its roots and values that have lasted two millennia and have contributed to our European civilization. But isn't it remarkable that although Christians represent 33.2% of the world's population, they have won a total of 65.4% of all Nobel prizes between 1901 and 2000 (Wikipedia, 2018)? According to the same source, we have a list of Catholic churchmen throughout history who have made important contributions to science. Catholic scientists include Nicolaus Copernicus, Gregor Mendel, Albertus Magnus, Roger Bacon, Roger Joseph Boscovich, Marin Mersenne, Francesco Maria Grimaldi, Nicole Oresme, Jean Buridan, Robert Grosseteste, Louis Bertrand Castel, Christopher Clavius, Nicolas Steno, Athanasius Kircher, Giovanni Battista Riccioli, William of Ockham, Agostino Gemelli, and others […] This list includes priests, bishops (including popes), deacons, monks, abbots, and those who received minor orders in the Church (ibid.).

The Jesuit education is famous for its well-balanced approach to problems related to 'means' and 'ends'. In a world of specialized researchers who have more knowledge

A. C. BĂRBAT

about extremely narrowed topics, Jesuit universities are research universities and 'sanctuaries' for reflection, where students are taught how to understand the world and how to understand themselves. Since the foundation of the Society of Jesus, nearly 500 years ago, the Jesuits:

> [...] often took the message of science to people on other continents. For instance, it was a Jesuit who helped found the Indian Association for the Cultivation of Science. Jesuits also introduced Western astronomy to China during their travels there and in turn brought back original Chinese research back to the West. Most prominently, Jesuits have founded many influential schools and colleges – including Georgetown University and Boston College – which emphasize teaching and research in science. (Jogalekar, n.d.)

Jesuit missions and schools together have long provided an institutional framework housing both scientific education and research, giving the world an illuminating example of how science and religion can make progress together (Udias, 2015). Udias' study gives a comprehensive history of the Jesuits' contributions to science by following an uncommon path to the frontiers where the Christian message had not been yet known (the author, a Spanish Jesuit, born in Santander, Spain, in 1935, has published on the topics of earthquake source mechanism, on science and religion, on Teilhard de Chardin and the history of Jesuits in science).

The Jesuit school highlights five core educational principles:

- the passion for quality;
- the commitment to lifelong learning;
- the preoccupation with questions of ethics and values;
- the importance given to the religious experience;
- the person-centered attitude (Loyola University Health System, 2008).

THE ISSUE OF PUBLIC HEALTH

Without a doubt, medical ethics has concentrated on the ethics of clinical medicine. Meanwhile, the ethics of public health has been neglected. This fact is surprising, because public health measures are often the most effective and efficient means of improving general health. Furthermore, public health care measures ensure that health care is distributed justly and fairly. They are based on three main pillars: the *prevention* of diseases and disabilities, the *treatment* of potential diseases and disabilities, and the *medical care* for the chronically ill and/or the disabled (Trancă, 2015). Public health regarded as an essential collective responsibility involves:

- public services (provision of clean water, suitable urban and rural sanitation systems);
- laws regarding hygienically measurable parameters of used air, water, soil/ measurable parameters of pollution (including the electromagnetical and psychological ones);

THE NORMATIVE VALUE OF HEALTH

- (inter)national and local agencies responsible for law enforcement (occupational health, consumer product safety, control of infectious disease);
- (inter)national and local educational activities and campaigns (oral care, smoking habits, alcohol and illicit drug consumption, screening tests for risk groups);
- (inter)national and local sanctions and penalty measures;
- (inter)national and local incentive actions.

WHO (World Health Organization) claims that health professionals have a responsibility for promoting health training programs and adequate measures in education to address general health care needs in the 21st century:

- Be country-owned, country-led, context-specific, and embedded in the broader socio-economic and development characteristics of communities and populations;
- Respond to population health needs and expectations, and adapt to evolving epidemiological profiles and burden of disease; [...]
- Be aligned with national health objectives and strategies and human resources for health plans (evidence-based, cost and sustainable); [...]
- Apply a combination of context-specific interventions, applicable in both the public and private sectors, in broad areas such as: governance; education and training institutions; regulatory frameworks; financing; and planning [...] (WHO, 2012).

CONCLUSIONS

It is a fact that transdisciplinary as a research strategy needs to be integrated more often in our academic learning environment. Academics can thus address problems that cross disciplinary boundaries; otherwise our research cannot develop harmoniously in an open dialogue with other research fields and we will lose confidence in our research products.

University research and teaching will only flourish under global conditions in those places where universality, transdisciplinary, identity in plurality, and equality are assured. If this is not the case, the paradigm of the school replaces that of the university. (Mittelstrass, 2006, p. 181)

The quality of the work carried out by future therapists depends on the amount of useful theoretical knowledge available and the type of field placement education they have received (Vlaicu & Bălăuţă, 2017, p. 54).

Medical education has always been defined by its universal character. However, today medical universities seem to concentrate more and more on how to 'privatize' their knowledge in the interest of financial enterprises. Researchers and scientists are, to some extent, exhorted to 'sell' their knowledge. The question is whether we should continue to encourage this approach.

If unfair educational politics are yet to be implemented, the foundations of science as well as our rational culture will be seriously threatened. With regard to health

193

A. C. BĂRBAT

education, one of the worst effects is the emergence of an unscientific approach to health and normalcy:

> Science is the expression of universal claims to validity, and this [...] both in the sense of being a special form of knowledge formations as well as in the sense of being a scientific ethos, which is also the moral form of science. The orientation toward truth typical of the first of these follows the orientation toward truthfulness of the second. This is to say, quite simply, that truth determines the scientific form of knowledge, whereas truthfulness determines the moral form of science, which as a result belongs to the form of life of the scientist, to his ethos. (Mittelstrass, 2006, pp. 188–189)

REFERENCES

Battyn, B. (2006). The ethical implications of patenting academic research. *Ethical Perspectives, 13*(2), 165–160.

Beck, M. (2008). *Symposium "Medizin, Ideologie und Markt"*. Retrieved from https://www.youtube.com/watch?v=1t1CgsvgMxw&t=812s

Beck, M. (2017). *Braucht die Medizin die Philosophie?* Retrieved from https://www.youtube.com/watch?v=1t1CgsvgMxw&t=812s

Burns, L. (2017). What does the patient say? Levinas and medical ethics. *The Journal of Medicin and Philosophy: A Forum for Bioethics and Philosophy of Medicine, 4*(2), 214–235.

Califf, R. M. (2017). Clinical trials. In D. Robertson & G. H. Williams (Eds.), *Clinical ant translational science: Principles of human research* (2nd ed., pp. 25–52). Retrieved from https://www.sciencedirect.com/science/article/pii/B978012802101900003X

Denier, Y. (2005). Public health, well-being and reciprocity. *Ethical Perspectives, 12*(1), 41–66.

Frankl, E. (2000). *Man's search for ultimate meaning*. New York, NY: Perseus Publishing.

Heart Math Institute. (n.d.). *The mind body spirit connection*. Retrieved from http://www.holistic-mindbody-healing.com/mind-body-spirit-connection.html

Jagalekar, A. (n.d.). *Jesuits, science and a Pope with a chemistry degree: A productive pairing?* [Blog post]. Retrieved from https://blogs.scientificamerican.com/thecurious-wavefunction/jesuits-science-and-a-pope-with-a-chemistry-degree-a-productive-pairing/m

Jurca, E. (2016). *Psihopatologie și psihoterapie*. Timișoara: Editura de Vest.

Lipton, B. H. (2013). *Epigenetics: The science of human empowerment* [Video]. Retrieved from https://www.youtube.com/watch?v=kqG5TagD0uU

Lipton, B. H. (2017). *The biology of belief change subconscious programs to reprogram your mind* [Video]. Retrieved from https://www.youtube.com/watch?v=c1k2AuneJ4g

Loyola University Health System. (2008). *Medical education and health care in the Jesuit tradition*. Retrieved from http://www.lumc.edu/depts/ministry/education.htm

McCraty, R., Atkinson, M., & Bradley, R. T. (2004). Electrophysiological evidence of intuition: Part 2. A system-wide process? *Journal of Alternative and Complementary Medicine, 10*(1), 325–336.

McCullough, L. B. (2017). Philosophical provocation: The lifeblood of clinical ethics. *The Journal of Medicine and Philosophy: A Forum for Bioethics and Philosophy of Medicine, 42*(1), 1–6.

Mittelstrass, J. (2006). The future of the university and the credibility of science and scholarship. *Ethical Perspectives, 13*(2), 171–190.

Negruț, V., Pavel, C., & Negruț, L. (2012). E-learning – An alternative to traditional education. *"Ovidius" University Annals, Economic Sciences Series, 12*(2), 463–467.

Rogers, W. A., & Walker, M. J. (2017). The line-drawing problem in disease definition. *The Journal of Medicine and Philosophy: A Forum for Bioethics and Philosophy of Medicine, 42*(4), 405–423.

Török-Oance, R. (2013). A study of risk factors and t-score variability in Romania women with postmenopausal osteoporosis. *Iranian Journal of Public Health, 42*(12), 1387–1397.

THE NORMATIVE VALUE OF HEALTH

Trancă, L. M. (2015). Die professionelle Ausbildung von Sozialarbeitern in Rumanien. In J. Sagebiel, A. Muntean, & B. Sagebiel (Hg.), *Zivilgesellschaft und Soziale Arbeit. Herausforderungen und Perspektiven an die Arbeit im Gemeinwesen in Rumanien und Deutschland* (pp. 254–274). Munchen: AG SPAK Bucher.

Udias, A. (2015). *Jesuit contribution to science. A history.* Retrieved from http://www.springer.com/us/book/9783319083643

Vlaicu, L., & Bălăuţă, D. S. (2017). Perceptions of actors involved in social work field placement at the West University of Timisoara. *Social Work Review/Revista de Asistenţă Socială, 2,* 53–60.

Weinhold, B. (2006). Epigenetics. The science of change. *Environmental Health Perspectives, 114*(3), 160–167.

Wikipedia. (2018). *List of Christian Nobel laureates.* Retrieved from https://en.wikipedia.org/wiki/List_of_Christian_Nobel_laureates

Wikipedia. (n.d.). *List of Catholic clergy scientists.* Retrieved from https://en.wikipedia.org/wiki/List_of_Catholic_clergy_scientists

WHO. (2012). *Guidelines development group. Transformative education for health professionals.* Retrieved from http://wahoeducationguidelines.org./sites/default/files/uploads/WHO_EduGuidelines_20131202_Chapter1.pdf

WHO. (2018). *Constitution of WHO: Principles.* Retrieved from http://wwhttps://en.wikipedia.org/wiki/List_of_Christian_Nobel_laureates

INDEX

A

academic distress, 174–180
adult education, 9, 28, 83, 84, 91, 94, 99–102, 105, 153, 154, 157, 159, 161, 162

B

beliefs, 15, 17–19, 27, 28, 59–61, 67, 68, 70, 71, 104, 126, 185, 186, 188, 189

C

citizenship, 9, 39, 46, 47, 83–86, 92, 101, 134, 167, 170
collaborative learning, 137, 139–141, 144, 149, 156, 158, 161
community development, 3, 36, 37, 40, 42
critical analysis, 59, 61, 62, 65, 66, 69, 71, 156
critical thinking, 8, 17, 32, 59–64, 70, 71, 127, 130, 135, 156
cultural heritage, 8, 27, 35–42
culture, 1, 2, 19, 25–33, 36, 41, 42, 46–48, 50, 53–57, 84, 88, 92, 94, 100, 109, 111, 113, 114, 120, 126, 133, 142, 143, 154, 156, 158, 162, 166, 167, 169, 170, 193

D

democracy, 7, 9, 15, 16, 18, 20–24, 46, 47, 83–86, 91, 93, 96, 105
didactics, 83, 95
digital communication, 73, 80

E

Education for Sustainable Development (ESD), 123, 127–135

enculturation, 8, 25, 26, 28, 29, 32, 33
epistemology, 16, 20, 94, 95
European cultural identity, 19

G

generation Y, 10, 123–128, 130, 131, 133, 135 (*see also* millennials)

H

healthcare, 189, 190
heritage education, 40
higher education, 7, 10, 11, 55, 86, 109–111, 113, 120, 132, 137, 148, 157, 161, 167, 172
human rights, 16, 51, 52, 55, 56, 84, 92, 191

I

inclusion, 49, 54, 55, 83, 87, 91, 93, 142, 143, 167
Initial Teacher Education (ITE), 138, 139, 141, 149, 150
internationalization, 100, 137, 139, 144, 145
community learning, 11, 40, 156, 161

M

mental health, 11, 165, 172–174, 178–181
millenials, 135 (*see also* generation Y)

N

neo-liberalism, 85, 100, 101
new learning environments, 91, 96

INDEX

P

pedagogical leadership, 139–141, 144, 147, 149, 150
personalized learning, 139, 141, 144, 149
philosophy, 8, 16, 18–20, 24, 26, 31, 161, 170
psychological disorders, 175, 177

R

Roma community, 8, 45, 46, 48–57

S

social capital, 2, 8, 36–39, 42, 118, 123, 155
social phenomenon, 79
social system, 30, 46, 47, 49

V

vocational social workers, 190

W

well-being, 2, 4, 6, 11, 23, 90, 92, 124, 165, 168, 170–181, 185, 186

Printed in the United States
By Bookmasters